Dearest Riju

Many happy returns of the day!

Lots of love
Shinu
(Nov 2018)

never let me go
a memoir

Nicole Lowe

The people, places, and events described in this book are real. However, in some cases the names and identifying characteristics of certain individuals have been changed to protect their privacy.

Copyright ©2016 Nicole Lowe

All rights reserved. No part of this book may be reproduced, stored in a retrieval system, or transmitted in any form or by any means without prior written permission from the authors, except for the use of brief quotations in a book review.

Published by Glass Spider Publishing

www.glassspiderpublishing.com

ISBN 978-0-9979825-0-3

Library of Congress Control Number: 2016951915

Cover design by Jane Font

Edited by Vince Font

Publisher's Note: We endeavor to provide you with a book that is of the highest professional quality and free of printing errors. If the copy of the book you have purchased contains any printing errors, please contact us at info@getmystorypublished.com to arrange for a free replacement of this product.

Dedicated to my children, who have taught me to love and find beauty in the world.

Map of Travels

As teens, we explore our surroundings and ourselves. What most of us discover is that we do not have to venture far for the answers we so desperately seek, and the further we go in our search, the more evasive the answers become. My story is heart-wrenching and terrifying, but most of all, it is filled with hope. I kept journals throughout my adolescence, and this book and its poetry are reflections of those pages. Names have been changed to protect the not-so-innocent, and conversations are the closest approximation my rattled memory contains. The courtroom scenes are a composite of actual cases I have worked on.

the descent of the sun

When a placenta is ripped from the uterine wall, our children and their dreams are either strong enough to fight for breath, or they suffocate within the womb.

Nicole Lowe, 2014

opening statement

My rolling briefcase *click*, *click*, *clicks* across the white marble of the Matheson Courthouse, occasionally catching the heel of my flat-bottom dress shoes. So long as it doesn't catch hold of my nylons, I don't care much.

   I pull the eight-foot almond doors open and take three steps to the second set of doors. The bailiff's face appears in the window of the door. A bright smile spreads across his face. I'm the first attorney to arrive.

   Passing the few rows of benches, which remind me a bit too much of going to church as a child, I step across the invisible barrier patrolled by the bailiff to where the parties of the case sit. I weave my way through the three black-topped tables and cluster of chairs in the well of the courtroom.

   I pause and take a breath. I'm not sure how I ended up at the state's counsel table and not the parent's. Honestly, I should be dead. But for whatever reason, whatever higher power there is, it saw fit to plant a seed within me that refused to die despite the lack of sun and rain. A miracle? I smile. Doubtful.

"What's up Nicole?" The bailiff, Maxwell, makes a sweeping gesture with his hand, indicating the empty courtroom. "Are we having a trial today?"

"Most likely," I say, pulling off my red-pinstriped black blazer and hanging it on the back of my chair. "At the last pre-trial, the mother said she wanted a trial."

I grasp the frayed edges of my briefcase and unlatch the gold locks on each end. I pull the inches-thick Utah Court Rules book free. My hand is barely able to hold onto it. It thunks onto the table. Next, I struggle with the five-part file bursting with yellow and white pages telling the story of a little girl. I slide it gently onto the table, careful not to lose a piece.

"Is there coffee in the back?" I ask.

"For you?" Maxwell says. "Yeah." He waves me back.

I follow him past the blue flag of Utah and the U.S. flag hanging limp on either side of the state emblem behind the judge's bench. Institution white and grey plaster the back hallways. The chambers for all six Salt Lake City juvenile court judges are tucked in at regular intervals. Once in the breakroom, I pour myself coffee and tip some creamer in, watching it swirl in a spiral. I learned to appreciate mediocre coffee — even bad coffee — long ago.

"I don't understand these parents who don't do any of the services, but want a trial," Maxwell says.

"I think they can't bring themselves to give up and walk away."

I know the parents feel like they're giving up on their kids, but that's not how I see it. It takes an incredible amount of strength to recognize that you're unable to provide what your children need and to release them from your grasp, allowing them to fly to heights you could never take them.

The children's attorney, Carl Johnson, is setting out his laptop and case files when we re-enter the courtroom. Three-year-old McCartni ducks in and out of the cherrywood table legs. Her auburn hair is laced with the rays of the sun, and her cheeks have been kissed many times over by the same.

"How many witnesses do you have?" Carl asks, watching his child-client clamber into each charcoal chair.

I hold the back of my chair to prevent it from rolling or turning as McCartni explores. Carl wriggles his tie until it hides the buttons of his shirt. His suit hangs pristine, with creases down the front of each leg.

"Just three. The mother, the social worker, and the foster mother."

The trial will take less than three hours. The fewer the witnesses, the less the parents did to address the reasons the state took protective custody of their child in the first place. The more services they've engaged in, the more witnesses we will have to testify about their ability to parent. It's my opinion that the termination of parental rights is equivalent to, if not worse than, a death sentence in the criminal courts.

Carl shakes his head. "What about Jake? How many does he have?"

"Just his client."

McCartni stretches across the tabletop, makes a pop with her lips into the overhead sound system, and clamps her hand over her mouth. From head to pink ballet slippers, she only stands the length of my leg.

"You should take her out through the back," I say.

"I thought Judge Cruz would like to meet her before we start."

It's good for all of us to remember why we're here; to look into the wide, curious eyes of the child whose life our decisions will impact until the day she draws her last breath.

The courtroom doors open and Jake, the mother's attorney, walks inside. He's carrying a stack of files and notebooks, squeezing his cell phone between his ear and shoulder. "You were supposed to be here at nine. How long until you're here?"

He listens, looks at Carl and me, and smiles.

"The judge only waits fifteen minutes. You need to get here." He hangs up and sighs. "She's on her way. Getting off the train now."

Never Let Me Go

```
I look up at the clock on the wall. 9:07 a.m.
   Carl takes McCartni's little hand and they
disappear through the door behind the judge's
bench. Her sea-green dress waves behind her.
   Many of the attorneys who practice in juvenile
court have been doing so for a long time. At
twenty-nine, I'm just a kid. More than half of
the parents who pass through here are older than
me. They see me as someone who could never
understand the situations or decisions that have
brought them here, fighting for the right to
raise their children. But that is not true at
all...
```

My parents' house was a cage.

I bit my lip as I stared at my reflection. *I've got to get out of here.*

A thin eyeliner pencil glided around my predominately green eyes in Cleopatra style. The pencil followed the smooth curve of my lips, like smoldering coals surrounding a fire. The walls of my bedroom pushed in around me, squeezing at my chest.

The wire hangers screeched across the metal bar as I pushed aside my lace dress, skull leggings, and full-length skirts. Black velvet leggings slid off a hanger. Pulling them on, I decided on the burgundy velvet blazer. I untucked the ruffles of my antique white shirt and slid my feet into my combat boots. I tightened the laces, tied them, and tucked them inside.

My fingers closed around the strap of my velvet gothbox purse. Flicking the bedroom light off, I stepped into the dark hallway and waited, listening. The sounds of my mother's light snoring drifted across the hall. The dog's tags clinked as she raised her head quizzically. Moonlight caught in her golden eyes. We stared at each other across the empty expanse. Then slowly, I crept down the dark hallway.

Nicole Lowe

I lowered my foot onto each creaking stair as I descended to the main floor. I refused to look at the smiling faces of my mother, father, older brother, and younger sister hanging on the wall as I passed. I pulled the front door closed with a practiced silence and stepped away from the house where they all lay sleeping, wrapped in their warm beds.

The crickets chirped. I unzipped my gothbox and the strap slid off my shoulder. I reached inside, feeling around for bus money. I pushed my rune stones, crystals, and makeup to one side of the gothbox, and then to the other. My cigarettes crunched. *Damn it.* The coins clinked together at the bottom. At last, my fingers closed around the cold metal I took from my mother's turtle-shaped coin bank.

Placing a cigarette between my lips, I flicked the lighter and pulled the nicotine into my lungs. My trench coat brushed against my calves as I followed the yellow glow of the streetlamps down the hill to catch the last bus into the city.

I cloaked myself in shadows and disappeared into the darkness. I didn't know when I would return to my parents' house. All I knew was I couldn't stay there any longer.

Fourteen seemed too young to be walking away from the shelter of home in the middle of the night, but I'd been doing it for a year already. Home was not a shelter to me. It was an icy pond and I was at the bottom with a chain clamped around my ankle, watching the bubbles drift to the surface. The friends who surrounded me were more like parasites and cockroaches. Their frantic scurrying along the walls, hiding from the light, distracted me from my fabricated, soul-sucking existence.

I was a member of what some believed was a cult, but we called it the Charade. I felt nothing for the world I was in, or its people. Each day, I watched it slowly crumble with decay.

Most of the time, I chose to live on the streets of my hometown, Salt Lake City—the Mormon capital of the world, with its castle-like temples and *love one another as Jesus loved you* shit. I flicked the ashes off my cigarette and took another drag before flicking the butt to the gutter. The streetlamp overhead trembled and a bus came to a stop before me.

Like so many nights, I had no set destination once I reached the city. It all depended on who I could find when I arrived.

Nicole Lowe

into the dark of night

In 1994, drug use among eighth-grade students increased from 11.3 percent to 21.4 percent in the United States.

chapter one

Judge Cruz's face is impassive as he takes his place on the bench. He rarely reacts to what's said by anyone in the courtroom. These cases never get easy, but their facts soon fail to shock you.

Everyone eases into their seats once the judge has taken his. Everyone but me.

"Any preliminary matters?" His studious eyes move over each of us as one by one, we respond with, "No, Your Honor."

"Your first witness, Ms. Lowe."

"Your Honor, the state calls the mother, Sabrina Hardy, to the stand."

"Ms. Hardy, will you step forward and raise your right hand, please?" Judge Cruz says.

Sabrina presses her lips together and stands, her chair rolling back easily on the charcoal carpet.

Her big toe has worn a hole in her right sneaker; bright-pink nail polish peeks out, matching her fingernails. Auburn roots have pushed the blonde hair away from her head. A faded blue- and white-checkered dress hangs lifeless over her thin frame and clings to itself as it brushes back and forth over her bare legs. Crude, colorless tattoos peer out as the collar shifts around her slender shoulders.

The court clerk stands. "Do you swear to tell the truth, the whole truth, and nothing but the truth?"

"I do," Sabrina says.

As she takes her place in the witness box at the front of the courtroom, Maxwell pours her a Dixie cup of water from the waiting pitcher.

I wait for her to arrange herself. When her eyes meet mine, I begin.

"Will you state your first and last name for the record, please?"

She leans forward, nearly placing her lips on the microphone. "Sabrina. Hardy."

"How old are you, Ms. Hardy?"

"I just turned twenty-two."

"Where are you living?"

"I'm staying with some friends."

Mascara shadows her lower eyelids, deepening her forlorn expression.

"How long have you been staying there?"

"A week."

"How long have you known these friends?"

She looks at Jake, her attorney, who sits at the table directly across from her. He meets her eyes, but gives no reaction.

"A few weeks."

"What are their names?"

"Bear and Sasha."

"How many children have you given birth to?"

"Two."

"How many of them live with you?"

She looks to the empty back corner of the courtroom. "None."

The questions I ask are always difficult to answer. Not because the parents don't know, but because they do. They are even harder when the parent understands the damage the answer does to their case.

"Where are they?"

"My son was adopted by his foster parents two years ago, and my daughter is with her foster parents."

"How old is your son?"

Her eyes seek the upper corner of the courtroom as she counts on her fingers. We watch and wait. "Six, now."

"Why was he taken into state's custody?"

Jake gets to his feet. "Objection; relevance. I don't see how this relates to why we are here today."

Judge Cruz turns his steady gaze to me.

"Your Honor," I say, "it shows the history and depth of the mother's drug addiction."

"I'll allow it, Mr. Lundberg," the judge says. Jake sits and nods at his client.

"He tested positive for cocaine when he was born," Sabrina says.

"How old is your daughter?"

Her eyes light up. She scoots forward to the edge of her chair and smiles. "She just turned three last week."

Whether or not she loves this child is not a question in the mind of anyone in the courtroom.

I smile back at her. "What's her name?"

"McCartni."

"When was McCartni placed into state's custody?"

"Two days after her first birthday." Her eyelids flutter and the muscles of her jaw contract.

"Why was she placed in state's custody?"

"Our apartment was raided by the police and McCartni's hair tested positive for methamphetamine."

Early August, 1992.

A month before my fourteenth birthday, my older brother's girlfriend bought me acid as an early gift. Michelle's mom worked evenings and went straight to bed, so it was the perfect place to drop the acid into our mouths.

Nicole Lowe

The little square of paper dissolved on the center of my tongue. Thirty minutes ticked by, and then my hands grew sweaty and clammy. The way the light fell on Michelle's face—or the touch of my own hand, as if it wasn't mine—sent me into convulsive laughter. A rising vibration of energy made me bounce on my toes and pace around. It needed to get out.

We stared out the window, looking at the stars and listening to The Cure, our favorite band. Overhead clouds swirled and contorted into faces that melted away or took shape as animals, prancing and soaring free among the stars. We danced and spun in circles, watching rainbow-hued tracers stream from our hands and skirts. We were caught in a whirlwind of happiness. It was something I had not felt in a long time.

Michelle flopped to the floor in a heap. Her copper hair splayed like a mop. She flung her head up, grinning, and I swayed as if the copper strands were reaching out for me.

"We need orange juice," she said.

"Why?"

The moonlight captured the golden flecks at the edges of her green eyes. "You'll see. Let's go."

She dropped into the driver's seat of her mom's beat-up Oldsmobile and turned her alabaster face toward me, smiling and wide-eyed. Laughing, she pounded her hands against the steering wheel and slid Skinny Puppy's *Bites* album into the CD player.

It didn't take long to get to the 24-hour grocery store two miles away and back to her house. We stripped the top off the frozen orange juice concentrate and ate it with a spoon. It was supposed to intensify the high.

We lay on her front lawn, watching the clouds. I reached for them, curling them between my fingers and stretching them like taffy. The light of the sun oozed across the sky, obscuring the stars and forcing us into an agitated sleep.

We rose late in the afternoon. The muscles of my face and stomach ached from laughing and smiling. Michelle took me to a gothic dance club called Confetti. The minimum age to get in was sixteen, but if you were goth, no one asked.

Never Let Me Go

Goth wasn't just a style of dress, but a state of mind. We wore black, burgundy, purple, and white. We looked like vampires with our pale skin, red lips, and dark eyes. We were suspicious of others and enthralled by the nefarious side of life.

Out on the dance floor, the goths were captivating as they danced with everyone and no one at the same time. Their movements were enigmatic and smooth. They wrapped the shadows around their fingers and it tangled with the mist of their souls. I watched from a corner for a time, then joined Michelle on a side-stage in the main room.

The night breathed its life into me. As the darkness descended upon my mind, I felt free. The dark cooled my skin. It sheltered me from the disapproving, condescending stares of mothers and fathers. Strangers. I was at home when cradled in its arms, swaddled by the stars and moon. There I could rest, secure in my absolution.

```
                    forever done

          i ache with sublime wretchedness
         craving the deprivation of my soul
                death never close enough
               cradled in its loving call
                peace among destruction
                  calm within the storm
       devour my heart's intent and be forever done.
```

The first time I ran away from home was a few weeks before the start of eighth grade. I hid at my friend Ralph's house in downtown Salt Lake City. Ralph was fourteen. He had thin, gangly arms and legs. We shared the mattress on the floor of his basement bedroom.

Two days passed before my mother showed up. It was eight on a Saturday night. The metal screen banged against the doorframe and rattled the glass. Her silhouette darkened the translucent curtains. My hands and knees hit the hardwood, and I scurried under an oak table. I snagged my nylons on a sliver poking up from the floor.

21

Ralph pulled the front door open. "Can I help you?"

Her feet were inches away from me as she stepped through the threshold. The lace tablecloth acted as a mourning veil between us. She mourned the loss of a child and I, the loss of my soul.

"I'm looking for my daughter, Nikki."

"Patrick's sister?"

My mother nodded. Her eyes flicked through the room, lingering here and there. They were shadowed by puffiness, beaten by my betrayal and her own sorrow.

"She was here yesterday," Ralph said. "Do you want to look around?" He pushed the door all the way open, sweeping his arm out.

She shook her head and turned to go, then stopped. "Tell her to come home, if you see her?" She turned a last glance toward the inner shadows of the house and then stepped out the door.

We waited until we were sure she was gone and then got dressed for Confetti.

Ralph and I found some space on the center dance floor and intertwined ourselves with the other goths. My movements slowed with the rhythms of sound. I saw my brother, Patrick, sitting at a table as I moved along the outer edge of the dance floor. He stood to greet two goths who came into the main room.

I continued to dance with Ralph. Spider, a close friend of Patrick's, bent his spindly legs and wove his way onto the floor to join us. Patrick pointed in our direction, and the heads of the other two swiveled along the same plane.

A conversation I had with Patrick a few days earlier surfaced...

The dark in the room was broken by the spark of a lighter until it caught hold of its flame. Patrick lit the candle sitting between us.

"What's the Charade?" I asked. I'd heard the goths whispering about it in coffee shops and in the bathroom at Confetti.

Patrick stared at me, his eyes searching mine. "It's a parallel world."

"It's what?"

He sighed. "Let me try to explain. Souls from the parallel world—*our* world, which is called Saedric—were ripped from their bodies and caught in an energy stream that planted them in *this* world, which is what we call the Charade."

I stared at him, wanting to understand, wanting to be a part of it.

He waved his arms, indicating all that surrounded us. "In this world, we are not what we seem to be. Our souls, trapped within these human vessels, are very old and powerful beings. This world is a false world to us—it's not ours. Saedric is our home."

"Is everyone from Saedric?"

"No, but Brenden and I are not sure how many are here." There was no twitch of a grin at the corner of his narrow lips or his grey-blue eyes.

"How do you know who is?" I said.

"Brenden and I see the strands of the shifting reflection of what exists in Saedric. It's woven into the fabric of this world and must be combed through on the astral plane to reveal who someone truly is. We confirm each other's view of the true identity of those in the Charade."

Patrick's manner of speaking always took on a formal, almost regal air whenever he spoke of the Charade.

"Are you one of them?"

His hand raised to shelter the flame from a breeze trying to claim its life. The fire danced in his pupils. He looked back up at me.

"Yes. Brenden, Michael, Deanna, Shelly, and you."

"Who am I?"

"I can't tell you any more until Brenden has a chance to meet you."

"Why not?"

"Because. You just have to wait."

I rolled my eyes. He was being dramatic and cagey. It was stupid, but whatever. I didn't know what to believe. It was all so unreal. It was difficult to believe, if not impossible.

"When will I know?"

"I'm not sure." He unfolded his arachnid legs.

As I stood, the rough tread of my combat boots caught on my skirt, pulling it down on one side. I clutched at the elastic at my hips. "Are you going to Confetti? Will Brenden be there?"

Spider stroked my cheek, bringing me back to the present. The song had changed to "Sweet Dreams (Are Made of This)" by the Eurythmics, and I continued to dance.

My heart told me it was Brenden sitting at the table with Patrick. "Cry Little Sister" from *The Lost Boys* soundtrack came on next, and I couldn't bear to leave the dance floor, even though I thirsted for answers from Patrick and Brenden.

I became lost in the words of the song. They stripped bare a deep longing within me. An ache ravaged my body with the words. I closed my eyes as the song came to an end. Taking a deep breath, I stepped off the dance floor. All three stood as I approached. I hugged Patrick.

When we parted, he ran his long, bony fingers through his hair. He wore it in a mohawk, but never spiked it up. Instead, he ratted it up in a tangle or combed it sleek to one side. He was tall, six feet and slender, but always walked with a slight hunch.

"Brenden and Michael," he said, "this is my sister, Nikki."

Brenden was the leader of the vampire coven, the Black Hand. Michael was the protector of the Black Hand, keeping its secrets and members safe. He straightened his white button-down shirt. The cuffs hung open, too small for his wrists. Michael was more gutter punk than goth.

Brenden took my hand. "I know your brother well. He is a brother to me, too." His chin-length, raven hair framed his narrow face. He was two years older than I was, and six inches taller.

Michael acknowledged my presence with a nod of his shaved head. He cocked his head as his eyes surveyed my body. He was older than us all, in his early twenties.

Brenden pulled me into the harbor of his arms. My mind was cleared by the scent of clove that clung to him. My cheek brushed the shoulder of his tailed suitcoat.

"You are as familiar to me as a child of my flesh," Brenden said. His pale cheeks pulled his lips into a sardonic grin as he turned toward Patrick. "You've kept her from me, brother."

He held me out at arm's length, cocking his head to look me over.

Patrick stared at me, not responding.

Brenden raised an eyebrow and smiled. "Interesting."

A shadow closed around Patrick's sharp features, contradicting the flare of excitement in Brenden's dark eyes.

A single pace behind Brenden, Michael stood like a Marine on duty, scrutinizing the mass of bodies moving in the dim club lighting. Brenden released me with a graceful wave of his arm.

"But I have—" I said.

"We'll talk later."

I danced and watched Brenden until it was closing time. I lost sight of him for a moment, and he was gone. Patrick caught up with me and shook his head back and forth as I jumped into the car of someone I'd just met.

"You need to come home and let Mom know you're safe."

I returned to my parents' house the following day. My mother grounded me, but she couldn't enforce it when she worked fourteen hours a day. We communicated very little. If we spoke, it was always the same questions from her and the same answers from me.

What have I done?

Nothing.

Why do you hate me?

I don't.

When she was home, I sat in my bedroom closet and listened to music. The blackness offered me the space to be anywhere but there. I rolled Brenden's words around in my mind, wanting to know what he saw.

Over the next few days, Patrick helped me to understand the Charade and my place within it. Understanding it was critical to understanding who I was. From the outside, the Charade appeared to be a cult. Those with a role in the Charade had lived an entire life on our parallel plane of existence.

In Saedric, there were many races: dark elves, vampires, werewolves, and humans—to name a few. Blood feuds raged between the races in Saedric. The worst was the feud between the vampires and the werewolves. The relationships between the races in Saedric carried over into this world and had an ongoing influence on our interactions with one another.

The gothic way of life proved to be the most accepting of our situation. It allowed us—all those involved in the Charade—to hide in the shadows and to perform the magical ceremonies which would get us back home.

My knowledge of the Charade came from Patrick, Brenden, and my own recollection of our lives in Saedric. Memories came like pieces of a puzzle to each of us, and together we formed the whole.

In the world of Saedric, I was the princess of the dark elves and heir to the dark elven throne. During a hunt for a rogue dark elf mage, Brenden and I fell in love. Our love was forbidden by my people, because he was both human and vampire. To complicate matters, Brenden was married and loyal to his wife... in a sense.

During a battle with the dark elf mage, I was run through with a blade and mortally wounded. Brenden couldn't bear to watch me die, so he gave me a vampire existence against Michael's advice.

My mother, the queen, banished me from the dark elven realm. I sought solace with Brenden and his vampire coven. My brother and sister followed me, rather than stand by my mother's draconian following of the dark elven laws. My banishment, along with my siblings' rejection of my mother, caused a rift among the dark elves. I was the only one who could reunite them.

In addition to the turmoil between dark elves and vampires, the longest-standing war in our world was between the vampires and the werewolves. No one recalled when or why it began.

Never Let Me Go

The wolves and vampires continuously hunted one another, and the transfer of souls to this new world had not diminished that hatred. In fact, the wolves were the greatest threat to our coven in this world. Brenden and Michael were constantly on the lookout for them, and cautioned me on a regular basis to not be alone in the city.

We could not disclose our identity to anyone outside the coven. If the wolves were to destroy one of us here, the rest of us might never be able to return to Saedric.

To outsiders, our belief in the Charade may have bordered on the absurd. To us, it was everything.

```
             to be or not to be

             is their god my god?
          do they see the same as i see?
        will they ever live the life i lead?
      does their god cry as he watches them die?
          souls ripped from their corpses,
    just whisked away, for not accepting me, just
                    rejecting me
   they will never understand that all we want to do
                      is be.
```

Nicole Lowe

In 1994, 2.8 million children ran away from home in the United States.

chapter two

McCartni's mother picks at the chipped pink nail polish adorning her fingers. Maxwell slides unobtrusively toward her from his bailiff's post and places a box of tissues within her reach.

"When did you first begin using illegal drugs, Ms. Hardy?" I ask.

Her eyes shift to Carl, McCartni's attorney. He arches an eyebrow and she looks away. Her attorney looks up from his yellow pad of paper and gives her a small smile.

"When I was thirteen."

"What were you using then?"

"Marijuana and alcohol, mostly."

"Anything else?"

"Well, I used LSD a few times, and ecstasy after I turned sixteen."

"Who were you using with?"

A wry smile pulls the left corner of her mouth up. "My mom." Her tongue twists the words in concert with her smile.

Judge Cruz raises an eyebrow. It's one of the few reactions anyone gets from him. Only the attorneys see it. Sabrina is watching me, but gets no reaction for her efforts. Mothers providing drugs to their children and friends is nothing new to me.

"And when did you start using methamphetamine?"

Once again, her eyes rest on Jake.

"A few months before my son was born. I knew you guys would come take him away, so I just didn't care."

"Have you tried to stop using?"

She swings her head around to me. Her hair slices through the air. "Of course I've tried. But it's not like you can just stop. It's a disease, you know. I've been to drug treatment three times."

"Have you ever completed the programs?"

"I finished the first one and was clean for six months."

"Why did you start again?"

She cocks her head to the side, considering her answer before she delivers it.

"You can't stay clean when everyone around you is using."

I pick up my pen and scribble on my question sheet. Without looking up at her, I ask, "Why didn't you find other people to be around?"

She flings her next answer at me like a dart. "Would you just leave your family?"

I don't take the bait. She continues.

Nicole Lowe

```
"Everyone in my family, other than my sister,
is an addict. I could get anything I wanted. I
tried to get away, but I had nowhere to go
besides the streets. Do you think I should have
lived on the streets as a teenager?"
I don't respond.
```

Rosa had cornrows sweeping back from her round face. We had a common friend, Hunter, and we'd been crashing on his floor the last few nights. I was on the run again. Rosa and I walked to the 7-Eleven on 300 East, asking for spare change from strangers along the way. We needed money for cigarettes and drinks.

We were a collision of two worlds, Rosa and I; her with chocolate skin, cut-off shorts, and a pink tank top; me with pale skin, black leggings, and a black blazer. Rosa was just another kid on the street. She sat on the sidewalk outside the 7-Eleven with her knees pulled to her chest. I stood with my shoulder pressed against the brick wall above her as we tried to get the last little bit of money we needed.

A black man in his twenties strutted past with his hand on the waist of his sagging jeans. He let out a low whistle. "Damn."

Rosa snapped her thighs together. "You got five dollars?"

"You show me a little more of what you got, and I'll give you five dollars," he said, running his hand over his shaved head.

Laughing, she pulled her panties and shorts to the side, exposing her vagina for him to see.

"Mmm-mmm, very nice." He handed her a crumpled wad of money from his pocket.

We got our cigarettes and started walking toward the hotel where Rosa's boyfriend was staying. "Hey, don't tell anyone about that. I'm not like that, you know," Rosa said, staring at the cracks in the sidewalk. Her foot propelled a small rock into oncoming traffic.

I shrugged, saying nothing. I got smokes and a Dr. Pepper. I didn't care what she did to get them.

"He's a cheating bastard and I'm done with him," she said as we walked.

Rosa's boyfriend was staying on the north side with another girl. His Cadillac was parked in the shadow of the LDS temple in front of a shady motel. We crossed the street to the motel. Rosa flicked her knife open and slammed it into his front tire. The air rushed out with a loud *pshhh*.

She clicked the knife closed and tossed it to me. I slammed it into the rear tire and tossed it back. Rosa's knife traced the sun's glow down the side of the Caddy. People stopped and stared at us. A man in a brown tweed jacket swayed on his feet, fell, and puked in the gutter. He stayed down. Men in black and blue suits blew by, one after another, on their way to Temple Square, pretending none of us existed—their minds locked on the celestial kingdom promised to them by their god. I stopped listening to Rosa, but she babbled on and on as we walked back to Hunter's.

I sat in Hunter's room and watched the world from the bare wood-framed window. Headlights brightened and revolved into taillights, one after another. I lit another cigarette and picked at the chipped paint on the sill. I blew the smoke against the glass. It mushroomed and dispersed.

Hunter was laying with his head in my lap. His blond roots were showing at his scalp, while the length remained raven's feathers. My finger traced his lips and jawline. He smiled up at me. The opposing octaves of Depeche Mode's "Master and Servants" played in the background. We fell asleep and Rosa was gone when we awoke.

It was the last time I saw Rosa. Everyone I met, especially on the streets, slipped below the surface or faded into the shadows. Nameless faces, each with their own story of why they were out there. Some were searching. Others were escaping. Most were lost in a tangle of both threads. If you loosen one, it tightens the other.

At my parents' house, my mother asked, "What's wrong? What have I done to chase you away from me?"

"Nothing," I mumbled, not meeting her eyes, trying to slip past her to avoid more questions.

She didn't ground me this time. Instead, she asked me to promise to stay home and go to school.

"I'll try, Mom," I said.

I kept my head low at school. I didn't like to draw attention to myself and most everyone ignored me, teachers and students. I was failing all my classes. My teachers never said anything to me about how much school I missed or my missing assignments. I stayed for a week, long enough to tell myself I tried, just as I told her I would.

I left school at lunch and caught the bus to Shelly's. Shelly and her pot-smoking dad lived in Rose Park. Her dad had restrictions on when we could hang out: after 4 p.m. and weekends. He let me stay with them once or twice a month, but he thought I was a bad influence on Shelly. He knew my school attendance was lacking and suspected marijuana was not the thing that poisoned my veins. He was right on both accounts.

Shelly and I were often mistaken for twin sisters. In Saedric, we were sisters. Our faces didn't really look alike, but everything else did—hair length and color, height, and build. The same clothing style and makeup design. Her eyes were green. Mine were hazel. She had deep acne scars. I didn't.

Once we were out the door, Shelly opened her hand. Four little squares sat in the center of her palm. We each placed two hits on our tongue and climbed on the bus to Confetti. We were high by the time we strolled through the glass doors and down the black-walled corridor, where we found our vampire coven, the Black Hand, lounging around the fireplace.

Brenden sat reclined on the burgundy couch as we crossed the last threshold. Deanna, ever watchful, was at his side. Brenden and Deanna were beautiful. They radiated the presence of an old-world vampire couple—cunning and melodious. Michael, the sentry, was leaning against the wall in mock ease. His eyes followed us as we came in. His solid, lean form towered over the other goths. His worker bees fed him information, which he would then provide to Brenden.

Deanna and Brenden rose as we approached. Deanna wore a striking black and red velvet dress that made her green eyes cut through the dim lighting. Brenden's movements were eloquent. His ruffled sleeves fluttered as he came toward us, motioning for us to go onto the dance floor.

We danced with them while Michael reclined at a table, surveying the crowd. Brenden's hot breath flowed across my neck. His teeth scraped my skin and I tilted my head, inviting his bite. His soft lips pressed just below my ear before he glided toward Deanna, circling her and biting her neck from behind as well. He beckoned me toward them.

Deanna's eyes narrowed and I turned to Shelly, running my hands along her upstretched arms and through her hair. We laced our fingers together and twisted into each other's arms. Back to back, we moved with the rhythm of the music. We took a few steps in opposite directions, then turned to face one another, sliding our feet in crisscross pattern over the smooth floor until our bodies pressed together.

Brenden left the dance floor, and Deanna drifted over to dance with Shelly and me. The heat of their bodies and the smell of their perfume enveloped me. Deanna slid in behind me. Her hands glided along the curve of my body and grasped at me.

Michael materialized from the dark, standing over us. He whispered to Deanna, but his eyes never left mine. She turned to me, smiled, and slipped through the bodies after Brenden. Michael's fingers brushed my sleeve as he turned away. I watched him stalk off the dance floor, and I turned back to Shelly.

We danced, lost in the music, until closing time. Brenden, Deanna, and Michael had already left. Shelly and I caught a ride downtown with some Confetti regulars and walked the last few blocks to Gary's, the guy who sold her the LSD.

Gary lived in a red-brick, three-story apartment building a block down from the Cathedral of the Madeleine. We buzzed the door and waited.

His voice crackled over the speaker. "Who the hell is it?"

"Shelly."

The door buzzed open and we climbed the three flights to his apartment. We laughed and made fun of him on the way up, repeating his words in our best "Gary" voice. He opened the door just as we reached up to knock.

He was in his late thirties, about six feet tall. Gangly arms and legs, receding hairline, and thin, patchy brown hair. He waved us inside, stuck his head into the hallway, glanced both ways, and closed the door. The deadbolt hammered into place.

"It's still cool if we crash here, right?" Shelly asked.

"Of course," he said. He bowed with a flourish of his hand. "You ladies hungry or want a drink?" His smile exposed the black gaps where teeth should have been.

It was a one-bedroom apartment. A dusty bookcase full of CDs and movies hovered next to the door. A dingy couch and chair squatted in the living room. There was a small, metal dining table and three chairs in the kitchen. The bathroom and bedroom were down a short hall. The institution-white walls were barren. A lamp stood in the corner, casting deep shadows across the room.

"What do you have?" I asked.

Gary was bent over, looking in the fridge. "Vodka cranberry, bloody marys, screwdrivers, whatever you want."

Shelly set her gothbox on the arm of the couch. "Vodka cranberry for me."

"Water," I said.

His beady eyes peered at me over the door. "Water? Really."

"I've been dancing with my boyfriend. I need some water."

Shelly rolled her eyes, but said nothing. I didn't have a boyfriend. He closed the fridge, mixed Shelly's drink, and got me some tap water. He handed it to me with a smirk, then sat on the couch and patted the cushion next to him. "Have a seat. You girls must be tired from... dancing."

I remained leaning against the far wall.

Shelly sat next to him on the couch. He brushed her stray hair out of her face. My stomach tightened. I sipped the water and set the glass on the counter. I didn't want to stay here. I didn't want to sleep here.

Gary went into the bathroom. A lighter flicked three times, he coughed, and something metallic clattered on the linoleum.

I glanced at the bathroom door and took the few steps over to Shelly. "We should leave."

She glared at me. "Stop being paranoid."

The bathroom door opened. Gary ran his hand up my back and gently tugged on the end of my hair as he passed.

"Come sit with us," he said in his silken voice.

I sat on the chair in the far corner of the room. I wasn't hallucinating anymore, but the electricity of the acid still ran beneath my skin.

Shelly talked about dancing at Confetti and told him how nice it was of him to let us crash.

"Oh, it's not any trouble," he said, smiling. "Do you want another drink?"

She handed him her glass.

He stood, looked over at me, and raised his eyebrows.

I pointed to my glass on the counter. "I'm good, thanks."

While he was in the kitchen mixing Shelly's drink, I waved to her and mouthed the words, "We need to go." She frowned and shook her head. He came back and sat close to Shelly, practically on her lap.

He handed her the drink and rested his hand on her thigh. "You two are so beautiful."

I got up, walked across the room, and locked Shelly's hand in mine. "I need to use the bathroom."

Shelly tripped over her own feet two or three times on the way, and was laughing by the time I got her into the bathroom and shut the door. My foot slid on a blackened spoon. I kicked it. Air tinged with a chemical taste burned in my lungs.

"We're leaving. Where is your gothbox?"

She was laughing so hard she had to sit down on the toilet. Taking her by the hand, I opened the door. Gary was hovering in the hallway, blocking our path.

"Where are you going, Beautiful? If you two are into each other, I can just watch."

35

"We're leaving," I said, and moved toward him.

"I think you two owe me a fuck." He reached for my arm.

I ducked under and pulled Shelly along with me. She was quiet now and just trying not to fall over herself as I dragged her toward the door. I scanned the room for her gothbox but didn't see it. I kept moving to the door.

"I can't believe this!" Gary said.

The deadbolt turned in my fingers and I reached for the doorknob. Shelly pulled against my grip. I looked back. Gary had taken hold of her arm. I took two steps toward him, grabbed his arm, and sank my nails into his flesh.

"Go fuck yourself," I said.

He released his hold on Shelly and I hurried her out the door, down the stairs, and out of the building.

A few blocks away, we slipped into the courtyard of a burnt-orange stone Presbyterian church encircled by a black iron fence. Shelly lay her head in my lap, and I stroked her hair until she fell asleep. I caught myself drifting off and bit my lower lip to stay awake. We were going to have to go back for her gothbox. Brenden would not be pleased if he found out.

The glow of the sun stretched, devouring the night sky, and a yellow sliver crested the mountains.

Shelly woke, stretching. "Did you sleep?"

I shook my head.

We walked deeper into the city. We passed the LDS temple. Women and men were milling around in suits with name tags; Sister this and Brother that. I stared at them and they looked away. The temple's granite spires pricked the sky. The golden angel Moroni with his trumpet looked down upon the city from the highest.

We continued down the double-wide sidewalk along Main Street, past the department store windows that lined the street. The buildings acted like curtains, concealing the mountains and all but a slender strip of soft blue sky above our heads.

We found Brenden, Deanna, and Michael at Grounds for Coffee. We just called it Grounds. Shelly began telling Deanna what happened at Gary's. Michael and Brenden ceased their discussion to listen.

"It's your duty as coven leader to go with us to reclaim Shelly's gothbox and teach Gary not to mess with your coven," Deanna told Brenden.

"It has all my crystals, Brenden," Shelly pleaded.

Brenden looked at Michael, who nodded and said, "Why not?" A slight smile came to his thin lips.

Shelly buzzed the door of the apartment building. Gary's muffled voice came over the speaker.

"Who the hell is it?"

"Shelly."

"That bitch of a friend with you?"

"It's just me."

The door buzzed to let us in.

We climbed up the stairs. The door to Gary's apartment was slightly ajar, waiting for Shelly. Michael and Brenden went in first. We heard Gary tripping over stuff and swearing. We waited a second, then Brenden invited us to come in.

Michael's hand was around Gary's throat. Gary was stretched on tiptoe, his back against the wall. His boxers hung on his knobby hips, and his stomach extended and retracted. Michael had a menacing jack-o-lantern smile lighting his face. Brenden pulled the fridge open and disappeared behind the door. He emerged with a box of pizza. He pulled a slice from the box and took a bite as he wandered over to where Gary hung on the wall.

"You've been messing with my girls. My coven."

Gary rattled his head in the negative as Michael lifted him an inch higher. I slid up on the counter, swinging my legs and staring at Gary, who was averting his eyes.

Shelly found her gothbox behind the couch in the living room. I slid off the counter. Deanna spit on Gary as we walked to the door. Michael released Gary and he crumpled to the floor. Brenden's black combat boot connected with his stomach. Gary curled into the fetal position, his hands over his head.

"Don't ever look at them again," Brenden said through clenched teeth, and kicked him again. Deanna took Shelly by the hand and walked out. I followed behind them. We heard more blows and scrambling over furniture, and then it was quiet.

Michael and Brenden strolled out and closed the door behind them, pizza in hand.

When I first became a part of the gothic scene in downtown Salt Lake, I was quickly absorbed by the Black Hand. I still maintained acquaintances on the fringe, much to Brenden's displeasure. It exposed me to danger from the wolves, so he said. The people on the fringe of the goth scene were usually drug addicts living on the streets. They knew we used, and we knew where to find drugs on the street. Most of us only used recreationally. It wasn't a daily thing like it was for others.

Misfit, who was in her early twenties, was one such acquaintance. Unlike my coven family, I had no loyalty to those on the fringe, and they were not a part of the Charade. I didn't like or dislike Misfit. She was a source of entertainment when there was nothing better. She was useful when I needed an adult with identification. Sad and shallow, I know.

I sat on a grey concrete planter beneath a tree outside of the Crossroads Mall. Nordstrom's windows reflected my image in the glass. Misfit sat on the sidewalk, frizzy-haired and twitching from withdrawals. She picked at the freckles and scabs that marked her skin. She twisted her tangled, dirt-brown hair around her finger. Her t-shirt was discolored from days of wear, and sagged at the neckline.

She glanced at me and I gave her a crooked smile. She stood and took a few steps in my direction. A middle-aged white man in a grey suit cut her off.

"Excuse me," she said as he nearly knocked her on her pudgy ass.

Misfit was an addict who would do anything for a fix. Crystal meth was her drug of choice, but she used anything she could get.

He turned to her. "I'm sorry."

I looked up with a cigarette pressed between my black lips. No one ever said sorry. They usually just ignored you.

"Do you have any spare change?" Misfit said. "I'm trying to get money for food."

He smiled. The sunlight ricocheted off his bald head. "Why don't you come have dinner with me? I have a hotel room out by the airport."

I flicked my lighter once, twice, and it ignited.

He wanted some female companionship, and in exchange he would give her a couple of hundred dollars. He took a step toward Misfit and said something I couldn't hear. She nodded her head, the cadence increasing as he spoke. He pulled a business card out of his breast pocket, along with a sleek black pen. He scribbled on the back, wrapped it in cash, and handed it to her. He glanced up and down the street at the apathetic faces floating along, then darted to the bus stop and stepped on the first bus that pulled to the curb.

Misfit bounced over to me. "What you doing?"

Smoke rose from my mouth and nose. "Nothing."

"You want to come with me to meet that guy? I'll give you some money."

I shrugged. "How much?"

"Twenty?"

"Fifty."

She pursed her lips and nodded her head once. I sprang to my feet and flicked my cigarette onto the otherwise clean sidewalk.

A couple of hours later, we called a taxi and rode out to the hotel. The room was nothing special, two queen-size beds with faded quilts and a TV. Stale cigarette smoke permeated the room and yellowing blinds hung in the window.

He ordered Chinese food for dinner, which mixed with the smell of the room and created a nauseating potpourri. Misfit took a shower. I sat watching TV. I didn't speak a word and picked at the food on the paper plate. He fingered the remote and paced the room.

When Misfit came out, he told her about the conference he was in town for and dropped his little bomb. His wife had left him. He wanted sex. Misfit was just getting the drift of what he was saying, and turning the idea over in her mind. She was so slow. Addicts accepted money before they knew what the exchange rate was and whether they were willing to pay.

He excused himself to the bathroom.

She moved in close to me. The thick fragrance of hotel lotion threatened to choke me out. "I know he wants me to fuck him."

I grinned. "Figured that out, huh?"

She gave me the *shut the fuck up* look. "I've never had sex for money. I'm not sure I can do it."

"It's easy," I said. "You just spread your legs. I'm sure as shit not having sex with *that*."

She stared at me. "What are you going to do if I have sex with him?"

"I'll go for a walk." I wiggled my fingers in a walking motion and laughed.

He came out of the bathroom wearing Fruit of the Loom tighty-whities. His hairy belly hung over the overstretched elastic. Tufts of hair adorned his chest and back, and his skinny white legs stuck out the bottom of his barely-visible briefs. I looked at Misfit with my eyebrows raised.

"Oh shit, I can't do this," she said.

He looked back and forth between us, both eyes getting wider with each turn of the head.

She grabbed my arm with one hand and money out of the man's wallet with the other. She led me out the door. We walked to a hotel down the street and called a taxi to take us downtown. Worst of all, the man didn't have much money. There was about eight dollars left after the cab ride.

"You owe me smokes," I said, snatching the pack of cigarettes out of her hand.

Every year, over 1.2 million students drop out of high school in the United States alone. That's one student every twenty-six seconds—or seven thousand a day.

chapter three

The fact Sabrina had no way to get free from the drug community was no surprise to anyone in the courtroom. Especially me. Having nowhere to go and needing to get away is a constant tug-o-war in the lives of many addicts and street youth.

"Ms. Hardy, when was the last time you were employed?"

"When I was sixteen."

"Where did you work?"

She ran her fingers through her hair. "McDonald's."

"How long did you work there?"

"Two months."

"Did you graduate from high school?"

"I got pregnant and Jackson was going to take care of us." She rolled her eyes.

"Who is Jackson?"

"The father of my children."

"Both of them?"

"Uh, yeah." She looks at me like I'm an idiot. "We're married. Of course he's the father of my children."

"When did you get married?"

"My mom signed the papers so I could marry him when I was sixteen."

"Was he taking care of you?"

She laughs. "Nope."

"Why weren't you working?"

"No one will pay a high school dropout more than minimum wage, and I made more money on state assistance than I could by working for minimum wage."

"Why didn't you go back to school?"

She shrugs.

"Ms. Hardy, you need to answer aloud for the record," Judge Cruz says.

"I didn't have time."

"What were you doing with your time?"

"Helping my mom and watching Jackson's other kids."

That gets a raised eyebrow from Carl, the guardian ad litem.

My skin itched to rid itself of the infection that was me. I hated everyone, but mostly myself. I was disgusted and appalled by the world and all that crawled upon its surface. Some said it was a nightmare to fall asleep and not wake up. To me, that would have been a dream come true.

September brought the beginning of eighth grade. It was three weeks before my fourteenth birthday. At school, I floated through the halls in a trance, one foot in front of the other. Heads followed my movement. Tongues whispered. I slid into a desk at the back of a room. My pen roamed the paper. I turned the combination lock left, right, left. Books in. Books out. The cold yellow metal door closed with a click. I sat among the skaters and mods at lunch. I watched them eat. I heard their words. But nothing registered. I was not part of their world.

I spent hours each day in the counseling center. When asked, I said I was waiting to see Tina, my counselor. If she wasn't in, I sat in her office, so still that the motion lights turned off.

Tina had seen the cuts on my wrists and legs. She wanted to help me and tried to get me to talk to her.

"Everything is fine at home," I would say, because I didn't exist. "My classes? No. They're not too difficult. My teachers? Sure, I like them just fine."

They didn't bother me. I didn't bother them. I never opened up to Tina. This went on for two weeks. I even showed up to about half of my classes.

I didn't want help. I didn't care what happened or who it hurt. I was leaving this world as soon as Patrick and Brenden figured out how to get us home. It was time to run again.

———

I sat stiff at the back of the bus, lost in the conversation I'd had with my mother that morning.

"Will you be home for your birthday party, if I plan one?" she asked.

"I'll be here," I said.

"Promise?"

"Yes, Mom, and I'll stop staying out all night."

She should have known it was all lies, like every time before. When the words fell from my lips, I knew they were a lie.

Nicole Lowe

Two days later, I jumped into Hunter's arms and wrapped myself around his slender frame as he walked into Paisley Park. I hadn't been home during those two days.

"Happy birthday," he whispered in my ear. My heart's pace increased with the touch of his lips and warm breath on my neck.

"I brought you something." He set me on the ground.

"You are my gift," I said.

He painted his face like Jason Lee in *The Crow*. His chin-length, black hair fell forward around his thin face when he bowed. He handed me a 44-ounce cup with a grin and sparkling blue eyes.

"What's in it?" I asked.

"Dr. Pepper and Everclear."

Despite my promise to my mother, my fourteenth birthday was spent with all the goths, street kids, and gutter punks. We congregated at a grass-free red-brick park known as Paisley Park. Red leaves rustled in the autumn wind. A dried-up fountain provided seats. The sounds of cars bounced between the buildings, hemming in the park. A narrow alleyway allowed quick departure should unwanted guests arrive. The park was about an eighth of a city block. It was directly south of the Crossroads Mall. The park was the city's attempt to create some green space outside of Temple Square. What it actually created was a communion space for us street kids.

Alcohol hadn't saturated my brain in a while, and the Everclear burned my nostrils and warmed my stomach. My body swayed with a wind only I could feel, and walking was an impossibly complex task of movement and balance.

We sat on the sidewalk in front of the mall. It was twilight by the time I had a moment of awareness. What was this sparkling moment of clarity? I was going to vomit. All the food I'd eaten surged up my throat and splattered, decorating the ground.

Downtown Mom pulled her long, silver hair into a ponytail. She wrapped her chubby, wrinkled hand around my bicep and hoisted me up from the sidewalk. I leaned into her, a wave of icy sweat breaking from my skin.

She looked at Hunter. "This is your mess. You clean it up."

Downtown Mom tried to keep an eye on us younger ones on the street. She knew Hunter would take care of me, and that I would get them all busted if I stayed there much longer. Shelly led me, shivering, into the Crossroads food court bathroom. Hunter followed and waited outside. The cool water brought my mind back and I spat into the sink.

Hunter guided my floppy body to the apartment he shared with his on- and off-again girlfriend, Kim. He led me by my hand to the bathroom and turned on the shower.

"Coffee?"

I nodded and started pulling off my clothing. He closed the door and I got into the water. I stood there with the world spinning, letting the warm water pelt me in the face and run down my body in little rivers. I turned the tap to ice cold and gasped as it stole my breath. I turned it off and stepped over the side of the tub. The world spun like an out-of-control merry-go-round. I was glad there was nothing left in my stomach.

There was a knock at the door.

"Come in," I said.

Hunter opened the door enough to poke his head through and set the coffee on the sink. A pink towel loosely wrapped my body. He handed me one of his t-shirts and a pair of sweatpants. Our eyes met, but there were no words. He closed the door with a soft click. My stomach sank into my pelvis. I pulled the t-shirt over my head and cinched the sweats around my waist.

I found Hunter lying on the hardwood floor of Kim's bedroom on a bed of blankets and pillows. I climbed between the blankets next to him and looked up at Kim sleeping on the queen bed. She was wrapped in a blue and purple quilt. She breathed, slow and even.

He had his own room at the other end of the apartment. Kim wanted to be with him, but he didn't want to be with her. Not right now.

"Why are we in here?" I whispered.

"She has nightmares if I'm not with her."

Nicole Lowe

Hunter grew up in California. He was twenty-three when we met. When he was growing up, his mother sold him to couples who were unable to have children. She used the money to support her heroin addiction. The couples always brought him back because he would bite, hit, and start fires. He said that sometimes she would sell him for other reasons, too. He eventually became addicted to heroin, just like her.

He took my face between the palms of his hands, his blue eyes drilling into mine. "Promise me you will never use heroin."

"I promise."

"It makes you feel more amazing than I can describe. It starts in your center and wraps you in a blanket of bliss. It's all I have," he said. "But you can be anything. You're beautiful and intelligent. Don't get stuck in all of this. From the moment I first saw you, I have burned for you, but I am not going to have sex with you unless it is what you want. Is it what you want, honestly?"

When he asked, and I stopped to think about it, I wasn't sure.

He nodded his head. "You can be so much more than what I am. More than all of us."

We lay in the dark, listening to the song "Return to Innocence" by Enigma.

"This is your song." He ran his fingertips over my face. I closed my eyes. "Don't get stuck. Promise me you won't get stuck."

"I promise." I drifted off to sleep.

My eyelids fluttered open to the burning sun peering in through the west windows. Crawling out of the makeshift bed, I felt like I had weights around my ankles, wrists, and neck. The apartment was empty. The ceiling boards creaked from the feet overhead. Muffled voices were in the hall outside the apartment.

On my way to the bathroom, I shoved a handful of Frosted Mini-Wheats into my mouth. I glanced at my reflection. Not pretty. I scrubbed the remnants of last night from my face, redid my makeup, and pulled my hair up in a tight bun. I left my long bangs

Never Let Me Go

hanging down, framing my face. I stuffed another handful of cereal into my mouth and headed out the door.

I smoked my last cigarette and rummaged through my gothbox for money as I walked downtown. There was one store downtown that sold cigarettes to minors. Not that I didn't have friends who would buy them for me, but I liked to do things on my own. I stopped at the corner market on State and Market and bought a pack of Camel Wides.

The gutter punks, with their ripped-up jeans and studded leather jewelry, clogged the entrance to Paisley Park. I pushed through and found a few goths. Among them were Shelly and Michelle. As it got closer to dark, we moved to the front of the mall and sat in the shadow of Nordstrom's on the sidewalk, the scene of my sidewalk art from the day before. The black glass of the storefront provided a mirror for fixing makeup.

It was Saturday. We stood waiting for the 8:15 p.m. bus to Confetti. I heard my name and looked up. It was my mother. She hobbled toward me.

"Oh shit," Shelly said. "Run!"

I got up and walked into the mall. I started to jog and my mother started to run after me, calling my name. She had multiple herniated disks and had her lower back fused. Walking caused her pain; running must have been excruciating. Why wouldn't she just stop?

My palms hit the glass doors of the food court and I pushed through. I slowed when I saw the cop car parked on the curb. My mother was still behind me, running, tears falling down her face. She was shouting my name. When she saw the cop, she yelled for help and he stopped me. She finally stopped running. Some of my friends had followed.

"That's my daughter!" she shouted. "She's a runaway."

I glanced back to see her limping across the road.

The cold metal cuffs clicked around my wrists.

"Hang tight while I talk with your mom," the officer said.

I slouched in the back seat as the metal dug into my bones. I folded my hands into themselves and stripped the cuffs off.

47

Nicole Lowe

Shelly's voice was muffled by the windows, but I could still understand. She was telling the cop that my mother abused me, and that was why I was running away. I knew she was just trying to help.

No lies, I decided. My mother didn't need any trouble. She hadn't done anything wrong, other than produce me. She was a good mother. She wanted what was best for me. I just... I didn't know. There was something wrong with me.

The officer opened the back door. He stood in front of me with one meaty hand on each side of the doorframe.

"So, tell me what's going on?"

"I ran away from home and she found me," I said.

"Why?"

"Because I don't want to be at home."

He raised his unibrow. "Why?"

"I just don't. I don't really know. I just can't be there."

"Your friends say you're abused. That true?"

"No. I just can't be there."

"I see," he said. "Well, you can either go home with your mom, or I can take you to Youth Services, and you and your mom can get some help working this out. What do you want to do?"

"Youth Services," I mumbled.

He shut the door and went to talk with my mother.

He drove me to Youth Services and checked me in. They gave me an itchy, thin grey blanket and guided me to a room with two sets of metal bunk beds. I climbed up onto the top bunk's flat mattress and lay down. It smelled musty and old.

Sinking beneath the surface of my own thoughts, I replayed the night in my mind. Why did I run? I didn't know. She had never done anything to hurt me. It was stupid. I should've just gone with her and then left again tomorrow. Now I had to deal with Youth Services bullshit.

Shelly shouldn't have told the officer that my mother abused me. She didn't, and I didn't want anyone to think she did. My mother tried to do everything she could to help me. She gave me everything she possibly could. She had to work a lot because she had credit card debt from overspending on my siblings and me.

Never Let Me Go

Why did I make her run? It must have hurt her. What was wrong with me? Why would I hurt the only person who still gave a fuck what happened to me? What's worse, I knew this would do nothing to change what I was doing. I couldn't stop. The running, the drugs, not going to school, having sex—I wasn't going stop any of it.

I lay there in the dark, smiling. I hated myself.

```
                         empty

         alone in a world far from my own
    awoke in a room with no exit, no windows, no hope
                    of getting out
      only walls as friends, not even any dreams to
                discover or stars to wish on
     no sound. not even falling rain. crying in a
               corner takes nothing away
          do i even exist? am i really even here?
```

The next morning, I melted into a grey-green armchair tucked in the corner of a therapist's office. It was the only space in the room not bathed in sunlight. My mother sat in a similar chair across the table from the therapist.

"Hi, I'm Martha. I'm the therapist assigned to work with you all. I'd like to start by getting some family history, if that's alright with you?"

"Where should I start?" my mother asked.

I said nothing.

"Wherever you'd like." A pad of yellow paper sat in front of Martha, and she began scratching her pen across it as my mother spilled out our story.

"Okay." My mother shifted in her chair. Still hurting from last night, I imagined. "Kurt and I have been married since we were eighteen. We met in high school. He entered the Air Force and we were living at Mountain Home Air Force Base in Idaho when Patrick and Nikki were born. I wanted to be a stay-at-home mom, but I've always worked. After my first child was stillborn, I was told

I couldn't have any children. So, Patrick was a gift when he arrived. Nikki was a wonderful surprise. Patrick is fourteen months older than her. Our other daughter, Kara, is four years younger. We moved back home to Utah on Nikki's first birthday."

Their voices faded to the back of my mind like some intrusive, hovering fog. As a child, I believed I was able to achieve anything I set my mind to. I was not sure what happened to that little girl, but she died. She fell asleep one night, and I woke up in her place.

The change in voice sucked me back to the therapist's office.

"Any drug or alcohol use with you and your husband?"

"No, none."

"Tell me about Nikki's development." Martha glanced at me in the corner. I met her eyes, my face expressionless.

"She did everything early. We never had any concerns about her." My mother continued tossing out facts, waiting for Martha to offer some insight or new revolutionary fix for whatever they decided was my condition.

"She hated to be swaddled. I tried to wrap her in blankets because Patrick loved to be wrapped really tight, but she would kick and scream her little head off. She and Patrick have always been close. They had their own language. He would have to tell me what she was saying. She walked when she was ten months old. She has always made her own way in the world. She was defiant from the moment she could talk, telling me 'you can't make me cry' when she was in trouble, even as the tears spilled over her face."

"And as she got older?"

I stared out the window, the heat of my breath fogging it. I cleared a line with my index finger and watched as the remaining fog faded. It wasn't a sole event that had made my world dark. It was a rapid descent of growing comprehension, based on comparing my actual experiences in the world to what my family and other institutions had scrawled on the steamed-up glass. Words like *love conquers all* and *people are inherently good and kind*. When the words faded from the glass, I began to challenge their beliefs—and my challenges shattered their beliefs, without resistance.

They were still talking.

"When we moved back to Salt Lake from Idaho, we lived with Kurt's father. Kurt's mother had passed away a few months before Nikki was born. Kurt and his siblings were raised in the Mormon Church, and we've raised our children in the Church too. When Nikki was three, she developed an incredible belief in the Church. Just like her Grandma, Mildred. Mildred, Kurt's mother, had an unwavering faith in the Church. She would take in strangers off the street and make sure they were fed and had somewhere to go before she was through with them. She had foster children and adoptive children. She was the true model of unconditional love. Nikki would run around the house singing 'Jesus Wants Me for a Sunbeam' for days after church. She would tell anyone she met that she was a child of God."

She paused, waiting for Martha to say something, but she just smiled.

"We have always spent a lot of time with aunts, uncles, and cousins on the weekends. She played softball and danced jazz, tap, and ballet. She was always very active, riding her bike, roller-skating, and building forts with Patrick. She and Kurt used to watch baseball together and play chess. Until she was ten, and then they just didn't do things together anymore."

"How does she do in school?"

My mother looked relieved to have gotten a question. "Nikki has always been an excellent student. Up until this school year, she's gotten straight A's. Her teachers love her."

Martha wrote something in her notebook. "What about friends?"

"She's always had a few close girlfriends who she had sleepovers with. Up until this last year, they all seemed like nice, normal girls. She doesn't hang out with any of them now. I don't know her current friends."

Martha glanced up and asked, "Any history of trauma?"

My mother didn't respond immediately. Instead, they both looked at me. I turned away. They didn't want answers from me, not really. They wouldn't like what I had to say, anyhow. They didn't want to know how I thought of killing myself every day. How I hated not only myself, but them. And how I liked the hate. No, I loved it.

I had become just another pebble at the bottom of the river. I had no value, other than allowing the water to flow around me with as little resistance as possible. I sat at the bottom of the river and the water passed over me. I sat at the bottom of the river and began to drown.

"No," my mother said, "none."

"Is she sexually active?"

"Of course not," my mother said.

I was thirteen when that started.

"No sexual or physical abuse?" Martha asked, her voice quieter.

"No."

"No violence in the home?"

"None."

"Drug use?"

That started at thirteen, too.

My mother's eyes filled with tears. "I don't think so. All this started with Patrick running away, and then she started running too. I don't understand."

Martha slid a blue box of tissues toward her.

We set an appointment for the following week and left. On the drive home, my thoughts wandered the labyrinth of my mind. This darkness inside of me had crept in long ago. At first, when I was eleven or twelve, it only showed up every once in a while, maybe for a day or two at a time. It got longer and darker after that. Now it was what I had become. It was who I was. I loved it. I cherished it. I fed it.

At school the next morning, I caught sight of a goth girl turning the corner in the hall. I was the only goth in my school. She was sitting at the back of my second class. She lifted her head as I slid into the desk beside her.

Never Let Me Go

"Oh my gosh!" a girl in a cheerleader's uniform exclaimed. "Are you two sisters?"

I closed my eyes and breathed. I wanted to punch that bubbly blonde in the teeth. When I opened my eyes, I turned to the goth.

"I'm Nikki."

"Abigail." The word came out with as much feeling as a sunbaked worm on the sidewalk. She pressed her black lips together and picked at the chipped black nail polish on her pinky finger.

"You move here?"

She nodded. "Parents are divorcing. I live with my mom now."

"That'd be nice."

Abigail looked over at me.

"You want to get out of here?" I asked as the teacher walked into the room.

"After class."

When the bell rang, we slipped through the crowded hallways and out the east doors. All of the other students were marching into the cafeteria from the pale-yellow mobile classrooms to get a good spot in the lunch line.

We caught a bus a few blocks from school.

There were a couple of gutter punks lurking around in the food court at Crossroads Mall. Our eyes met and I guided Abigail toward them.

"Brenden and Michael are looking for you," said the girl with hot-pink hair and short, studded black leather skirt.

I shrugged. "You seen Hunter or Shelly?"

"Nope. Brenden and Michael are at Grounds." She looked Abigail up and down.

"Got it."

I took Abigail's hand and we wove our way through the white tables and pushed the glass doors open. I couldn't see anyone in Paisley Park across the street, but we crossed anyway. Two bike cops turned and slid to a halt when they saw Abigail smoking.

"How old are you two ladies?"

"Sixteen," I said. There was no way we were passing for nineteen.

"Is that your only cigarette?" one of them asked.

53

Abigail pulled out the pack of cigarettes rolled into the top of her long black skirt and gave it to them. We needed to work on her honesty and innocence. The bike cop crushed the pack in his hands and threw it away.

"Is that it?" he asked, nodding toward me.

"I don't have any," I said.

"Can we take a look in your backpacks?"

"Sure," Abigail said, handing them her frayed pack. They searched her bag and found nothing. One of the cops reached for mine, and I pulled it away.

"No, you can't search my bag," I said. They looked at one another. And I waited.

"You can go." They mounted their bikes and continued on their way.

"Fucking pigs. Let's go."

We continued through the back alley. Abigail was a step behind me. We walked around the corner and ran into a dealer I knew. He twitched as he spoke. He had acid, three dollars a hit.

I swung my pack around to my front and unzipped it. "Will you trade two hits for a bottle of vodka and a pack of cigarettes?" I said.

Abigail's eyes flashed wide, then looked behind us. He made the trade. I gave Abigail a new pack of cigarettes out of my carton.

"Seriously, Abby, you can't let them push you around like that." I offered her one of the hits of acid. She shook her head no and asked where we were going next. She didn't want to take any acid, and I didn't pressure her. I wasn't a pusher. Drug use needed to be a conscious decision.

We walked a few more blocks to the Gallivan Center, another park. No one was there, so we went to Grounds. Michael and Brenden weren't there. Abigail and I sat and drank coffee. I didn't want to see either of them, anyway, but I wanted to say I made the effort.

It was after school hours, so Abby called her mom and asked if she could stay over at my parents' house. Abby wasn't comfortable with just taking off for the night.

I dropped both hits of acid when the sun started sinking. I always took two or three hits of acid at a time. Each hit cost two or three dollars, depending on the quality and availability. A trip lasted eight to twelve hours.

My plan was to wander the streets, maybe go to Dee's for coffee, then spend the night at Memory Grove, a park nestled between the capitol building and the Avenues. Nighttime tripping was so much better than daytime; the dark made the light more vivid. Some of my friends had bad trips and totally freaked out, screaming and crying, and we had to hold them down. I'd never had a bad trip and I never would. When I was high, I knew I was high, and I knew I would come down.

The acid crawled under my skin like rows of marching ants. Their pace quickened to a frenzy. The streetlights transfigured into fire fairies flickering their smoldering wings in the night. The colors of the world smeared like melted crayons dumped down a wall.

I laughed, startling Abigail. Buildings looked like Toontown in Disney's *Roger Rabbit*. You could always tell that someone was tripping because their pupils expanded, obscuring the irises. Grins were permanently slapped on their faces.

"What time does the last bus leave?" Abigail asked.

"11:30, why?"

"I don't want to get into trouble with my mom," she said, rubbing her foot on the cement.

We walked to the bus stop and I waited with her. This friendship was not going to work out.

"We can tell my mom we decided to stay at my house instead of yours," she said. "She won't mind. We can tell her your mom brought us over. She'll be fine with that. We can hang out in my room. She won't know you're tripping. She doesn't know anything about drugs."

"I'm not coming over, Abby."

Abigail got on the bus. I watched it pull away from the curb.

I spent the rest of the night in Memory Grove, listening to the leaves rustling in the wind and the water smoothing the stones along the bottom of the river that flowed through the center of the

Nicole Lowe

park. I lay on the grass and let the cold of the ground suck the warmth from my body.

The stars twinkled to the rhythm of the night. I imagined myself lying on the bottom of the river, the stones pressing into my back, the water flowing over my face. I opened my eyes and looked up at the stars distorted by the water. Leaves, branches, and water striders danced on the surface above my face. I remained motionless on the bottom, watching the world awaken with the rising of the sun. I opened my mouth, feeling the icy water rush over my lips, flooding my mouth. My body convulsed and I sat up, gasping for breath. Another dark day was before me.

Thirty-six percent of sexual assaults occur when the victim is between the ages of twelve and seventeen.

chapter four

Sabrina finishes off the water from her cup and pours another. It clicks on the wood as she sets it in front of her. I wait for her to finish. I want her full attention on the questions. I don't want her emotional reaction concealed through action.

"How have you supported yourself?" I ask.

"Selling drugs and other stuff." She takes a sip of water, staring at me over the lip of the paper cup.

I often wonder what parents think of me as I stand here at the state's table in my dress suit and shiny shoes. They must think my life has been so different from theirs, that there is no way I could understand what they have been through, or what it means to be an addict.

I look down at the list of questions I prepared for today. My next question isn't there. The list is only a guideline, anyway. Many times, I improvise. My fingers dance across the silver shaft of my pen.

I meet her gaze and don't look away. "Other stuff?"

Carl doesn't look up from his laptop.

"My ass," she says.

"Can you clarify your answer, please?" My intent is not to humiliate her, but for the court record to be unambiguous.

The others' heads sink an inch or two. Their eyes cast downward. In my mind, there is no shame in what she's done. It's an old business, and at times your body is the only commodity others will buy. It's a harsh reality for many kids on the street and poverty-stricken women. I meet the specter of shame clouding the courtroom. Brushing it aside, I see the woman before me.

"I was a whore."

"When was that?"

"When I was eighteen and Jackson was in jail."

"Is that the only time you have sold drugs and yourself?"

"No, I've done it off and on, whenever I need money or a fix."

―――

Every couple of weeks, I surfaced at my parents' house to get some fresh clothes and to make sure my mother knew I was still sucking air and not a maggot buffet. She searched for me when I was out there, just as she searched for Patrick the first time he took off. She cried a lot when he was gone. Back then, her agony made me ache for her.

I had tried to comfort her, telling her he would be okay, he would come back, and I would never do that to her. But I broke that promise, too. I took off more often, and for longer periods of time, than my brother ever did. The nights she spent looking for me were probably much the same, only now my sister stood at her side instead of me.

One morning in November while I was at home, my mother asked me if I was going to school. I told her I was. It was our shared reoccurring nightmare, and it always ended the same. She sat me down and explained how I was ruining my chances at getting into a good university. She asked her questions. I told her my answers. She couldn't understand how a bright-eyed, straight-A student and athletic girl with tons of friends could have changed so much in so short a time.

"What happened to the doctor and the lawyer dreams?" she asked.

To make the questions stop, I told her what she wanted to hear. There was a small piece of me that felt bad about what I was doing, but I shoved a dirty sock in its mouth, duct taped it, and hung it from a tree.

"I'm done with street life, and I will go back to school. I promise."

I made it through half a day of school.

It was 4:30 in the afternoon when I got off the bus at Shelly's. She was finished with her homework and chores. I had four hits of acid in the plastic cellophane around my cigarettes.

"We're staying at Deanna's tonight," Shelly called to her dad as we walked out the door. He thought Deanna was a nice girl, even though she "dressed weird" like the rest of us.

"Brenden's been looking for you," Shelly said as we interlaced our arms.

I rolled my eyes. "So I've heard. What does he need?"

My love for Brenden had not paled since the day I first saw him in Saedric, but I knew who came first in his life: Deanna. Together, he and I would have been unstoppable. The thought sent an icy thrill through me. If he would just leave her. But he never would. I was alone.

"I'm not sure. I think he just wants to make sure you're alright and can be found when he wants you."

"Patrick can always find me." My brother and I had a connection; he could always find me when needed, and I him.

Nicole Lowe

"Brenden hasn't seen Patrick since he went to Ogden with Spider and Ogre," she said. "We'll find Brenden tomorrow."

I nodded in agreement. Spider and Ogre were mages for the Black Hand, working on restoring us to our bodies in Saedric. Most of Patrick's time was spent with the other mages of the coven. They were part of the Charade. Spider was a dark elf and Ogre was a vampire.

At the moon's rising, Shelly and I dropped the acid. Shelly took one hit, and I placed the other three paper squares on the center of my tongue. We went to Dee's on 400 South to drink coffee and eat cheese fries until it kicked in. I started to tingle, as if I had lightning loose in my veins. Every nerve in my body became alive and awake. I ran my hands through my long hair, and it felt like it was stretching out. I laughed and Shelly looked at me, grinning. We paid our check and began walking around downtown.

People were ugly when I was on acid. My eyes became microscopes, able to see every pore on a person's skin. I noticed little differences in the color of their skin, the imperfections they tried to balance with foundation and powder. I saw the lines and oils that covered their faces.

I never looked in the mirror when I was high. It was just one of my rules. Another rule was that I never looked at the ground for more than a second. If I did, I started seeing a countless mixture of bugs swarming at my feet. The centipedes were the most unnerving, as they braided their bodies together and tangled their legs into a squirming mass. I knew the bugs were not there, or if they were, there were only a few, but it still unsettled me. My mind would become obsessed, and I would start seeing them everywhere and could not get them out of my head.

I noticed my arms swinging at my sides like Mary Poppins marching over rooftops. The song "Chim Chim Cher-ee" began playing inside my head as Shelly and I walked to the Gallivan Center. I nearly choked on my unexpected laughter.

Shelly asked, "What's so funny?"

I started singing the song, and she started laughing too.

Mid-laugh, I realized we were both standing on Main Street, laughing wildly. People would notice and think something was wrong. I tried to cork my laugh hole and ended up snorting like a pig, causing us both to double over. I took Shelly by the hand and kept walking until we reached our destination.

The Gallivan Center was an inner-city park between Main Street and State Street on 300 South. We trundled through the middle of the park, passing the empty stage. We jumped into the empty ice skating rink, then back out. The echo was why we went there. The echo happened when you stood in a specific spot in front of the small amphitheater. Only the person standing in that spot could hear the echo.

I stood there and marveled at the clouds behind Shelly's head—how the wind swirled, dipped, and laced them through the buildings. I was lost in the wonder of the world. A child seeing the stars for the first time.

Shelly was a follower, even when in our world. She complied with her father's rules just as she did with our mother's, the dark elven queen. We were so different in that way. It was my fault that she found herself banished and trapped in this world. She wouldn't have been at risk if she would have stayed away from me, even in the world we found ourselves in. She would have been safer far from me.

We lay on the grass and I brushed the palms of my hands over it. I watched the water cascading down through the water-walk. Rainbows lanced out from the streams of falling water and collided with one another before the sun scorched them into nothing. Two children scuttled through, giggling and bouncing around. The water ran over their round faces. They stretched out their stubby little fingers, feeling the water pour through them.

"Look, Mommy, a rainbow!" said the young girl. Her dark-brown hair was stuck to her head and face. She pushed it aside with a clumsy hand, losing her balance. Her mother reached for her, catching her before she hit the ground.

"I see them, aren't they beautiful?" She brushed the wet hair from her daughter's face.

I didn't remember such love. Even if it was there, the memory of it was lifeless.

I looked over at Shelly and back at the children, but they had faded into the night.

We left the park at two in the morning. Two goths wandering the streets at night would attract police attention, so we walked back to Dee's on 400 South. We receded to a back booth, drinking coffee and smoking.

"Shit," I said, putting my cigarette out and sinking into the booth. Shelly turned.

I moved to sit next to Shelly. Michael slid in next to me. Brenden and Deanna slid in on the other side. We sat in silence. The waitress came around. Three more coffees were ordered and brought to the table.

Brenden stared at me over the lip of his coffee mug as he took a sip. "If you two insist upon roaming the streets high as a kite, you must take Deanna or Michael with you. Preferably Michael, who could protect you in the event you ran into wolves or something equally as dangerous."

The giggle fits, which were a theme of our acid trip, continued to sprout up, but they were beginning to wilt.

Michael shared Brenden's sentiment. "You two cannot take these types of risks. You are lucky I heard the two of you were here. You place the entire coven at risk with your bullshit."

"We're not your pets," I said.

"No, but you are my children. Deanna, get them home so they can sleep that shit off," Brenden said, ending the conversation.

Due to my position, the coven family watched and "protected" me. I wasn't sure the protection bit was so much for my sake as for their own. I wondered if Brenden's pursuit of me had always hinged on my status as heir to the dark elven throne, rather than who I was without the throne. Without me, he would not be able to reunite the dark elves. Without me, his people would never achieve the strength to be free of the cages others placed around them. Without me, their knowledge of magic would fizzle.

Deanna escorted Shelly and me to Shelly's house. Her dad had left for work. I was wired, but no longer hallucinating. I lay awake for a long time, staring at the ceiling. Coming down off acid was the worst part. You still felt it in your system. You ached from head to toe, like after a fever, as the chemicals worked themselves out of your muscles. Grease and grime oozed from your pores. You were physically exhausted, but your mind couldn't sleep. You were in that state for an hour or two before falling into a fitful sleep, eventually entering a more restful sleep.

Thoughts circled in my head in that space between. We lived in a world of desire, a world that cried out what we were supposed to be with such ferocity that the song of who we truly were was devoured. A battle raged within my mind. My childhood dreams of who I could have become were fighting for their existence against the hordes of death and destruction that thrived within me. I didn't know which side would prevail. I didn't care. I just wanted the war to end.

Angry and on the verge of destruction, I disappeared from Brenden's oppressive gaze for a few days.

It was morning, but I didn't know what time. I didn't know what day of the week it was. It didn't matter. It was late fall. My breath formed clouds with each exhalation. I trudged across the deserted street and into a Chevron gas station. A bell clinked as I pushed the glass door open.

The man at the counter was the father of a girl who went to school with me. His family went to the LDS church near my parents' home every Sunday. His daughter was involved in the Church's young women's program. We had gone to church camp in the summers together. His wife had given me a ride to school a few times. I asked for the bathroom key. He glanced in my direction, slid me the key, and turned back to the TV behind the counter.

Nicole Lowe

My fingers scraped along the rough brick wall as I walked around to the back of the building and unlocked the bathroom door. There was a sink, mirror, and toilet. It smelled damp and earthy, like a crypt. The light flickered before holding a dim glow.

I walked to the sink to wash my hands and set the key on the edge of the sink. A girl stood before the mirror. She had long, burgundy hair a few inches past her shoulders. She looked to be about a hundred and twenty pounds, a little over five feet tall. She was dressed in black velvet leggings, black boots, and a burgundy blazer, which fit her slender body. She had on a white, ruffled dress shirt under the blazer.

I didn't recognize her. Her makeup was streaked across her face, as if she had been crying. She had the remains of what appeared to be black lipstick on her mouth. Her hair was tangled and matted with vomit. She had bruising and bite marks on her throat. She couldn't be much older or younger than I. She looked at me, but did not see me. She looked through me. Or was it I who looked through her?

...It's dark. I can't move. Something is holding me down. I see him, broad shoulders, thick blond hair. He reaches for me. I can't breathe. I'm choking. My throat. I reach for my throat. His hands are clutching my throat. I can't breathe. It's so dark...

I turned my back on her and finished washing my hands and face, rinsed my hair, put it in a tight bun, fixed my makeup, used the toilet, and washed my hands again. I left the girl in the crypt. She was nothing to me.

I walked north on State Street until I found a bus stop, and then I waited. I couldn't recall the past few days. I had vague recollections of meeting some new people at Confetti, friends of friends. Drinking whiskey. Even those memories caused a wave of vomit to fill the back of my throat. I gagged.

The bus arrived. I stepped on and found a seat in the back. I got off at the ZCMI Center in downtown and lit a cigarette. It was midday. I needed to find someone in the coven. I ached all over. I felt sick. Something was wrong, missing, left behind somehow. I looked over my shoulder. No one. I shook my head to clear it. Was someone there? It felt like it. I decided to go to Paisley Park first, and then Grounds.

    I staggered into the park and scanned the faces. No Brenden. Michael stood with one foot up on the red brick, leaning his elbow on his knee. He was speaking to a couple of goth girls at the back. One of them put her hand to her mouth when she saw me standing at the entrance.

    Michael turned his shaved head toward me. His eyes narrowed. He straightened to his full six feet and his black pants fell back over the tops of his combat boots. The hem caught on the boot knife. He raised his leg to fix it, never taking his eyes off of me.

    He had come to Utah six or seven months earlier from California, where he had a baby mama and a child. Michael was twenty-four. The rumor was that he was a skinhead and had spent time in jail. He walked with an exaggerated stride and leaned into each step. It was a fluid motion. I couldn't suppress the urge to step back from his commanding form.

    He was within inches of me in a few long strides. He took hold of my chin and I grabbed his forearm. His muscles bulged in my hand. He moved my face back and forth. "Who did this to you?"

    "I don't know." My eyes avoided his.

    Michael's jaw clenched and a crease formed between his eyebrows. He spun me around in one quick motion. Off-balance, I grabbed his bicep to steady myself. He turned me to face him again. "You look like you've been attacked by a wolf. Where is it?"

    "I don't know. I took off this morning and came straight here to find you. I don't know what happened. I don't remember."

    ...It was dark. I was on the ground, on my stomach, my hair caught behind me. I couldn't get it loose. I screamed and thrashed my arms around. He was on top of me. "SSHHHHH," he whispered in my ear. I could feel his hot breath. His mouth on my neck. His teeth tore my skin. He ripped off my clothing. It was so dark...

    "I remember drinking and then I woke up. He left to go get food, and I snuck out." My eyes burned and didn't leave the ground.

Other people at the park were gathering around. Michael's hand encircled my bicep and he led me away. "You will stay with me from now on. This will not happen again."

I accepted my place within the Charade and nodded my head. I was too hollow to argue with Michael. Segments of that night infected my thoughts throughout the day, images of the wolf on top of my naked body, thrusting himself inside of me. I needed a shower, to wash his filth off my skin, but even that wouldn't erase what the wolf had done.

Michael's hand swallowed mine. "Let's go."

Michael's behavior toward me had always vacillated between distaste and desire. My belief was that he was waiting for Brenden to reject me in this world, as he had done in Saedric.

Brenden had delivered that rejection two weeks earlier, leaving me free to be claimed and conquered. We were lying on the lawn of the LDS hospital, which was wedged in among the foothills of the Salt Lake Valley. The clouds gathered and diverged from one another as they moved across the night sky.

Brenden rolled up onto his elbow and I turned to face him, cocking my head questioningly. He placed his finger on my lips and traced a line down to the small indentation at the intersection of my collarbone and the base of my throat. He slowly moved his finger down my chest, between my breasts, and stopped at my belly button.

"Patrick is like a brother to me, making you more of a sister in this world. I cannot be with you as my sister."

I turned back to the stars. It didn't matter which world we were in. Brenden would create the most stunning wall of thorns between us and present it to me as a gift. I craved Brenden's affection and touch. I had held on to a twist of the thorned branches, hoping our love would smooth out the barbs. It wasn't his rejection that tore at me. It was his desire, because it would not be me who satisfied it. I lay next to him that night, wrapped in his arms, and he kissed my mouth and neck.

I was positive Michael knew Brenden had built his wall of thorns. Gathering information was his specialty.

Michael pulled me along behind him. I took two steps to every one of his as we made our way through the city. He was staying with his friends. He knocked once and opened the door. Torn blankets were pinned over the windows. The only light came from lamps dimmed by more blankets.

Mohawks and shaved heads dominated the horizon. Torn-up jeans, leather jackets, safety pins, chains, and metal-studded clothing adorned the bodies. A swastika was spray-painted on the wall and a Confederate flag flew in a window.

"My room's in the back." Michael nudged me to go in front of him.

People were passed out on the floor, in various states of nudity and entanglement. Unfocused eyes peered out from the fog of whatever drug soaked their brains. The place smelled like vomit and stale sweat. The meager furniture was broken and well-worn.

I stepped over shattered and whole glass bottles. Cigarette butts poured over the edges of ashtrays. White powder sprinkled the surface of mirrors. Needles lay scattered on the sole upright table.

We didn't talk to anyone as we passed through. A full-size mattress stuck to the floor in the corner beneath the window in his room. A pinned-up black sheet was pulled back, allowing the evening light in through the window.

Michael unbuttoned his shirt and tossed it into a laundry basket in another corner. His chest and arms were pale and muscular. I stood there looking around, lost. He took my gothbox and set it beside the mattress.

He brushed my cheek with his thumb. "You want to wash your face or anything?"

I nodded and pressed the inside of my cheek between my teeth. Tears slipped from my eyes.

He led me back down the hall to the bathroom. I washed my face a few times to get the makeup off. I thought I got it all, but I didn't want to look into the mirror. I opened the door to find Michael waiting, his hands in the pockets of his black slacks. We went back to his room. He opened the window and pulled the sheet over it.

"You look like shit," he said with a smile, and brushed my hair behind my ear.

"Will you stay with me?"

Each time I started to drift off, I jolted awake, gasping for air.

"It's alright," Michael whispered. His reassuring hand rested on my stomach.

I lay there, detached, for hours, until sleep took me.

I came to with the rise of the moon.

Michael was right beside me when I awoke. "I was starting to worry. You've been out for two days. Didn't even stir when I had to go out."

"Two days?"

"You've been in and out. You got up once to use the bathroom and drank some water. But that was yesterday."

Another promise to my mother, shattered. Why it hit me at that exact moment, like an atomic bomb, I would never know. I gave up all hope of turning around after that. Nothing mattered anymore.

unzip

```
the blade unzips my skin,
 life spills out my sin
    futile to love,
 what is filled with hate
 uninhabitable is my skin,
barren of warmth from within
  darkness at the core,
   death is my whore
  tortured by shame,
 crazed, unable to tame.
```

Females between the ages of sixteen and twenty-four are roughly three times more likely than the rest of the population to be abused by an intimate partner.

chapter five

Sabrina's attorney stands and waits for her to finish her answer. Judge Cruz looks over at him, raising his eyebrows and scratching a single finger down the length of his broad nose. "Mr. Lundberg?"

"Your Honor," Jake says, "can we take a short break to allow my client to collect herself?"

"Make it short, Mr. Lundberg," says the judge, standing.

"All rise," calls Maxwell.

Sabrina strides from the witness box and flings the doors open. Jake follows her out.

I flip through my pad of paper, reading over my notes and talking to the caseworker next to me.

Sabrina takes the stand after a five-minute break.

"We're back on the record regarding McCartni Hardy," Maxwell says.

The judge pulls his sleeves up a bit and prepares to take more notes. "Alright, Ms. Hardy is back on the stand and under oath. We have Ms.

Lowe, Mr. Lundberg, and Mr. Johnson all present. Ms. Lowe?"

"Why didn't you complete drug treatment the second time you entered, Ms. Hardy?" I ask.

"Because I was going through a difficult time."

She bites her lip, leaving an arched red line. She closes her eyes. When she looks up, tears wet her cheeks. Her voice shakes as she continues.

"Jackson, my husband, had gotten out of jail again."

"Why was that hard for you?"

She looks away from everyone, staring into the empty back corner of the courtroom. I know that look. She is not here anymore. I know that feeling. Separation from things you'd rather not remember. Ever. Sometimes, when you recall horrible things, the part of you that was damaged has to go away while the rest of you tells others what happened.

Her voice is empty of emotion and inflection. "He would beat me when I wouldn't fuck his friends for money. He would beat me with whatever he could reach. He wouldn't stop until one of the neighbors called the police or I was unconscious."

She turns her face toward me. Her eyes are red and the tears fall one by one, but she is still far away, somewhere safe. "The last time, he said he would kill me when he got out. He said he would take me out in the woods, shove his gun up my ass, and pull the trigger."

I take a slow breath. As much as I want to tell her it won't happen, I know I can't protect her. I know I can't offer her any solace. I know as soon as he's out, she will run into his arms because he is sorry and he loves her. And he'll promise it will never happen again. I know that if she leaves him, the chances of him killing her are more real than the chair she sits on.

"Where is he now?"

"Prison."

"How long has he been there?"

"Since I was first pregnant with McCartni."

I make a note. Before the trial, I filed a motion requesting to bifurcate Jackson and Sabrina's trials so she would not have to testify with him in the courtroom. The motion was granted.

"How many times has he hit you?"

She leans her head back and blows out a breath, ballooning her cheeks. "I don't know, too many to count."

"When was the worst incident, in your opinion?"

"Christmas, two years ago. Four months before he went to prison."

"Were you pregnant at that time?"

Sabrina lowers her head. "I was six months pregnant."

"What happened?"

"He hit me in the face and stomach with a baseball bat. I had to have my jaw wired back

```
together and the baby died..." Her hand cradles her
stomach. "...inside of me."

"Are those the charges he is in prison for
now?"

She nods.

"You need to answer aloud, Ms. Hardy."

"Sorry. Yes, that's why he's there now."

"When will he be up for parole?"

"In four days."
```

Michael claimed me as his own. I silently consented. I couldn't live through another wolf attack. With Michael by my side, I was safe from that particular threat. He found us a new place to stay. He didn't want me at the other house.

"Not appropriate," he said.

Sunny and Megan, members of the Black Hand, invited us to stay with them. It was a one-bedroom apartment within walking distance of Shelly's, which made me happy. I slept between Michael and the back of the couch, springs pressed into my hip and shoulder. I lost myself in the pages of my books when Michael wouldn't let me out of the house. He walked me to Shelly's and then picked me up a few hours later. If he went out to handle Black Hand business, Megan or Sunny were home with me. Overseers, but they never admitted it, even when I confronted them. More often than not, we were out in the city together.

A couple of weeks after we moved in with Sunny, Shelly came over and told me the police had arrested Hunter for having a pipe in his pocket.

"Misfit can get us in to visit him," I said. "I haven't seen him in a month."

Shelly and I were standing out on the balcony, smoking. In order to get into the jail, we needed someone who was over eighteen with identification.

She lit another cigarette. "Michael will never let you go to the jail to see Hunter."

I glanced back through the sliding glass door. Michael was on the couch, sharpening his boot knife. "We just won't tell him that's what we're doing."

"It's your ass if he finds out."

Michael abhorred Hunter.

I flicked my cigarette. It sizzled in a puddle from the rain the night before. I pulled the sliding glass door open. Shelly followed me inside and slid the door closed. I stood in front of Michael and he pretended not to notice me while he finished with his knife and slipped it into his boot. Then he grabbed me and pulled me onto his lap.

"What do you want?"

I kissed him on the neck and pressed my lips to his. "Shelly and I want to go shopping and to coffee."

He looked at her. "Who else is going to be with you?"

Shelly rolled her eyes. "It's just us going."

"No acid and you can go."

I kissed him again and we bolted for the door. He caught my wrist when I had one foot out. I came to an abrupt stop. I turned back to him.

"No acid." He opened his hand and I was gone.

———

We found Misfit on State Street where the prostitutes walked.

"Hunter's in jail and we need you to get us in to visit him," I told her. She agreed to take us if I could find her a fix afterward. We walked to the jail and they let the three of us in with Misfit's ID.

Hunter smiled when he saw us. He was zipped into an orange jumpsuit with white loafers on his feet. He looked like hell and the ridiculous jumpsuit just made it worse. A sheen of sweat glistened

Nicole Lowe

on his forehead. His skin was grey. He sat on a black stool behind the Plexiglas and his hand shook as he picked up the phone receiver that hung on the wall.

I pressed the phone to my ear. "I'm going to do whatever it takes to get the money to pay your bail."

He shook his head. "I'll be released tonight, but it's good to see you. You haven't been around much. Is everything alright?"

I nodded my head, not trusting my tongue.

"You been going to school and staying home?"

"Yes," I lied.

"That's my girl." He put his hand against the glass. I reached up to touch him and he blew me a kiss.

I went to Hunter's house the following afternoon and found him curled up in a corner, shivering and sweating. I couldn't get him any more heroin because Michael would find out for sure. I placed cool washcloths on his forehead and brought him fresh water.

"Why aren't you at school?" he asked, his voice weak with exhaustion.

I looked away from him. "Things have changed downtown within the coven," I said.

He nodded knowingly, brushing my hair from my face. His eyes were sad, but he smiled a little. He knew about the covens, even though he was not involved with the Charade. You overheard things when you were on the fringe and unnoticed by many.

I stayed with him until Kim got home.

```
          the facts

      depression is setting in
    the darkness is coming through
         the light is gone
      happiness is only a dream
           love is lost
         hate is not new.
```

After leaving Hunter's, I headed over to Grounds to find Michael. The scent of fresh-roasted beans and ground coffee filled my nose and lit up my eyes. My body let go of some of the tension over facing Michael's anger. I had been gone for a couple of days. He was not going to be happy.

Grounds was on the second floor above a tavern on Main Street. The front of the coffeehouse had nice tables, chairs, and a big front window. There were paintings lining the walls, landscapes and flowers with dark wood frames. The front was where the "suits" drank their coffee.

I ordered. The guy at the counter slid me a mug of black coffee. I dumped a bunch of sugar and creamer in and stirred it with a thin red straw. I took a sip before passing through the bead door and into the back.

The goths and gutter punks hung out in the back room. There were two card tables, a handful of chairs, and three couches. One wall was dedicated to our written musings. Another had concert posters tacked on it. Michael was not there when I arrived, but Brenden and Patrick were.

Brenden raised his eyes and shook his head. "Nice of you to join us. Michael will be here soon. Sit." He pointed to a white plastic patio chair.

Patrick patted the seat next to him, and I plopped into it as if I'd just been sent to time-out. As a mage, Patrick studied the occult and read Tarot cards for members of the Black Hand, as well as others.

"Michael's been worried about you," Brenden said. "He's been looking everywhere for you, but no one has seen you, which, of course, makes him even more concerned."

"I was with Shelly," I said. "He knew that. I left with her and he said it was fine."

"And we have had that discussion before?" he growled.

"I was fine, nothing happened."

Brenden turned back to Patrick. They were discussing the next rituals and meetings for the Black Hand. We performed the rituals in places where the magic energy was contained in the land or the buildings, like Memory Grove and some cemeteries. The purpose was to rip the veil between the two worlds. My participation in the rituals was minimal, as I was primarily a warrior, and my focus wasn't on developing my magic ability. Thus, the rituals were left in the hands of Brenden, Patrick, Spider, and Ogre.

Brenden and Patrick went outside to smoke. I followed them through the back door and down a long flight of metal stairs to a space about twelve feet by twelve feet. There was a walkway between the two buildings leading back out to Main Street.

The back door swung open and Michael stepped onto the small landing. He spotted me before the back door had time to close behind him. His lips formed a straight line. He clenched and released his jaw. He took his time dropping each foot on the next metal stair, causing heavy clomps. Michael said hello and hugged Brenden and Patrick without even looking at me. Then he stalked toward me, sniffed, and wiped his nose: thumb, finger, thumb.

I didn't back away, which was what I thought he expected. I stood my ground and looked straight at him, one predator to another. He closed the space with two long strides. I felt the heat of his body.

Patrick stood watching. He flicked his cigarette and pressed it into the ground with his toe and leaned against the wall, waiting. Patrick was not fond of Michael. He tolerated him because Brenden accepted him and found him useful. My vision constricted to only Michael.

He grabbed my chin and turned my head from side to side. He lifted my hair and looked at my neck. He saw nothing.

He kissed me hard, forcing his tongue into my mouth, then pulled back. "Where the hell have you been?"

"I was with Shelly. I told you I was going with Shelly."

Michael spoke through clenched teeth. "You did not say you would be gone for two days. I was..." He paused. "...concerned. I've been looking everywhere for you."

He kissed me again and backed me up against the wall. He grabbed the back of my head, lacing his fingers in my hair. Patrick and Brenden resumed their conversation. Michael kissed me again.

"I'm sorry. We just needed some girl time." I stuck my lower lip out.

He smiled and released a deep laugh. He grabbed my hand and walked me back upstairs, taking them two at a time. I stumbled as he dragged me behind him. He bought me a bagel and a mocha. We sat together on the couch as he watched me eat.

Once a week or so, Michael would get high on crack. I knew when he was using because his nose ran, and he wiped it in a particular way—right side with his thumb, left side with his index finger, and then the thumb again. He smiled in his Jack the Pumpkin King way. He was rougher with me when he was high, and would grab my arms and pull me to him. He would kiss me roughly, pressing my teeth against the inside of my lips. He always told me not to touch crack, or he would kick my ass. I believed him.

"Things have been tense with the wolves lately, and I was worried about you." He wiped his nose again and scanned the room. The room was empty and he was high. He pulled me toward him.

"They have been hanging around more than normal and started a fight yesterday. There are new faces in the city all the time."

I took another bite of the bagel. I couldn't remember when I'd eaten last.

"I need to know where you are at all times. I worry, and you know why. We don't need a repeat of *that*."

He was talking about the rape. I looked at the ground and shook my head. No, I did not need to repeat that lesson.

Returning to my own world with the dark elves and bringing an end to the Charade was my sole desire. I wanted to go back to my true world all the time, where I could run through the woods laughing and hunting with my friends, and spend nights lying next to rivers, letting the cool water run through my fingers and kiss the tips of my toes. In this world, I was no one. I had nothing. The darkness had colonized my mind. I wanted death to rescue me from all that I found in this world. I was not sure I could hold out until Patrick could get us back home.

A week later, Michael and I were at Sunny's. There was a knock at the door. Sunny looked through the peephole and saw my mother. Patrick was with her. Michael growled and pulled me into the bathroom with him. He turned on the shower, but we could still hear their voices. Steam filled the room, fogging the mirror. We listened as Sunny invited Patrick and my mother inside.

"Have you seen Nikki around over the past few days?" Patrick asked.

"She stayed here the night before last," Sunny said.

"Will you let her know I'm looking for her?"

"Of course."

We heard the door close. Their voices were gone. Sunny knocked once. "You're good."

Hiding in the bathroom was a minor inconvenience compared to having to go home for a few days, answering questions, and skipping out again.

Michael started to kiss and caress me. He ran his fingers through my hair, stopping at my lower back to pull the lacing loose at the back of my dress. His hand continued down my thigh until he reached the bottom of my dress. Taking hold of the black fabric, he slipped it up and over my head. He kissed me on the neck, chest, and breasts. His kisses were tender. It caught me off guard, made me want to push him away, but I knew making him angry would be a mistake. Tenderness was never what it appeared to be.

Relationships and sex were a means to an end. Love had nothing to do with either. I wasn't sure love was even real. It was something people talked about and desired, but it was impossible to hold onto. Relationships consisted of you benefitting me, and me benefitting you. When that ended, we ended.

Sex was control and manipulation. Sex was primal, violent, and coercive. Emotions came and went. There was no choice in their arrival or departure. There was choice in responses to emotions. Lust and desire were real. Anger was real. Sadness was real. Hopelessness was real. Compassion was real. Excitement, joy, and pleasure were all real.

Love was not an emotion. Thus, it was not real. It was an action—like fighting and running. It was a choice. And I chose not to participate.

———

Hours melted away on Confetti's dance floors. The vibration of sound began in the center of my being and moved throughout my body, expressing its rhythms and waves through me like a physical medium. I could have stayed there forever, lost in the sounds that expressed how I felt better than any words falling from my mouth. If I couldn't be high, at least I could be there.

Michael was more at home in the mosh pit than on the dance floor. Ministry and Skinny Puppy crashed over the moshers from the black boxes overhanging the pit. Watching Michael circle filled me with pride and trepidation. His authoritative stride, those arms whose strength I knew so well, pushing, shoving, and slamming into all the other males.

Few females stayed in his line of attack. He pulled me in whenever he saw me in the shadows, positioning me in front of him. He changed his stride to match mine. His reach was long enough to continue on his warpath around me. It filled me with a sense of power and control. I understood his love for the pit. I knew from whence my power and control arose. As long as he was with me, I was safe from everyone else.

One night, my mother came into Confetti looking for me. I was at the back of the mosh pit. I watched her through the circling,

Nicole Lowe

colliding bodies. Strobe lights flashed across her face. I wished that kind and loving feelings filled me when I laid eyes upon the woman who brought me into this world—fed me, clothed me, and loved me. But they didn't. Instead, it was a malicious annoyance. I coddled and fed it, as my mother had done for me.

Fifty percent of young people who experience rape or physical or sexual abuse will attempt to commit suicide.

chapter six

"Ms. Hardy, have you ever been admitted to a mental health institution?" I ask.

"Twice."

"When was the first time?"

"When I was sixteen."

"Why were you admitted?"

"I tried to kill myself by overdosing."

Judge Cruz makes some notes.

With each topic of inquiry, Sabrina's path in life parallels mine in many ways. Yet, somehow, I stand outside the witness box.

"When was the second time you were admitted?"

"A month after McCartni was born."

"Why were you admitted then?"

"I didn't see the point of living anymore."

Some questions have to be asked, even if they seem rude or insensitive. "How did you try to kill yourself the second time?"

Her eyes lock with mine and I wonder what thoughts are circling in her mind. "Hanging."

Hanging sends two clear messages to the world: *You can't hurt me anymore; I have control now.*

"Ms. Hardy, what is your diagnosis?"

"Bipolar disorder, post-traumatic stress disorder, and addiction."

"What were the discharge recommendations?" I ask.

Jake, her attorney, pops to his feet like a jack-in-the-box. "Objection, hearsay."

Jake knows I can rephrase this, but he has to do his job and make me do mine.

Judge Cruz turns to me. I try to avoid objectionable questions. I don't play attorney games. Jake wants this information left out, because Sabrina is not following the recommendations.

"Your Honor," I say, "let me reword the question."

The judge nods. Jake sinks into his chair. Sabrina graces me with a smug smile.

"After you were released from the hospital, did you meet with your caseworker?"

"Yes."

"Why were you meeting with her?"

"To schedule a visit with McCartni."

"Had you missed a visit?"

"Two, while I was in the hospital."

"Did you meet with her for any other reason?"

"She wanted to talk about my service plan."

"Did you agree to add anything to the service plan at that time?"

"Weekly therapy, and taking my medication."

"Why did you agree to add those to your service plan?"

She rolls her eyes and exhales audibly. "Because that's what the hospital said I needed after I left."

"Are you attending therapy and taking your medication?"

"I'm taking the medication."

"Is it helping?"

"I believe so. I'm more stable."

"Why aren't you in therapy?"

"Because I don't want to talk about my past. It's over and I want to leave it there."

I woke up screaming, drenched in sweat. The wolf had come for me again. Many times, I had woken up crying with its teeth clamped around my throat, but never like this. This time was different.

I was alone at my parents' house. Vomit rose in my throat. Trembling, I crawled from my wet sheets. The sun's rays burned through the blinds.

My legs shook when I tried to stand. I made my way down the hall toward my parents' bedroom on hands and knees. Gipping the doorframe of their closet, I pulled myself to a stand. I probed through layers of blankets and old clothes until my hand brushed against the cold barrel.

Nicole Lowe

Pulling the gun from its hiding spot, I sank to the floor. It sat in my lap, cold against my bare legs. I choked on my snot and the tears running down my burning cheeks.

...It's dark. I'm on the ground. My face is wet with tears. My arms won't move. There's a weight on my hips. My body is being jerked up and down along the floor as he forces himself inside of me again and again. I'm going to be sick. I feel the vomit rise from my stomach. Taste the burning in my throat, the back of my mouth. It's so dark...

My breath caught in my constricted throat. I didn't want to breathe. No one was home. The cylinder pushed free. Empty. Trembling, I crumbled into a ball of agony on the floor. Exhausted. When I woke, I showered, grabbed some clothes, and left the house.

```
         the only way to win

           stranded here alone
            left here to die
               no way out
               no way in
             no way to win
           stare at the stars
      wish impossible things  happiness
        to make all of this go away
             no way to win
           no way to get away
       no way for anyone to get in
    the ceiling crashes in, my body splattered
                everywhere
           the only way to win
         the only way to get free
         the only game left to play.
```

At sunset, I found Michael at Paisley Park with Brenden and Deanna. The sinking sun danced across Brenden's face and played in his tangle of black hair. A smile snuck into the corners of his mouth. I knew my desire for him was unrealistic and would bring only stark pain. We were together in a Chinese finger trap.

Their eyes never left me as I crossed the street. On tiptoe, I kissed Brenden's cheek. His white, silk arms slid around me. Next, I kissed Deanna on the cheek. I wrapped my arms around her corpse. Then Michael gathered me up in his arms, kissed the top of my head, and breathed me in.

I looked up into his smiling face.

"I missed you," he said. "Are you well?"

I nodded. He stroked my hair, kissing me again.

We caught the bus to Confetti. Brenden and Deanna danced. They were beautiful together. I danced with them, moving my body in synchronicity with theirs, becoming one within the rhythm as the sounds bounced through the air. Our dance was fluid and graceful. There was no sharpness or coarseness to it. We flowed within the sound and with each other. We breathed the same breath. Brenden pulled me into his arms and turned me around, never releasing my hands. Deanna moved in a circle around us, pivoting with each graceful step.

Brenden breathed in the smell of my hair, kissed me on the neck, whispered, "Ever my sweet elven temptress," and released me.

Michael watched those who watched us, as much—if not more than—those who danced.

Deanna and I took a bathroom break. "Brenden is pleased that you and Michael are together," she told me. "He wanted that, and believes you're destined to be together. Michael has never taken another mate."

I turned on the hot water.

Moans of pleasure rode on the air. A slap rattled the stall door. It earned a flickering glance from the two of us.

Deanna hugged me and kissed me on the mouth. Her words, as always, were seeded with jealousy and suspicion.

We moved to the back room when Patrick arrived. One wall was purple; the others, black. Smoke entered my nose and lungs. My eyelids fluttered as I entered the blinding light dimmed only by the heavy smoke that filled the room. My chin rose at the scent of the clove.

Michael smiled and scanned the room. Like a bloodhound hunting a body, he easily sighted the person with the cloves. A few seconds later, he held the coal-black cigarette before me. Gently sliding it from his fingers, I placed it between my lips. He produced a lighter from his pocket. Cloves burned my lungs. I cherished each drag.

A chill lived in the room, even though it was as crowded as a junior high hallway. Patrick and Brenden were talking about a ritual and referring to arcane symbols on a sheet of paper Patrick had produced from his trench coat. Michael stood over them as they talked. I leaned against his chest, listening.

Patrick drew three Tarot cards to get a sense of the energy tonight: success and openness. It was a perfect night to pull our world closer. It would take many more ceremonies to close the gap, but this was one step closer to home.

We arrived at Memory Grove close to midnight. The full moon shone in the cloudless sky. We approached the black iron gate and waited. Red stone pieces were fit together into the shape of pentagrams in the sidewalk on both sides of the gate. Patrick moved ahead of us and stood over them, his hands flowing through the air, drawing an invisible pattern I didn't recognize. Then he motioned for us to cross the threshold of the park.

Spider and Ogre stepped from the darkness as we reached the meditation chapel, with its eight-foot iron doors and faint orange polished stones. Small headstones with the names of soldiers, those never found, covered the ground around the chapel. Thin strips of grass separated them.

Spider was seventeen years old. He bowed with a flourish to Brenden. His shoulder-length, dingy black hair dangled to the ground. His knobby legs seemed longer than they were in his black leggings. His silk, button-down shirt was cool on my skin as he embraced me. I rested, for a breath, with my head on his chest.

Ogre bowed next, his mountainous form sending his long ponytail flipping with the swift motion. He pulled me into his arms. My arms couldn't reach around him, so I tucked them in and smiled up at him. Spider, Ogre, and Patrick were like family. As a result, I had their love and protection.

We continued down the dirt trail as it wound back through the towering pines and aspen trees. The river's tumultuous melody filled the silence as we passed the bridge and falls.

Deeper in the grove, we came to a stop at the lower of the three levels of the altar. It was composed of roughly chiseled, faint orange stones. Patrick walked to each of the pentagrams puzzled into the stones surrounding the altar. He lit sandalwood incense and moved it through the air in a protection pattern above each stone. He placed four candles—three black, one white—on the altar and lit them.

Patrick posted Michael on the lower trail, where he paced back and forth in the dirt, keeping watch. Deanna and I were instructed to stand at the crossroads of the upper trail—Deanna in the north, and I in the south. I paused at the moon and sun formations pieced together in the stone landings of the altar before proceeding to my spot.

As I stood alone in the dark, the earthy scent of the sandalwood rose up to me. The candlelight flickered between the trees. The sound of the river drowned the voices I knew were below.

I stood still just inside the tree line, avoiding notice. Small animals rustled in the scrub oak. The temperature dropped. I wrapped my trench coat tighter around my body. I closed my eyes and inhaled, pulling the cold air into my nose and lungs. My eyelids parted slowly, reveling the world as I exhaled a breath into the frigid air.

I saw movement out of the corner of my eye. I knew better than to move—any motion could draw attention. There were rarely people on the upper trail this late at night, other than police. Moments later, I saw it again on the other side of the trail. Another cloud of incense confronted me. The animals stopped scurrying in the underbrush. Footsteps were coming up the trail. I held my breath.

Patrick. He stopped and lit a cigarette. I stood still for a moment. "Nikki," he said. "We're done."

I stepped forward, my fingers to my lips.

A quiet laugh slithered from his mouth. "Come on."

I started walking toward him. "I saw something move twice."

"It's alright." He continued walking the way he had come.

I lit a cigarette, cast a quick glance behind us into the mass of shadow, and followed him. We met up with the others at the lower level of the altar. Together, we walked deeper into Memory Grove and reached the five black stone pillars where we could relax and speak, unhindered by the presence of outsiders.

Michael reached his hand out to me, and I took it. He pulled me close to him. I stood in his embrace, listening to the ballad of the night.

I turned at the sound of feet rustling the fallen leaves.

"Come, speak with me, Nikki," Brenden said. Michael released me, and I took Brenden's outstretched hand.

"You cannot change her heart," Ogre called from the trees, laughing. Brenden waved his hand dismissively toward the mage. I turned and looked back. Spider stood just inside the tree line. He raised his hand to his mouth, blew me a kiss, and rested his hand over his heart—a sign of loyalty and love to the dark elves.

Deanna called after us. "Brenden?" She got the same wave of the hand that Ogre received.

Brenden was quiet for a few minutes as we walked. "Back home," he began, "there is a great rift among the dark elves. When I gave you my lifeblood, a war began between those who support you, despite the tainted blood, and those who supported your mother. Those who love you have joined forces with my vampires to protect your right, and the rights of others, to choose life, love, and equality. Your younger sister, Shelly, joined us as a vampire. Your brother, Patrick, followed—although he did not choose the vampire path.

His loyalty is to you, and he serves this coven because of that, as does Spider."

We stopped and sat on a fallen tree softened by the insects burrowed within.

I stared at the moonlight as it caught the leaves behind his silhouette. "You came to me on a night not so different from this one, Brenden, the silver moon high in the sky. We talked and danced under the stars. I was yours. I had no need of vampire immortality as an elf. You came back to me, over and over again, despite your words that it could never be."

"I have given my soul to another," Brenden said, "and despite our ups and downs, Deanna and I belong together. I told you this from the beginning, but your independent and defiant nature refuses to believe me. You were dying, and I could not let you go. Perhaps I should have listened to Michael. He told me many times to stay away from you, and that I had been caught in your elven charm. Maybe so, but our people can still be magnificent because of this. But only you can reunite the elven people and make them even stronger with an allegiance with the vampires. Together, we can control the powers of life and death."

"Why are you telling me this?" I stood and turned away from him. He didn't talk about the past without a reason. His talks always resulted in a fracture to my soul.

"So you understand," he said, wrapping his arms around me from behind, "why I must give you to Michael. Only he can protect you."

I closed my eyes. "But I am yours," I said, pleading. "You made me. You loved me, took my blood, and gave me this life."

"It is because I love you," he said. "You can never be mine."

"Then I will be no one's." I walked away from him, weaving my way through the trees.

He returned to the others and I watched them from the trees. His eyes strayed to my location every so often. The wind rustled the leaves. One leaf broke loose and glided to the earth on currents of air. It laid fallen, as I was.

Nicole Lowe

Michael fetched me when they were ready to find a camp for the night. Climbing up the steep slopes of the Grove in the dark was tricky—the underbrush caught our feet, branches grabbed at our clothes and clawed at our faces. We came to a small clearing where we had spent many nights. Patrick lit a small fire to warm our hands during the coldest hours of the night. The fire burned until it was just embers and smoldered for a few hours. We slept huddled together, with trench coats as blankets.

Teens who suffer dating abuse are subject to long-term consequences like alcoholism, eating disorders, promiscuity, thoughts of suicide, and violent behavior.

chapter seven

"How many times have you been arrested since your daughter, McCartni, was born?" I ask.

Sabrina waves her hand in the air dismissively. "I don't know. Three or four times."

The attorneys to my right and left jot down some notes.

"Why were you arrested?"

Jake is on his feet again. "Objection. My client will be invoking her Fifth Amendment right against self-incrimination."

That's her choice of course, but things are a bit different in juvenile court. Our goal is not to punish, but to protect the children and reunite families — regardless of what the public and the news media believe.

Parents can plead the Fifth in juvenile court, but the judge has the power to make a negative inference against them for their choice.

I clear my throat. "Your Honor, I'm moving the court to take a negative inference each time the mother invokes the Fifth Amendment and does not answer a question."

"Of course, Ms. Lowe."

Jake sits down.

"Ms. Hardy, what outstanding charges do you have?"

She looks from me to the judge, and then to her attorney. "I… I plead the Fifth?"

"Ms. Hardy, you cannot plead the Fifth when the answer does not incriminate you," Judge Cruz explains. "Stating your charges is not an admission. It's just the charges you are being accused of committing in the criminal court."

Jake stands. "Your Honor, I'm not sure that's relevant?"

Judge Cruz purses his lips. "It's relevant, Mr. Lundberg, sit down."

He sits.

Sabrina looks to Jake anyway. Jake nods his head slightly.

"Sex solicitation, possession of a controlled substance, fraud, and criminal mischief."

Carl arches an eyebrow. The charges mean his child client has been exposed to sexual activity and drugs.

―

Life crashed into me, crushing my bones, extinguishing my breath. I wished that my last breath would have escaped my hollow form, and that my heart would have lay silent in my chest during the night. The thought of another day of life was unbearable.

The dull blade caught as I pressed it deeper, splitting open my skin. The razor's crimson trail brought an intensified focus; it quickened my breath and increased the force of my beating heart. My arms, wrists, and ankles all bore the red linear scabs. I cut to feel. I cut to remind myself I existed.

The contents of my gothbox lay in a scattered pile on the glass coffee table. I stirred them around, searching for a clean razor blade. The blade slipped free of its cardboard sleeve. It looked clean, mostly. More importantly, it was sharp.

Michael lounged next to me on the couch watching *Bram Stoker's Dracula*. The corner of the blade pierced the flesh of my ankle, and I slowly dragged it along the black outline of a Celtic cross, leaving a thin line of red. I repeated the motion, taking my time to make it straight.

Michael leaned toward me, brushed my long hair away from my neck, and kissed me. I pushed him back and glared coldly at him. He laughed. The circle of the cross was more difficult than the lines. The razor was dulling and caught in the tissue, making the curves uneven. A bottle of black ink sat on the table.

I poured the ink in a slow, controlled stream onto my leg and rubbed it into the lines. A cloth lay beneath my leg, catching the dripping fusion of ink and blood. I let it air out and dry, just as I would if I were painting my toenails. The Celtic cross was a symbol of life and death, forever united. The circle, which lay below the intersecting lines of the cross, was the symbol of life. The cross itself, a symbol of death. I pulled my right leg up onto my lap and began drawing vampire fangs.

I passed through the space of the world, but I was not there. I interacted with others, drank coffee, ate, laughed, and walked from place to place—an actress on the stage of life. I watched my daily motions as a displaced apparition, silent and observing. I spent the days wandering without any real purpose.

Michael left the apartment and I sneaked out while Megan was in the shower. It was getting dark, and I needed to find somewhere to sleep. Michael wasn't my keeper. He wasn't my king. He wasn't Brenden. I didn't bend to anyone's will. I needed space. If I didn't get it, I'd create it, one way or another. Exerting my independence. Becoming a self-destructive, chaotic force.

I was walking north on Main Street, passing Crossroads Mall, headed in the general direction of Memory Grove.

"Nikki?"

I turned. It was Misfit.

"Have you seen Hunter?" she asked.

"No." I hadn't seen him in a week.

"You know where I can find some crystal?"

I faked a smile. "I don't, but you could find Michael and ask him."

She pouted at the idea. Michael didn't like her, and both she and I knew it. However, he could have found whatever it was she was seeking.

"Will you come with me to ask him?"

I laughed softly, knowing it would be a mistake. I shook my head no.

"What are you doing tonight?" she asked.

"I'm open."

"I'm going to drum up some money, get crystal, and head to an empty apartment I found near the Grove. You want to stay with me?"

I didn't have anything better to do. "Sure."

"Wait in the food court. I'll be back with money."

I shambled into the food court and found a table in a corner. I waited and I watched. I liked to watch people. I watched them shift between masks like a multicolored ballpoint pen being constantly clicked by an impatient teen. It was not just those of us in the Charade who walked the city streets pretending to be someone we were not. Deception of self and others was an epidemic.

I knew Misfit was probably giving some suit a blowjob, gagging on his dick and hoping she didn't throw up into his pants. It wasn't her first rodeo. If she needed to get high that bad, it was not my problem. If I benefited from it, I was alright with that. Misfit was a distraction at this point, and useful at other times. She had no role

Never Let Me Go

in the Charade and had no knowledge of it. She hung around with the goths because we had drug connections, knew safe places to crash, and watched out for one another as far as the cops were concerned.

About a half hour passed before Misfit walked back into the food court. She went straight to the bathroom. I strolled over and stood against the wall, waiting for her, running my fingers over the tiles, feeling the rhythmic canals between each smooth surface.

Misfit pushed through the bathroom door, releasing the smell of urine and cleaners. "Ready?"

I shrugged my shoulders and followed her. She found her fix. I stayed out of the transaction. Michael would have heard about it and been irate that I was speaking with a crack dealer. He would sink his fangs into me over this whole escapade regardless, but I figured why make it worse? I was cautious in my interactions when I was on my own, more because of the yellow-haired wolf than because of Michael. Michael wouldn't kill me; I was too valuable to Brenden. I found a sense of satisfaction when he was unable to find me.

Misfit led the way to an empty fourplex seated along the road to Memory Grove. Social interaction held no interest for me, so I set about finding a room for myself. Dark. Empty.

I awoke screaming and crying in the middle of the night. Another nightmare. A grey wolf chased me through the forest. I recognized the forest. My family went there every year, but this time something was different. I veered down a separate path, willing the wolf to follow. No more running; I turned to face him. Without slowing, he pounced on me. His front paws lay against my chest and his back paws straddled my thighs. I tried to push him off and got my feet underneath his soft, smooth belly. His fur was matted and coarse over the shoulders. Enormous teeth clamped down on my throat and ripped it out. I watched my life drain ruby red into the mud, creating a puddle. The wolf lapped it up.

Despite my screams, no one in the apartment stirred. I sat up, pulled my boots on, and left. I'd had the nightmare before, many times. Before the rape, I had always escaped the wolf's jaws.

Nicole Lowe

It was raining. Not a heavy downpour, just a cold drizzle. It was close to four in the morning. I walked to Memory Grove and crossed the creek to the east side, where the dirt trail meandered through the trees. The rain pattered the leaves and the water.

A half mile in lay the remains of a single-room stone house with a dirt floor. Small circles of trees pushed through the earthen floor. There were no walls. Only its foundation and corners still stood, half-buried in dirt.

I lay atop the exposed foundation, face to the sky. Rounded stones pressed painfully into my spine and shoulder blades, preventing sleep. I welcomed the discomfort. Sleep brought the wolf, and I wanted none of that.

Cold raindrops hit my face and hands. My thoughts chased one another, an endless stream of self-hatred. I needed to get out of this place, this city—just walk into the woods and never look back.

I hated my weakness. I hated my vulnerability. I hated my dependence on others for survival. Tearing against that shrapnel in my spine, I raged against myself.

```
                mirror

    sink the silver blade to the hilt
          of weakness i am built
         just an echo in the glass

   lay waste to my unprotected heart
           crucify my compassion
           suffocate my empathy

              shadows remain
           fearless destruction
             dauntless rage.
```

Dog tags knocked against one another. A whistle followed. I sat up on the wall. A Golden Labrador jumped up and licked my fingers. The wet dog smell climbed up my nostrils. The vitality in the soft, golden-brown eyes chased away my dejection. I smiled. I was quite a sight, makeup smeared by the rain, but the dog's owner said nothing as he strolled past.

A growl rumbled in my stomach. I stopped at the bathrooms on my way into the city, splashed cool water on my face, washing away and reapplying my mask. Avoiding Michael was at the forefront of my mind, but my feet betrayed me with their habitual steps. Before long, I was back at Grounds.

My guts clenched each time the bead door jangled. I had a few cups of the house coffee before Ralph showed up. I hadn't seen him since the first time I ran away and hid in his house under the table. The memory brought a smile to my lips.

"On the run again, Nikki?"

I puckered my lips and smiled.

He laughed, straggly hair swinging with his head.

Ralph was a vampire and a member of the Black Hand. He was next in line for an apprenticeship as a mage, thus he spent most of his time with Spider and Ogre. I wanted to get out of Grounds to delay Michael's wrath for as long as I could. Ralph and I trundled through the ZCMI Center, trying on clothes and shoes, then headed over to Paisley Park.

I stayed at Paisley when everyone else set off for coffee. Someone would tell Michael I was here, so I waited and strategized. He was going to be furious. Fear and anger welled up within me. I didn't want a confrontation in front of everyone, and the confrontation was unavoidable. They shouldn't witness my submission to placate his rage.

I was sitting toward the back under the crimson trees as his unmistakable footfalls grew louder. I turned to face him, tears already falling down my cheeks. He slowed. I reached for him, and he pulled me into his embrace.

He raised my chin and wiped my eyes. "Where have you been? Why did you take off from Megan?" He spoke in a whisper, but the undercurrent of rage was there.

My tears had caught him off guard.

I bowed my head. "I went for a walk. I needed to breathe. My mother was patrolling the neighborhood. She saw me, and I had to go with her. The nightmares won't stop." Slow and easy, my eyes rose to meet his. "If you're not there, the wolf comes for me. I'm afraid he's coming back." I buried my face in his chest.

He held me for a long time, stroking my hair and back. My eyes closed, and I relaxed. Then the tension in his body began to creep in. He extended his arms, pushing me away from him, and squeezed my shoulders.

"Don't you fucking leave without my permission again. Do you understand?" He jerked me once as he spit out the words.

I nodded.

He pressed his fingers and thumbs into my shoulders. "Do you understand me?"

"Yes," I said, looking him full in the face. "I understand."

"Let's get you cleaned up."

Everyone was getting ready to leave for Confetti when we arrived at Grounds. Brenden and Deanna were seated at the first table past the bead door. Brenden raised an eyebrow at Michael.

"We've got it straightened out," Michael told him.

Brenden looked me up and down. I wrapped my arms around myself.

"Better than I expected," he said.

He did not expect submission. I was defiant, but not stupid.

"She needs me more than she's willing to admit," Michael said. "But she will."

I glowered up at him, teeth clenched to keep my tongue in check.

"You are beautiful when you're angry," he said flatly.

abandoned love

you haven't a chance
you're just a toy to me

i abandoned my love
tossed it away
the tears no longer consume me

won't you ever see?
the devil lives inside of me

discarded like trash
forgotten in life
no more pain waiting for me

just playing games
it's only a chase to me.

After dancing at Confetti, we needed a place to crash for the night.

"I know a place." The words tumbled from my lips before my mind caught a grip of what my tongue was uttering.

Some part of me was compelled to return to the wolf's den.

"There is this old paint factory just down the street."

Michael and I entered the building first. Patrick and Sandi trailed behind, followed by a small group of her friends. Sandi was infatuated with Patrick and would have followed him anywhere.

Broken glass crunched and ground on the floor beneath our feet. Sandi and her friends were talking and laughing.

"Shut up," Michael snapped.

They slowed their pace and their voices dwindled to whispers and stifled giggles.

We kicked up dust with each step and coughed into our sleeves. Michael pushed some electrical wires aside. Large hulks of machinery cast long shadows as the moon shone through broken windows and walls. We explored until we found an office space on the second floor that looked comfortable enough.

The others wandered off to check things out. The rising urge to be sick flattened any curiosity I might have had. Michael sat up against a wall, legs outstretched. I was between his legs with my back against his rising and falling chest. I absorbed his strength.

"You're shaking. Are you cold?" He wrapped his arms around me. I nodded yes, but I wasn't cold.

"You should not be hanging out with people I'm not familiar with. You should stay with one of the elder members all the time."

What he meant by elder members was Patrick, Brenden, Deanna, Spider, Ogre, or himself. I was desperate to push him away and pull him to me and never let go.

"I know you would like me to," I said, "but sometimes I just need a break from all the supervision. I need my space."

"I worry about your safety. I don't need you to be seen hanging out with the wrong people." What he meant was that he didn't want to look like he couldn't control me. His ability to choose words that hid his intent was an endearing quality, and I hated him for it.

"It's not like I go hang out with the wolves. I'm usually with Shelly." That wasn't true; I rarely spent time with Shelly, but he didn't see her enough to confirm that statement. I was confident she would lie for me, so long as the questions came from Michael and not Brenden. She would not lie to Brenden.

"Consider your position," he said. "You're valuable, and they know it. They will take advantage of any opportunity."

I was afraid of him, yet clung to his strength. "I can protect myself."

He gently placed his hand over my mouth. Footsteps were coming up the stairs. I moved away from him and crouched low to the floor. He rose to his feet and stepped between the doorway and me. Beams of light drove back the darkness.

Cops.

They shone their lights on the two of us. We stood, hands out. They pointed the flashlights directly in our eyes, trying to figure out if we were high. We weren't.

"You two are trespassing. Do you have ID?"

We spoke at the same time. "No."

"We'll need your names and dates of birth."

Michael gave them his information. They ran his name and found nothing. They asked for mine. I gave them my name and date of birth, but the wrong year. I made myself seventeen to protect Michael.

"You're out after curfew," the female officer said to me. "Do your parents know where you are?"

"Yes."

The male cop pointed to Michael. "You can go." Michael didn't move.

"I'll be fine," I assured him. "I'll see you in two days."

He hesitated a second more, then nodded and left. I wanted him to get the others out before they were caught.

The officers hauled me to the police station. I asked to use the bathroom and hid my ID in my combat boot. They called my father and he confirmed the birthdate I'd given them. I asked to be released to Melanie, my old friend Julie's mom. He consented. He didn't know the day I was born and he didn't want me home. I couldn't say I blamed him. I wanted to forget I existed, too.

Melanie picked me up and took me to her house, which was only a few blocks away from my parents. The window of her car was cold against my face. A few other cars drove through the streets. I needed to escape the conflict in my skull.

Metallica's "The Unforgiven" met me before anyone else in the pale-yellow house. Julie's house was where my life diverged from its white picket fence path. It was there where I began smoking and drinking, despite Julie's pleas not to.

We met in the last term of seventh grade. Julie and I were inseparable, until she moved to Arizona to live with her father. After she left me, her house lost its sense of home. I returned a few times during my transition from gangbanger to goth, but those visits became less frequent as I began to believe in the Charade.

I pulled the door open and the smell of cigarettes, stale food, and dirty litter boxes assailed me. Four guys with mullets, tight jeans, and faded t-shirts huddled around a circular glass table. Four shot glasses stood before each, and there was a bottle of vodka at the center. They were bouncing quarters into the shot glasses. Each miss equaled a shot.

I interrupted their game by snatching four shots and sending them down my throat, one after another. I followed its warmth through my chest and into my stomach.

"Hell yeah!" Nick said.

I'd always had a thing for Nick. He was on the high school football team and drove a 1970s Chevelle.

I hadn't seen any of them in weeks. There were lots of hugs and questions about where I'd been. I climbed the stairs and stood in the doorway of Julie's room. A memory shimmered in the shadows. Julie and I, sitting on the floor amid dirty clothes, shoes, and schoolbooks. She tossed me a razor blade. I pierced my flesh with the corner of the silver blade, carving red letters to form the names of boys I'd had sex with—Steve and Rick—on the inside of my ankle. I squinted in the dim light and wiped the blood away with my fingers.

The room still smelled like her. I ran my fingers over the clothes still hanging in the closet. I walked out and closed the door behind me.

The vodka ran out, but not before I was saturated and freed from reason. Chris, who wore his mohawk flat and combed back, was lying on the couch. He beckoned to me with his hand. My fumbling feet caught the carpet and I tumbled into his waiting arms, boiling over with giggles. He rested his chin on my head as I tucked myself between him and the back of the couch. He ran his fingers through my hair as we listened to "November Rain" by Guns N' Roses. My lips formed the words of the song.

"We need some weed," Jeremy said.

Nick and Jeremy's eyes swelled with delight. "Jason!" they said in unison.

Chris sprang to his feet and I sank into the depth of the brown couch that was blackened with use. He grabbed my reaching hand and pulled me to my feet. I swayed and had to grab hold of his shoulders to stop the cyclone.

Snickering and snorting, they plunged out the back door into the dark. I followed.

Jason always had potent weed with a pungent smell. I thought he must have laced it with something, because everyone said it was better and stronger than any other weed they could get. We knocked on his door. He answered in a smart red t-shirt and sagging basketball shorts. A red rag was tied around his ankle.

He came back to Julie's with us and passed a blunt around. When it came to me, I passed it on. Marijuana had an odd effect on me; it made me "white out." Every time I smoked it, I would see a bright white light and nothing else. It was so disorienting that I'd fall to the ground, but remained conscious.

Jason sold a couple of dime bags to Nick and Jeremy. As he was leaving, he waved for me to come with him. We walked down the street and he opened the passenger door of his black satin Cadillac. I slid onto the leather seat. He walked around and climbed into the driver's seat.

"You don't like my weed?" he said.

"Weed's not my thing," I told him.

"You're pretty in a weird sort of way, in all that black. Mysterious."

I didn't respond.

"You ever have sex with a black man?"

I smiled. "No."

"I've never had sex with anyone like you, either." He meant a goth; his girlfriend was white.

"So do you really do black magic and sacrifice animals like everyone says?" he asked.

I shrugged my shoulders. "You can believe what you want."

103

He laughed and put his hand around the back of my head and pulled me in for a kiss. His tongue pushed into my mouth and slid alongside my own.

"Have sex with me," he whispered. "Right here. Right now."

"I'm not really interested," I said, getting out of the car. I started to walk back to the house and the car door opened and closed. I didn't turn around.

He called out, "Your loss, spell-caster."

I ended up passed out at Melanie's on a bed downstairs. I woke up fully clothed, but tangled up with Nick. I got up, used the bathroom, lit a cigarette, and walked to my parents' house.

My father had changed the locks and I no longer had a key, so I went in through the garage. The inside door squeaked, which was new. Our dog barked and came running into the kitchen. I let her out into the yard and then went upstairs.

My bedroom door brushed the carpet as I pushed it open. I stepped inside and found my pet rat waddling out from underneath my bed. He was mostly white, with a black head and a black stripe down his back. I fed him, cleaned his cage, and refilled his water. My father took care of him while I was gone.

I lifted him and he wrapped his scaly tail around my arm. The coat of stiff, coarse hairs tickled my skin. I wanted to take him with me, but I was afraid he would be lost or hurt out on the streets. I kissed his head and cradled him in my arm while I went through my closet, trying to decide what to wear.

Shadows draped my room, despite its west-facing window and the blinding sun outside. Purple and black curtains, made by my mother, blocked most of the light. The bedspread was black, purple, and green, with a black panther in the center. A poster of my favorite band, The Cure, was pinned to the wall. Five masquerade masks and a ten-inch statue of a mime adorned another wall. My mother had painted them for me. The masks reminded me to be wary, because everyone was false and pretended to be what they were not.

I pulled out some velvet leggings, a black blazer, and a white ruffle shirt. I needed bus money, which I found in my mother's turtle-shaped piggy bank. I picked out all the quarters and dimes. They cascaded to the bottom of my gothbox. I showered, got something to eat, and left the house.

When the bus arrived, I climbed inside and sat in the back. I never struck up conversations with others outside the goth community. I watched their interactions and I listened to their false conversations. My words and emotions were always guarded. People you thought were your friends collected information about you and used it against you as soon as it was beneficial to them. It was best just not to provide information to anyone in the first place.

People got on and off the bus, but no one sat in the back. I liked it that way. I wanted them to be afraid, and to stay away.

Dreams, goals, desires, ambition—I used to have those things. I lost them somewhere in the dank labyrinth of my soul. I wasn't even sure if they were still in there with me, if there was any "me" left. I didn't remember what they were, how it felt to strive for them, or how it felt to achieve them.

Who was I, anyway? What right did I have to claim a dream when so many had been robbed of theirs? Who was I to achieve more than the nothing I was? I breathed air that did not belong to me. I consumed food I had not earned. I was the infected. I survived just as any disorder or disease survived. I hid in the shadows, in the curve of the wall, under the benches, in the closet, and I waited.

In the United States, twenty-five percent of high school girls have been physically or sexually abused. Teen girls who are abused this way are six times more likely to become pregnant or contract a sexually transmitted infection.

chapter eight

I take a sip of my room-temperature water and set the bottle back on the floor by my feet. "Ms. Hardy, where were you living before moving in with your friends a week ago?"

Sabrina pulls her honey tresses up to put her hair in a bun, but the ends are tangled. She brushes them out with her fingers as she answers my question. "I was homeless."

"Were you staying in the shelter?"

"No way. There's so much crime and drugs around there."

"Where were you sleeping?"

"In a tent by the Jordan River." Finished with her brushing, she twists her hair into a bun.

"When was the last time you had a stable place of your own?"

"When Jackson isn't locked up."

"Is that your plan when he is released again?"

She hesitates.

Judge Cruz's eyebrows nearly disappear into his hairline. "Ms. Hardy?"

"No," Sabrina says, "I mean, I don't know what my plan is when he's released."

"Do you have a protective order against him?"

I want to scream at her and shake sense into her head. What in the hell does she mean, she doesn't know what her plan is when he is released? Run, disappear, and live should be her plan. But it's not, and we all know it. Eight is the average number of times a domestic violence victim leaves their batterer before they finally get away. Eight. The average.

"I been talking about that with my attorney. I'm going to get one." She nods.

"Ms. Hardy, have you ever separated from Jackson?"

"Once, after our son was born. Oh, and then when he's in jail. I guess we're sort of separated then."

One down, seven to go.

"Since he's been locked up, have you had a stable place to stay?"

She thinks for a few seconds before responding. "I stayed with Jackson's family when I was pregnant, but when you guys took McCartni, they kicked me out. So I stayed with some of Jackson's friends until one of them raped me."

"Did you report the rape to the police?"

She laughs. "They wouldn't believe me. They'd make me do all kinds of medical exams and drug tests. They never arrest the rapists. They probably wouldn't even talk to him. I don't need that. So I just left and went to stay by the river."

Butterflies fill my stomach. I stare down at my notes and take a few breaths. My chest tightens as I look back up at her — twenty-two years old, no education, no job, no home, and no family.

I ask, "Are you pregnant, Ms. Hardy?"

A part of me doesn't want to know the answer. I want to give her a bus ticket to get away from here. But the other part of me needs to know; needs to protect the child who may be growing within her.

She looks away. Is it shame, fear, or horror painting her face? All of the above, I decide.

"Six weeks." It's barely above a whisper, but it echoes in the quiet courtroom.

Patrick flipped the Tarot card face-up. "Death, a new beginning." The blue of his eyes connected with the hazel of my own.

"A new male will enter your life. He will take you where you need to go to learn whatever it is that you need to move forward in this life." A slight grin pulled at the corners of Patrick's lips.

Michael placed his hand on my thigh. Embers of anger continuously smoldered in his gut and burst into flames with the slightest breeze. I knew I was going to be burned. His jaw clenched and he ran his tongue along the front of his top teeth. He wiped his nose: thumb, index finger, thumb. My hand caressed his leg. It was so like Patrick to say such a thing to get under Michael's skin. What Patrick didn't understand was that Michael would only tighten his restrictions on me. Then again, maybe that was Patrick's plan to keep me "protected."

I pushed the cards toward Patrick. "Enough."

Brenden arched an eyebrow.

Patrick swiped the cards from the table and slid them into the deck with the tips of his fingers and shuffled.

"I'm curious—" Deanna began, but Brenden cut her off with a look. She slumped back and snuggled up against Brenden. I wanted to slap the grin off her face.

It was January, 1994.

Two white plates with melted cheese at the edges and five coffee cups with permanent brown stains crowded our table. I reached for my coffee and finished what was at the bottom. We were sitting in a back corner booth of the North Temple Dee's, where we wouldn't frighten the normal customers. We had been there for hours. We'd drunk at least ten cups of coffee each and eaten two plates of cheese fries between the five of us. It was midnight and time to go. Temperatures had fallen to the point where being outside all night was no longer viable.

"Where are we staying tonight?" I asked.

"What about above Dead Goat?" Patrick said.

Everyone agreed Dead Goat was best. Blades of icy wind cut us as we wound our way there. I pulled my trench coat tight and Michael wrapped his arm around me. I fit perfectly against him without jostling either one of us as we continued. Snow had yet to fall on the ground. If it had, it wouldn't have felt like Antarctica out there.

We got to Dead Goat and headed up the stairs. The smell of urine was strong at the ground level, but dissipated as we continued to climb. Dead Goat was a bar in an alleyway behind Paisley Park. There were offices above the bar, and a landing outside of each office on the different levels. The landings were about four feet by six feet. They were concrete, but out of the wind. Two or three of us could fit on each landing.

Michael put my hands between his own. My fingers barely reached beyond the palms of his hands. He rubbed them. "I'll get you gloves."

We laid down on the landing and he wrapped me in his trench coat with him as much as he could. I couldn't get comfortable. The cold seeped into my body. I lay awake most of the night.

In the morning, my hips ached from sleeping on my side, which was the only position I could lie in and still fit on the landing with Michael. No one slept much. The people who actually worked in these offices would want to get into them. The clouds had moved in overnight, trapping the sparse warmth close to the earth.

We headed back to Dee's for coffee and warmth. This time, we went to the one on 400 South. We traded off between the two downtown restaurants. Wait staff got sick of customers who didn't tip. Coffee, Confetti, and drugs were our primary objectives—tips didn't make the cut. No food that time, since the only money we had was what we could panhandle from the few people on their way to work.

My primary money source was asking random passersby if they had any change they could spare for the bus or for a phone call home. It was easier for people to hand over a little change if they believed it was for something wholesome, such as going or calling home. I stole cigarettes and went to the Catholic cathedral to get sack lunches from the nuns who lived next door, but cash was required for Confetti and acid.

"Patrick," Brenden said, "will you be going to Ogden soon?"

"Today, actually. I need to find Spider and Ogre."

"Michael, I would like to meet about the new wolves and other developments," Brenden said as he poured sugar into his coffee. Michael nodded.

"Nikki and I can have some girl time while you boys meet about business," Deanna said. "I need new leggings, anyhow."

I drank my coffee. I'd rather have stayed with Michael than go with Deanna. There was no way he was going to let me go after yesterday's Tarot reading, anyway.

He drummed his fingers on the table. "Have her back to me before sundown."

———

That evening, Shelly invited me, Deanna, and Brenden to stay at her house because her dad was out of town on business. It was around seven when we arrived. Michael and I sat on the couch while Shelly ordered pizza. Brenden was opening drawers and cupboards, looking for any leftover weed. After he finished with those, he started going through containers on the counters and in the living room.

Shelly slid the mouthpiece of the phone away from her mouth. "You know he took it all."

Brenden found a pipe, but no weed. The bowl was empty. Undeterred, he tried her dad's bedroom door.

Shelly laughed. "You've got to be kidding. Do you think he would leave his door unlocked?"

Brenden looked at her. "Not with you in the house."

Michael shook his head. "If you want weed, Brenden, I can get you some as soon as she's off the phone. How much do you want?"

"Dime is fine," Brenden said.

Michael made two calls. Twenty minutes later, he stepped outside and returned with a dime bag. The weed got there quicker than the pizza.

Shelly shook her head. "Fiends."

After we ate, they rolled a couple of joints on the table and went for walk around the apartment complex.

When they came back, everyone got into swimsuits and walked to the indoor pool. Laughing, I tried to push Michael in. He held me back with one hand, grinning. He grabbed my grasping fingers with his other hand, pulled me to him, picked me up, and tossed me into the water.

111

Michael cannonballed into the deep end and swam over to me. He picked me up by the waist and lifted me over his head. I dove in and glided along the bottom of the pool. I came up in front of Michael and wrapped my legs around his waist. His arms encircled me and he pressed his lips to mine.

We played water volleyball—Deanna, Shelly, and me against Brenden and Michael. We never had a chance. The boys just got through the water easier.

Back in the house, we made popcorn, settled onto the couches wrapped in blankets, and watched *The Lost Boys*. I fell asleep against Michael's chest, listening to his heartbeat while he ran his fingers through my hair.

Around noon the next day, we took the bus downtown. We asked for spare change along the way until we had enough for coffee.

We were standing in line waiting to order. My hand played across Michael's back as I watched a new guy come up the stairs. Michael turned at the sound of the door chime.

The guy had chin-length, light-brown hair, a stocky build, about five feet eight inches tall. He wore a black leather trench coat, black slacks, and a light turquoise button-down shirt. My curiosity was tickled and I watched him too long. Michael noticed. The guy was watching me too, and didn't even try to hide his interest.

Michael stepped in front of me, concealing me from view. I ordered my coffee and stepped around Michael to go into the back room. He caught my arm.

"Stay here."

Deanna snorted in her attempt to stifle a laugh and walked to the back room with a bounce in her step.

One last time, she turned and smiled, beckoning me to come. I looked up at Michael as he ordered coffee. He shook his head no. I pressed my teeth together, but didn't move. Deanna shrugged and walked into the back.

After we had our coffee, Michael prodded me down the hall. He pointed to a spot at the table where Brenden and Deanna were sitting. There were only three chairs, and Michael chose to stand behind me in the corner. The new guy was sitting on the couch, reading a book on runes. He looked at me over the top of the book every once in a while.

"I smell a dog," Brenden said.

Michael mumbled in agreement.

"You haven't even spoken to him," I said. "You can't know from just looking."

In my anger, I forgot who I was speaking to; Brenden was one of the few who *could* know, just by looking at someone.

He narrowed his eyes and cocked his head to the side. "Can't I?"

"I know from the smell," Michael said.

Brenden laughed.

Deanna smiled at me, but said nothing.

Misfit came in. When her eyes moved around my table, she sat next to the wolf on the couch. She knew better than to approach me when I was with Brenden and Michael—or even Deanna, for that matter. She started talking to the wolf in a whisper, which made Michael shift behind me. Brenden got up to go out back and smoke. He motioned for Michael to come with him.

"You're coming." Michael reached his hand out to me. I looked at his hand and then up into his face.

"Let her stay," Brenden said. "Deanna's here."

I smiled. Michael did not.

Deanna's face broke into a wide grin. "We won't move," she said.

I glared at Michael. He started to leave, then turned and focused on me. He pointed his index finger in my face. "Don't. You. Move."

I held his stare, mine just as menacing as his. He was starting to piss me off.

The wolf watched them walk out the back door. After a minute, Deanna looked at him, grabbed me by the hand, and walked over. She introduced herself, then me.

His name was Aaron. His eyes flicked to the back door.

Deanna smiled. "Don't worry about them. They'll be out there a few minutes. Where are you from?"

"I just got into town from Job Corps and I heard that this coffee shop was the place to meet my kind of people."

"And what, exactly, are your kind of people?" Deanna asked.

"Well, I thought people similar to you, but with the way your goons are acting, I'm not so sure."

Deanna shushed him with her hand. "They're just nervous around new faces." Her smile broadened. "They may warm up if they get to know you a little."

Yeah, they'll warm up, I thought. *While they rotate his carcass over a pit of hot coals.*

"I'm not so sure," Aaron said.

"I'd give them some space for a day or two," Deanna said, "but don't let them scare you away. You are so nice to look at." She looked at me and ran her tongue along her top teeth.

He smiled and let out a small laugh.

Deanna, still holding my hand, stood. "It was very nice to meet you, Aaron."

I grabbed a copy of Slug, a local punk and gothic magazine, on our way back to the table. About a minute later, Brenden walked in through the back door. Michael walked in through the front. He looked at the magazine, then at me. I smiled, daring him to say one word about it.

———

Aaron disappeared and Michael loosened up a bit again over the next week. I was able to get away for a few hours while he was out with Brenden, Spider, and Ogre. They would be back for Confetti, as always.

I got off the bus at Crossroads Mall and cut through to Paisley Park to see who was around. Bill and Mariah, a couple of hippies I sometimes helped find weed and acid, were there. The Job Corps kids—JC kids, we called them—were in town on a weekend pass. Many of them knew Michael because he hooked them up with anything they desired, so I didn't stay long. They created an interesting mix when they were in town and put Michael on high alert.

"Hey Nikki, where's your man?" Bill called out.

I rolled my eyes. "He'll be back around seven."

"Cool."

I continued my walk to Grounds and noticed Aaron across the street. He was keeping pace with me, occasionally glancing over as he walked. I smiled and spun around with my arms out. I was free—at least for a time. He smiled, laughed, and walked over.

I sipped the coffee he bought me as we walked down the street together.

"I see you're free from your entourage?"

"I am at this particular moment."

"And do they know where you are, at this moment?"

I laughed. "No, not really. I'm supposed to be going home to change."

Aaron had steel-grey eyes. His broad smile showed a row of straight, white teeth.

I blew into the lid hole of my coffee. "I've never seen you around, and I'm in Salt Lake a lot."

"I'm in the JC program learning a trade," he said. "I'm from Washington, originally. Everyone kept talking about the scene in Salt Lake, so I came hoping to meet people outside of the JC. Most of them are there just to get out of court charges."

My hand was twitching to touch his hair. "Do you want to go to Liberty Park?"

He smiled. "Sure. I have friends who live right over here. Do you like raves?"

"I've never been to one, but I like acid and dancing."

"You'll love raves, then." He took me by the hand. "There is a big rave in town tonight and some of my friends are going. Do you want to go?"

Michael was going to kill me. I smiled. "Yes."

We walked to his friend's house.

A wave of patchouli nearly bowled me over when the door opened. There were tie-dye tapestries hanging on the walls and over the windows. I felt like I'd walked into a kaleidoscope. Grateful Dead posters and peace signs plastered one wall. I recognized a couple of faces from Paisley. I silently hoped they didn't know Michael.

We walked to a tattoo shop in Sugarhouse a few blocks east of Confetti to get tickets for the rave. Aaron and I waited outside while his friends went in. They were told that tickets were sold out, which meant Aaron didn't have the right password. Rave locations were secret. Without the password, there was no getting in.

"I'm sorry you had to walk all over Salt Lake," Aaron said.

"I don't mind," I said. "But when we get back downtown, we can't be seen together."

The six of us smashed ourselves into a cab. I climbed into the back seat with Aaron and ended up sitting on his lap. I could smell his cologne. Michael's words—"I smell a dog"—echoed in my head.

Aaron pressed his face into my hair. "You smell like vanilla." He brushed my hair away from my neck and nuzzled me. I laughed.

When we got out of the cab, he kissed me on the cheek. "This is where we part ways."

I nodded and waved.

———

My feet made light clamps as I walked down the internal halls of Hunter's antique apartment building. I ran my fingers down the smooth white walls and stepped around the old-fashioned radiating furnaces from the early 1900s.

Kim answered the door.

"Hunter home?" I asked.

"No." She held the door closed to the width of her body.

"I just need to change real quick, and then I'll be gone."

She pushed the door open and walked away.

I'd planned to shower, too, but with Kim there I decided to just change my clothes. I went into Hunter's room. It was filled with the scent of him. I changed into a flowing, antique white silk shirt and a long, slender black skirt. I left him a note saying I was there and missed him.

When I pulled the door open, Kim was standing in the hallway with arms folded.

"How are things?" I asked.

She smirked. "Dandy."
"Thanks for letting me in."

I was halfway to Grounds when a thought slapped me in the face: I hadn't started my period. I was four weeks late. The last thing I needed was to get pregnant.

Michael and I weren't doing anything to prevent it from happening. I realized that was stupid of me. I considered my options. I'd heard that crystal meth would make you miscarry, and I knew Michael could get some. I also thought that if I could get someone to punch me in the stomach hard enough, I would have a miscarriage.

A baby was not what I needed. Michael was the last person I wanted to talk to about it. I pulled a cigarette out of my gothbox and lit it. If I asked him for some crystal meth, he would probably punch me in the stomach. Problem solved. *Fuck!*

I pushed through the bead door at Grounds with a coffee warming my hands. Michael stood and stalked toward me. He kissed me hard on the mouth, pushing my teeth into my lips. He wrapped his arm around me and guided me back with the rest of the goths.

"How was your parents' house?"

"No one was home. Thank god. I just changed, fed my rat, and left."

He kissed me on the forehead, then on the mouth, and moved to my neck. Then he stopped. He picked up a handful of my hair and pressed it to his face. "Who's been touching you?"

I hesitated. "No one." I shook my hair out of his hand.

"I'll find out who it was and they'll wish they never laid eyes on you," he growled.

"It's probably just from being at my parents' house," I said.

He didn't believe me. Once again, he took a handful of my hair and pressed it to his face. His grip on my arm tightened. I pulled away and joined a conversation with a couple of goths sitting next to us, trying to ignore him. The bathroom door opened and I looked up as Aaron came out.

Michael, already furious, hissed, "You got a thing for that wolf?"

He wiped his nose with his thumb and finger: right, left, and right.

I stared angrily at him. "What are you talking about?"

"He can't keep his eyes off you." His voice was vibrating with hatred.

"I don't care. I'm with you, and everyone knows that." I said it loud enough for everyone to hear.

"They'd better." He turned toward Aaron, then once again stood in front of me. The situation was getting intense.

"I need to talk with you," I said. "In private."

Michael motioned to the back door. He closed his hand around mine and we walked outside and down to the bottom of the steps. No one else was around. I lit a cigarette. "I haven't started my period. It's three, maybe four weeks late."

He lit a cigarette. "Is that why you have been asking around for crystal? You want to lose our child?"

A few days before, I'd asked someone if they had a connection. It wasn't for me, but that didn't matter now. Of course, he'd found out. I scowled at my own stupidity.

"I don't want a baby. I don't need a baby." My voice was icy.

"I find out you touch that shit, and you are going to regret it," he said, equally cold. "You should be happy. We are perfect for each other. We are strong together." He pulled me to him. "I'll always be here. I'll take care of you both."

"I don't even know if I am pregnant." I pulled away and turned toward the alleyway between the buildings, struggling with a rising urge to run or punch the brick wall.

He grabbed my hand before I was out of his reach. "You are mine. You have always been mine and always will be mine." He pulled me into his embrace and forced his tongue into my mouth.

"What have you had to eat today?" His voice became gentle and reassuring.

"Nothing," I said, giving in, at least for a time.

"Let's get you something." He took me inside, never releasing his hold on me. He stared Aaron down as we approached. His cologne hung around him in a cloud. Michael's pace slowed.

He turned to Aaron, grabbed his throat, and pulled him in close. "Fucking touch her again, and you're a dead doggie." Michael shoved him back down on the couch.

Aaron tucked his tail between his legs and held up his hands in surrender, nodding vigorously. No one there would have stepped between Michael and his prey.

That night, I watched myself sleep in a dark room with a single bed. The full moon's silver glow stretched across the walls. I was wrapped in a blanket. Something dark sat on the end of the bed. It was long and lean. It watched me sleep too. I could feel its apocalyptic emptiness. It moved toward my sleeping form, reaching for my exposed hand. Its blackness began to devour my hand and arm. I began to choke. It continued to eat. I awoke screaming and clawing at my arm.

Michael was at my side. "You're alright. It was a dream. Come here."

He opened his arms. I punched him in the chest. "Get away from me!"

He grabbed at me, but I pushed him away. He caught hold of my flailing arm and pulled me close to him, holding me against his body, stroking my hair.

"Shhh, it's alright."

I shook and cried.

He held me.

Nicole Lowe

my redeemer

death, my redeemer
whispers love songs
rescue me from my chaos
it's gone on too long

temple crumbled on the floor
couldn't take it any more
shattered skull, blood-splattered walls

i gave up everything
you made me fall apart
all you have left is my small, worthless heart.

Fifty percent of teens have never considered how a pregnancy would affect their lives.

chapter nine

"Have you gotten any prenatal care?" I ask.

Sabrina shakes her head.

"Ms. Hardy, you need to answer aloud," the judge reminds her.

She clears her throat. "Not yet, but I'm going to. I called yesterday, but no one answered."

"Who did you call?"

"The University of Utah."

I raise my eyebrows. "And they didn't answer?"

She shakes her head.

"Ms. Hardy…" Judge Cruz begins.

"They didn't answer," Sabrina confirms.

"When was the last time you used methamphetamine?"

"Two weeks ago, but I didn't know I was pregnant then or I wouldn't have used."

Now she has two reasons to leave the state to get away from Jackson and to keep her unborn child, but she won't go. If I bought her a plane ticket and put her on the plane myself, she would be back within a few days.

Why? Because she still has seven more times to go before she finally gets away. Maybe I'm cynical. Or maybe I'm just a realist.

"Who's the father?"

"I'm not sure."

"Are you in a position to care for McCartni today?"

"Not yet, but I'm working on things."

"What about the new baby, are you ready for that child?"

"I'm working on things."

"What do you think you need to do to become the mother that McCartni and the new baby need?"

"I need drug treatment, a house, and a job."

"What about domestic violence treatment?"

She looks to her attorney. Jake can't answer her unvoiced question.

"If the state wants me to do it, I will."

Not the answer anyone wanted to hear. Jake jots down another note.

"What about therapy?"

"Yes, I forgot about that."

"What have you done in the last nine months to accomplish those things?"

———

Michael became increasingly possessive over the next few weeks. I couldn't go anywhere without him. I hated it. I just wanted him to go away for a little while. It wasn't as if I was going to do anything. I just needed my space.

"I want to be with you and I understand that I'm yours," I told him.

"It's everyone else who needs to understand," he said.

"I can't control what others think, so why am I punished?"

"You're rebellious and independent. You don't listen to what I tell you. You always want to find your own way."

"You don't trust me."

He smiled and kissed me. "I don't trust others."

We were sitting on a red-brick bench at Paisley Park. Michael turned his head and looked across the street at the group of wolves congregated there. Aaron was with them.

"You have to understand how valuable you are to them," he told me. "Especially now. You need to stay close to me at all times. I need to know where you are and who you're with. It's just how it is."

"I have to use the bathroom. Are you going to follow me there, too?" Anger dripped from each word.

I stood and started to cross the street. He stopped me with a soft touch on my fingers. He tried to kiss me, but I turned away. He motioned for Deanna to go with me. She rolled her eyes.

"Humor him," Brenden said, without looking up from his book.

Deanna and I walked across the street and into the mall.

I slammed the stall door closed. "This is bullshit. I'm sick of being followed around like a child."

"I wouldn't let Brenden do that to me," she said.

I came out of the stall. "Brenden isn't twice your size," I said, matching her tone.

She shrugged her shoulders. "True." She tapped her chin with her finger. "And I'm not carrying his child, either."

A spiteful smile crossed her face and I wanted to punch her in the mouth. Instead, I glared at her. "I may not be carrying Michael's. Even if I am, it won't be for much longer if I have anything to do with it."

She shook her head. "That would be unwise."

I softened my voice, pleading with her. "Deanna, really, I don't need everyone to know."

"Only Brenden and I know."

"Let's keep it that way," I snipped, but then softened my voice again. "It's not for sure, anyway."

We walked out of the bathroom and Deanna nudged my arm with her elbow. I looked up. Aaron was waiting at the end of the hall.

"Good day, ladies." He was grinning from ear to ear.

"How are you?" I said. I moved to hug him, but Deanna grabbed my arm and raised her eyebrows. Michael would know. I covered my mouth and coughed.

"I've been better," he said.

"And what made you better?" Deanna asked. He didn't reply.

"I see you've made some friends," I said.

"Well, your friends were less than inviting. In fact, they seem to have gotten even more hostile." He looked at me questioningly.

"They're concerned about your associates. We don't all get along, and the pack you're running with is not compatible with us, you could say."

I wasn't sure how much Aaron knew about the Charade. Maybe he knew nothing and really was just looking for friends. Brenden and Michael would have told me it was a reckless assumption to make, which would get me killed. Even if Aaron knew nothing of the Charade, our friendship would get us attacked by both sides. Not mixing was the one thing we all agreed on.

"Are you alright? I've noticed security has been upgraded," he said with a nervous laugh and a quick glance at Deanna.

"Oh, I'm alright. We ought to be getting back, though. Nice seeing you again."

"You two friends?" Deanna said as we walked away.

"Not really. I just don't think it's a good idea to raise the hackles of the wolves with so much at stake. Keep your friends close and your enemy closer, isn't that the old adage?"

"Right," she said, drawing out the word in sheer skepticism.

I glanced over my shoulder at Aaron, who was watching us walk away. He waved. I turned back and caught Michael pouncing through the doors. He jumped down the four steps to the food court and spotted us.

"He talk to either of you?" he asked through clenched teeth.

I tried to play dumb. "Who?"

Deanna stared down at the square tiles on the floor. Michael looked at her, and then at me. I held his stare. "Oh, you mean Aaron?"

"Is that the dog's name?"

I was blowing on the embers in his gut and I knew it.

Sensing Michael's anger escalating, Deanna intervened. I was being reckless. She didn't want a scene. "He just said hi and asked how we were doing. No harm done."

Michael wrapped his hand completely around my bicep and dragged me out of the mall. I tried to shake him off, but his grip only tightened. Something had to give.

I waited for the moment when I could get free—not forever, just for a couple of days. Michael would be pissed, but I really didn't care. I felt trapped and caged. I knew myself well enough to know I was getting to my breaking point, and I was becoming self-destructive. Michael knew me well, too. I was rebellious, independent, and I cut my own path through the world.

I was sitting on the floor in the corner of the living room at Sunny's. Michael was asleep. I watched the steady rise and fall of his chest. The moon gave enough light for me to see the lines of his muscular arms, legs, and bare chest.

I thought about sneaking out, but he would have heard me and been angrier than I could control. It was better to make it look like I thought I had permission to go do something on my own, and then not return for a couple of days.

I planned to tell him I was going to the doctor. He wouldn't say no. My concern was that he would want to come. He'd ask what the pregnancy test results were. I could get a home test at the store, take it, and tell him I had one done. Whatever the answer was, I would tell him I was upset and needed some time alone to process it. He'd be mad, but I didn't think he would do anything to actually hurt me.

I crawled over to the bed where he was sleeping and slowly made my way up his body, kissing him as I went.

He stirred, then reached for me. "What do you want?"

"You."

The next morning, after breakfast, I said, "I think I should go to the doctor."

He finished chewing. "I agree. But I can't go with you. I want to be there, but people may be concerned about our relationship."

I hung my head and feigned disappointment. "I'm going to stop by my parents' house, too."

"Until tomorrow, my sweet." He kissed my hand.

"Tomorrow," I said.

Freedom at last.

I didn't waste any time leaving. I was worried that he'd tell me to wait for Deanna or something. I stopped at the Rite-Aid and picked up a pregnancy test. I went straight into the bathroom. I stood in the stall and read the directions. They said I had to pee on the stick first thing in the morning. I shoved it into my gothbox and left.

I took the bus to my parents' house. No one was home. I took a shower. I stood under the water and stared down at my belly. I rubbed my hands over it. I was all mixed up in a blender of fear and anger.

Stop it.

I changed my clothes and took care of my rat. It was late afternoon when I headed back downtown. I got off the bus at the Gallivan Center. Michael never came through there, so I felt safe to just hang out and relish my space.

Not many goths came through the Gallivan Center during the day, so I was surprised when Aaron approached with a bunch of hippies. I recognized all but one of them.

"Fancy meeting you here," I said.

He laughed. "Your boy let you out?"

"He's just protective, and my being out is my choice," I said in a tone that begged for a challenge.

Aaron shrugged. "Whatever you say. I've seen the way he is with you."

My eyes didn't move from his and I didn't say a word.

He looked away. "So, you up for some fun? My new friend, Sam, knows where to get some really good dose, if you're interested?"

Dose was another term for LSD. I smiled.

Michael didn't approve of my LSD use, but he knew he couldn't stop me. He told me that when I tripped, I bounced back and forth between silly, enticing, and intellectual.

"I never know what I'm going to get from you, and you change midstream," Michael told me once. "Why do you like it, anyway?"

He never quite understood when I tried to explain. I could feel it move through my veins. It made me feel alive and on fire. LSD enhanced my vision. Colors were radiant. Lines were more defined—at least until they started moving and morphing into something from deep within my imagination. Always, I would get lost in the maze of my own thoughts.

"I'm very interested," I told Aaron. "How much?"

"Three dollars a hit. It's double-dipped white blotter."

A smile claimed my lips, with mischief close behind. "I'll get two."

"We can all go over to the guy's house, but it'll go through Sam," he said.

Sam was a year or two older than me. He had chin-length, earthy-brown hair. He wore a Grateful Dead t-shirt and ripped-up jeans. Although not a vampire, he was definitely an elf. It was in his bone structure: narrow face, long fingers. He was a ragdoll moving with the flow of life, rather than against it.

Once Sam left to get the acid, I turned my attention to Aaron.

"We were just passing through when I noticed you lounging there in the shade," he said.

I smiled. "I appreciate you remembering your failed offer of good acid from a few weeks ago."

He laughed, then got up and went to the bathroom. We were sitting in a group on the lawn at Liberty Park. When he came back a few minutes later, he sat next to me on the grass.

"I don't get it. Why does your boyfriend hate me so much?"

"It's complicated," I said.

His eyelids sagged. His head drooped and jerked up suddenly when his chin hit his chest.

"How long have you been using?" I asked.

"Using what?" His eyelids drooped again.

"One of my good friends is a heroin addict," I said, tossing a rock across the road that circled the park.

He turned away from me. "A few years. I left the JC because they started asking questions."

"I didn't notice any track marks."

"I shoot up under my tongue."

Michael must have known about this, as well. He had an uncanny sense about who used what. Aaron was just another Hunter in Michael's mind. There was room for only one heroin addict in my heart.

After a long time, Sam finally strolled back. His laugh was tinged with a touch of guilt as he approached us. "Sorry. I lost track of time when he busted out this big old bong. You can't expect me to turn down free weed." His eyes were small, red slits.

Sam pulled the acid out of the cellophane around his cigarette box. He pinched each hit between his fingernails and gently separated them. Everyone but Aaron dropped at the same time: sundown. We hung out at the park until it began to tickle the base of our brains. We needed to move somewhere, anywhere. We started walking downtown.

"We need to stay away from Main Street," I said.

"That's cool," Sam said, glancing back at me with half-closed eyes. The acid hadn't counteracted the effects of the weed.

I felt alive; flames coursed through my veins.

Once we got downtown, Aaron said he was tired and was going home. He left us with a wave. I never saw him again.

I peppered Sam with a million questions as we walked. He was from Montana and had come to Utah looking for his brother, James, who came down to the JC about six months before. He hadn't found him yet, but he assumed he would show up downtown eventually.

Sam had grown up on an Indian reservation and his mom was a medicine woman. He and his mom had gotten into a big fight over his drinking. She cut his hair off, and he left home in search of his older brother. He hitchhiked from Montana to Utah. His plan was to find his brother and then follow the Grateful Dead for a while—go to Rainbow Gatherings and the like. I had never heard of Rainbow Gatherings. I knew the Grateful Dead was a band, but I had never heard any of their music.

We wandered aimlessly until we came to Memory Grove. It drew us into its sheltering shadows and hidden alcoves.

"I'm going to the bathroom before go any farther," I said, and rushed off.

I stared at myself in the bent mirror. I pulled the pregnancy test out of my gothbox and tossed it in the garbage. I didn't want to know.

We took the trail along the east side of the river.

Sam said, "What do you believe in, Nikki?"

"It's complicated." I thought that was probably the best answer, but he persisted.

"Try me."

"I believe in a parallel reality, which is separate, but tied to this world. We call it the Charade. In my world, vampires, elves, mages, and werewolves are real. People here may appear to be unimportant, but in our world, they have a significant role in our future."

"I'm a wood elf of the Silvermoon clan," he said.

"I'm a dark elf," I said. I was unwilling to tell him more without knowing his intentions. In my mind, Brenden and Michael stood watching.

"I came for my brother," he said, "but I also came to find the dark elven princess. She is here in Salt Lake, and she is the key to the future of the elven race."

He had my attention. Everything else around us faded.

Before I could say anything, he turned toward the river. "I'll be back."

I sat alone on a wooden bench as my thoughts shifted like a Rubik's Cube. I needed to stay with Sam, regardless of where he went. I needed to bind myself to him. Michael was going to freak out. I would have to leave him and my coven behind. I gazed up at the stars and the full moon. Beautiful circles of red, green, blue, and purple radiated from its center. I needed a plan. I was going to lose everything.

Sam returned after what felt like an age. He took me by my hands and pulled me up. We walked down the cedar trail, hand in hand. I didn't know how much to tell him, but it had to be enough for him to keep giving me information.

"I'm a member of a coven here in Salt Lake," I said. "I may be able to introduce you to others who know where to find our princess."

"I believe I have located her." He knitted his eyebrows together. "But that will take a few days."

I was stitching the pieces of an escape plan together.

"If your suspicions turn out to be incorrect," I said, "let me know, and I'll be more than happy to help you by speaking to my grande sire."

He stopped in his tracks. "You're in a vampire coven?"

I bit my lip. "Our coven has many races with many abilities."

"I'm generally not wrong about these things."

"I want to go with you when you find her. I know she follows the true path to unite us all."

I knew then that I would have to return to Michael. Returning wasn't the problem. The problem was getting away again. My feelings toward Michael were jumbled. I wasn't capable of love any longer. I felt something for him, but that something vacillated between hate and tenderness.

Our roles in the Charade united us. My leaving would be a choice between life and death. I wanted to die. But I wanted my death to come at my own hands, not Michael's. My desire to look the Angel of Death in the face grew more intense with every passing day. I longed to slip into the eternal darkness, wrapped in the fallen angel's soft robes. I wanted to find peace, to quiet the constant chatter of my mind. I found comfort in the thought of the end to my torment.

Nicole Lowe

In America, three in ten teenage girls will get pregnant at least once before age twenty. That's nearly 750,000 teen pregnancies every year.

chapter ten

Love is not enough. It's one of things I learned working as a child welfare investigator and an attorney. Every parent I have encountered in my career has loved their child. Every. One.

Foster parents are snared by the same belief: If you love a child enough, things will turn out just fine. But it's not true. Love will not fix a child raised in an abusive home. Love will not fix a child who has watched domestic violence or lived with drug-addicted parents.

Love will not save a parent from themselves. Love will not inspire a parent to change. So what is it that determines which parents will be reunited with their children and which won't? What separates the fighters from the victims?

I have absolutely no clue. It's different for everyone, and they each have to find it on their own. It's hidden deep within them, and not in the external world. That much I do know.

Sabrina takes a deep breath. "I know I haven't done what I was supposed to do, but I want to now. I want to be a mother to my children. I've never had a mother. I don't want them to not have a mother."

Never Let Me Go

"Why didn't you want to be a mother before three weeks ago?"

The question hangs there. It's a cruel question.

Sabrina musters what's left of her strength, takes another deep breath, and plunges. "When I found out I was pregnant again, it made me realize I was about to lose the only good things I had in this world. I've screwed up so many times. I've burned every bridge. But I can't let McCartni down. Or this baby." She wraps her arms around herself protectively.

"Everyone just wants me to fail." Her eyes fill with tears. "No one is helping me get my kids back."

"No further questions, Your Honor." I lower myself into the swivel chair.

Love is never enough. It takes so much more.

"The doctor said I'm not pregnant."

I watched as the disappointment came and went from Michael's face. He took me in his arms and kissed me on the top of the head.

"Not yet," he whispered.

I pushed away from him and looked up into his eyes. "Not ever." I took three steps backward before he stepped between me and my exit.

He grabbed my arms, kissing me on the mouth. "We were meant to be together, and you are meant to bear our children."

I laughed. I knew what he wanted, and I gave it to him. It was rough, ending with bloody scratches down his back. Exhausted and covered in sweat, he fell asleep. I slipped out of the apartment and went to the bookstore for a few hours before it closed.

Nicole Lowe

I welcomed the chilled air on my skin as I strode down the street. I jumped onto the first bus headed downtown. From there, it was a short walk to Golden Braid Books. When I pushed the door open, I breathed in the smell of the books. That smell was like a drug for me; the fact it was mixed with the scent of coffee made it intoxicating. I walked the aisles, reading the spines of all the books and running my fingers along them.

I slid my fingers between the pages of a book on druids. I stopped at a picture. The woman was slumped against a tree, bare-chested, an infant suckling at her breast. Her head was lying next to her on the ground, blood matted in her hair. One hand clutched a short sword; the other was holding her child. Celtic wars spared none.

I stared at the page for a long time. Who suffered the greater loss, mother or babe? A child would forever tie me to Michael, and I believed that was his intent. My end would be less poetic than the mother on the page.

Hours later, I slipped back into the apartment. The blackout curtains only let me see a few inches in front of me. I stood just inside the door, waiting for my eyes to adjust to the darkness. If I tripped, I would wake him. I heard breathing just beside me. He was waiting for me next to the door.

"Where have you been?" His voice was dead even. My stomach knotted.

Before I could answer, he grabbed my arm and threw me across the room. My ribs slammed into the arm of the couch. All of the air rushed from my lungs. I covered my face and head with my arms and stayed where I landed.

...I can't breathe. Stop. Stop. Stop! I hear myself scream, but the words have no voice. It's dark. I feel the vomit coming up the back of my throat. He's on top of me, his blond hair in my face and mouth. He pulls my legs apart. His hands are on my throat. I can't breathe...

I sucked in all the air from the room in a gasp. I could hear Michael pacing in the dark. He threw open the curtains. The moon's glow pushed back the darkness, leaving shades of grey.

"It's just you and me," he said.

I breathed in again, filling my lungs. I tried to control the air as I released it. I got to my feet.

"I was at the fucking bookstore! The bag is right there by the door with the book I bought." I pointed at the white mass on the floor.

He picked it up and threw it at me. I blocked it with my arm. While I was distracted, he came at me and shoved me against the wall. One hand pressed hard against my chest. The other was at my throat. We stared at one another, my toes barely touching the floor. I would not cry this time. If he killed me, then he killed me. It would be done. Forever.

He let go of me. Again, we stared at one another. My heart was pounding so hard that I was sure he could see it. I began to lower myself to the floor, but didn't look away. My hand brushed the carpet, searching until it found the plastic bag. I pulled out a book on astrology and stood back up.

"This is the one I was telling you about." I held the book out to him, my hand shaking. "I've wanted it since I went shopping with Deanna."

He took the book, stepped into the moonlight, and read the back. Then he handed it to me. "Don't leave without my permission."

"I'm sorry," I whispered.

———

My feet hit the ground, one after the other. My breath was ragged and my chest heaving. I chanced a glance behind me. The grey blur moved between the trees. I tried to slow my breathing. I had to stay in control. I started to run again. Faster.

Trees flew by and branches snatched my hair. My toe caught a rotting log as I jumped to clear it. I crashed to the ground in a cloud of dirt. I spit dirt and leaves out of my mouth.

I could hear him breathing now. Snarling. Growling. I rolled to get out of his way, but it was too late. His powerful hind legs launched him from the log. Saliva dripped from his jowls, onto my face. His lips curled, exposing white fangs and black gums.

Michael was shaking me. "Wake up. You're safe, it's okay." He spoke in a gentle voice.

I stopped thrashing and fought to get to my feet. My eyes moved, searching the room. I tried to run to the bathroom, but tripped over the blanket wrapped around my body. I hit the floor, sending a shock through my arms.

"Calm down, you're okay," Michael was saying from behind me.

Sunny came out of his room and flipped on the light. "What's going on?"

"Nightmare," Michael said.

I was bent over the toilet, dry-heaving, shaking, drenched in sweat. I pulled my knees to my chest and rested my chin on them. I stayed that way for the rest of the night, unable to sleep. Michael sat with me.

We spent the next day at home watching movies. I slept in his arms, waking every few hours to make sure he was still there. We never talked about what happened. It was an unspoken agreement. For days, I fought sleep—terrified of returning to the wolf's den.

Michael paced between the living room and kitchen. It had been three days. "You need to get out of here. Get dressed and make yourself look presentable."

"Where are we going?" I asked.

"Does it matter?"

"Grounds?"

He nodded. "Hurry up. I've got shit to do and I don't trust you here alone."

Sam was at Grounds with another guy. I assumed it was his brother, James. There were only a few people in the coffeehouse. Michael directed me to a table in the corner. I sat, drank my coffee, and read my astrology book.

Michael stepped outside to smoke and to talk with some people. I didn't know who they were and I didn't care. He opened the door to check on me every couple of minutes.

Sam walked past to get more coffee and slipped a napkin onto the table. Five words were scrawled on the napkin: *Three days. California. I know.*

I wrote a quick note back*: The plan. Acid. Escape.*

I stood and dropped it on his table on my way to the bathroom. When I returned to my corner, the napkin was under a magazine at my table.

Tomorrow. Here. Seven.

I stuffed the napkin into my gothbox just as Michael came back inside and sat down. I set my book down. "Why won't you get high with me?" I asked, pouting slightly. "You get high with everyone else."

He brushed the hair out of my face. It had been a rough couple of days, and he was eager to please.

"Is it that important to you?"

"It shows you trust me, and that you want to share new experiences with me. It's fine if you don't want to. I can just hang with other friends."

He scowled. "When?"

"Tomorrow? I need to get away."

He nodded his assent. I smiled and kissed him.

I gestured in the direction of Sam and his brother. "I'm sure you noticed the new elves in town. I know Brenden is always looking for new vamps and elves, especially with the recent influx of dogs."

He nodded.

"Have you talked to them?" I asked.

He turned his face to me. His jaw bulged and his eyes narrowed suspiciously. "No. Have you?"

"I know my place."

He walked over to where Sam sat and pulled up a chair. He turned it backward and straddled it. I went into the bathroom and flushed the napkin down the toilet.

While they sat and talked, I read and made small talk with the goths coming and going into the coffeehouse. Once he was finished, Michael gathered me up. I risked a quick glance at Sam. He smiled.

"Confetti?" I asked.

137

Michael shrugged. "Sure."

We went back to Sunny's to get ready for the club. Michael tossed me a black velvet blazer and leggings. I went into the bathroom, splashed water on my face, and began to scrub. I dried my face and looked into the mirror. Michael stood leaning against the doorframe. I eyed him. "The door?"

He waved his hand at me. "No one is here. Do your thing."

I hesitated, but he didn't move. As I changed my clothes, he explained that Sam was a wood elf from out of state looking for alliances. His elves heard there were elven vampires in Salt Lake, and he came to see what was going on and how the races had been joined in harmony.

I handed him my blazer so I could put my makeup on. He laid it over his arm. "Would you be upset if we tripped with them tomorrow night?"

"It's alright. I know how important this is." I bit my tongue to keep from smiling. I leaned against the counter and began outlining my eyes and lips in black.

Michael had arranged to hang out with them the next night. He wanted to see if they were worth the time to explain our ways, or to unite with under a treaty.

"With them high," he said, "I'll be able to figure out their motives for coming, and what their actual connections are in Montana."

There were two things I could always count on with Michael: his desire for power, and his desire for control.

I had more freedom than usual that night at the club. Michael spent the whole time talking with Brenden in the front room near the fireplace. I tried not to allow myself to hope this would work. I told myself we would fail, and that Michael would beat the hell out of me. The thought strengthened my resolve.

———

I turned the page of my astrology book. "Can we go in yet?"

"Soon," Michael said.

We were sitting on a bench in the shade across from Grounds, watching who came and went. We'd been there for two hours. I read my book while Michael stood, sat, and paced.

"I just want to be cautious," he said. "I don't know these two and I'm not going to risk you or the coven if they bring along anyone we don't trust."

"When we wake up tomorrow, can we go to Sam Wellers or Golden Braid? I'm almost finished with this book."

"Yes, of course," he said, barely looking at me.

His pacing increased the closer it got to the time we were meeting Sam and James. I laid the open book over my belly and watched him. This would be the last night we were together. I waited to feel something—anything—but there was nothing. Again, I wondered if I was even capable of love, or if it even existed. I decided it would be best if it didn't exist. I picked up my book and continued reading.

"There they are," he said. I got to my feet. He reached for me and I went to him. Wrapping his arm around my waist, he pulled me around to the front of his body. With my hands on his chest, I looked up into his storm cloud eyes.

"Not a word about who you are, understand?"

"Yes."

He kissed me. "You're everything to me."

Michael pushed open the glass door and guided me in, his hand on my lower back.

"Are we getting coffee?" I asked.

"Probably not. Just go to the back."

As soon as we pushed through the beads, Sam stood. "Ready?"

"Lead the way." Michael gestured toward the door.

We followed Sam to what I assumed was the same house he'd got the acid from the other night. Once the night enveloped our surroundings, we placed the little squares of paper on our tongues and waited. It took about twenty minutes for me to feel the acid marching through my veins.

I thought laughing and smiling were just part of experience, but Michael maintained his hard-as-stone face. Most of the time, he sat scrutinizing our companions. He cracked a few times, exposing his

Jack the Pumpkin King smile, but never once laughed or even snickered.

Our feet roamed the streets while we talked and laughed. Michael never let go of my hand. I was keenly aware that he was analyzing my interactions with Sam and James. Around ten, we made our way to the Dee's on 400 South.

"Coffee all around and a plate of cheese fries," Michael said. My hand wandered under the table to his inner thigh.

"Cream and sugar, please," I added.

The waitress set a cream-colored mug before each of us and poured the coffee. I shook the sugar to the bottom of the packets and tore them open: two creams and four sugars, every time.

Michael stroked my hair. "So, Sam, tell me about the elves in Montana."

Sam launched into explanation without hesitation. "The relationship between the wolves and vampires is much the same as here, I imagine. It was our home world. There are no mixed-race covens. Treaties between the elves and vampires have been in place for a long time, years, but I understand that here you've somehow mixed."

Michael nodded. "The dark elves and vampires mixed blood before the Rupture of Souls. Other than the wolves, we haven't had any conflict, even with pure-bloods."

"And the vampires have just accepted the mixed-blooded?" Sam asked.

"There's an understanding of the consequences to any who don't. We have some that quietly disagree, mostly elves." Michael sipped his black coffee.

Sam lit a cigarette, his third since arriving. "The fighting between the wood elves and the vampires has become fierce, including curses and spells. Territorial lines have cut each off from a few sacred places and are now strictly enforced."

"What caused the fighting?" I asked.

"Love."

James was quiet as he watched the cars drive by through the window. His breath fogged the glass. I had forgotten he was there.

I furrowed my eyebrows, and Sam continued.

"An elven princess fell in love with a vampire. The treaty between our peoples stated we would join together to fight the wolves, allowing the crossing of our lands, and allowing associations between the races—but mixing blood was certain death or banishment in both realms."

The waitress stood at the end of the table, wiping her hands on her apron, waiting for Sam to finish his sentence.

"Can we get some more coffee?" I asked. She turned back toward the kitchen, sending her ponytail swinging.

Smoke drifted from my mouth and curled to the ceiling. Michael wrapped his arm around my shoulders and played with my hair gently, tugging on the ends. I could see his mind working.

He ran his tongue across the front of his teeth. "So how'd that turn out for you?"

"The elves blamed the vampires for the treachery, claiming they used their powers of charm to draw the elf in. The vampires, of course, claim the elf came of her own free will and it was a matter of preordained, pure love."

Michael leaned forward and set his elbows on the table. "A similar situation arose between the dark elves and our coven many years ago in our home world. Most of those here have set aside their feelings on that to join energy and return home. There is one person who can repair the divide between the dark elves and the vampires, once we're home."

A group of goths came in and pointed to Michael. They began walking toward our table, but Michael held up his right hand, fingers splayed. The tall male nodded and they waited for a table of their own.

Sam covered his smile by taking a sip of coffee and lighting a cigarette. He waved the pack in front of James, who slid a cigarette out. Sam held out the lighter.

"Maybe this person can help my people since our divide took place?" Sam said.

"Maybe." Michael's face was stonelike.

"I'd like to speak with the sire of your coven. Perhaps enter into an alliance and bring members back to Montana to bridge the gap between our peoples."

Sam and I hadn't spoken of any of this—hadn't spoken at all, in fact, since the first night we met, yet he knew my coven's story.

My breath caught in my chest. I lit a cigarette and stood. Michael looked up, concern dipped in anger. My reflection stared back at me in his eyes. "I'm going out for some cool air."

He nodded. He knew; I saw it in his face. He knew my heart still ached for Brenden. Was there another like me who understood the rejection and loneliness of an elven princess? Someone who, despite years of being told that vampires were cold, compassionless beings, had found pure love in the heart of a vampire, who no longer echoed the heartbeat of the earth?

Once outside, I ran my fingers along the rough brick of the wall. I pressed my knuckles into the them. The pain grounded me in this world.

I didn't think Sam meant to reopen this hole. He wanted Michael to trust him. I forced the smoke out through my nostrils. Sam had been successful in that.

The cool air felt good on my face. I watched the tracers from a few cars as they fused the world by merely passing through. My thoughts flowed in and out with each breath. We were all from one essence, one soul, and one breath, linked together by an invisible thread. We were tied together—past, present, and future. It was what gave rise to intuition, *deja vu*, epiphanies, love at first sight, knowing without exchanging words, and touching without physical contact.

We tugged on one another as we moved through the world. Our thoughts and emotions traveled along this thread. Most people tied a knot in the string, stopping the flow from others to themselves and vice versa. They were the lonely, the depressed, and the hopeless. Others cut the string, severing their connection with all. They were the walking dead.

I propelled the smoke forcefully from my lungs and crushed the cigarette into the mortar between the brown bricks of the building.

The string that tied me to my coven needed to be cut.

Back inside, they were standing to leave. The conversation had shifted to prior acid experiences. Michael scooped up the check and walked to the register. He wrapped me in his arms as we waited for the waitress to ring us out. He tilted my head back by my chin. "Alright?"

Nodding, I asked, "Where are we going?"

He shrugged his shoulders. "Not sure yet."

We stood in a group just outside the doors. No one knew where to go next.

"It's cold." I pointed to people walking from the parking lot, bundled up against the night air. "I can see my breath."

None of us felt the cold. We were still high.

"We can go to a basement laundry room I know about," I said. "We can zone out, talk or whatever, but we'll be off the street and not drawing attention."

"Lead the way," Sam said, gesturing with his hand.

Michael took my hand and we led the way. Sam and James trailed close behind. They followed me to Hunter's apartment building. The laundry room entrance was never locked, and it was warm from the dryers that had been running earlier. No one was likely to be in there at two in the morning, and the four of us could stay out of sight.

The wood paneling on the laundry room walls breathed, in and out. It was easy to see faces and patterns in wood when on LSD. We laughed and described the things we saw. Michael pointed out faces and symbols to me, but I couldn't see what he saw. I acted as though I could.

We turned out the lights and waved our arms and bodies around in the dark, watching the light tracers dance around. I'd read somewhere that everyone has an aura—a faint glow of light that surrounds them, a field of colors that gifted people can see when sober—colors comprised of the full spectrum of the rainbow. The aura was said to be a visible projection of your current and past emotions. Things you dragged along with you, never letting go.

Nicole Lowe

Being high on LSD let us see these things. It opened our minds to things that were otherwise invisible.

Serious discussions were over for the night, of which I was grateful. Silence alternated with bouts of laughter. Michael sat close to me and ran his hands through my hair, watching intensely as it fell from his fingers, a few tresses at a time.

Once the sun began to suck the life out of the night, Michael got to his feet and pulled me up with him. "Do the two of you want to crash with us?" he said to Sam and James. "There are some people I would like you to meet once we've all had a chance to sleep."

Sam shrugged his shoulders. "Cool."

We walked to a house some of Michael's gutter punk friends were renting—the rainbow houses north of Liberty Park. The house was cluttered, but not with people. They had all gone to work. We cleared some space on the floor in the living room and sank down. My mind was racing at a hundred miles an hour.

There was no way I was going to sleep. Even if I could, I didn't want to. We were approaching the final stage of my escape. My eyes were closed, but I knew Michael was staring at me, perched on his elbow. He traced a line from my hair, down my nose, and over my lips. Then he lay down. It took him at least an hour to fall asleep.

When I thought he was asleep, I waited longer. His breath was even, but shallow, and so I waited some more. Finally, I rolled over and pushed away from him a bit. And there I waited for another hour. I knew it took a couple of hours for the restless-sleep phase of coming down from acid to end. Finally, his breathing became deep. He was asleep.

My feet slid into my black combat boots without a sound and I pulled them tight. I grabbed my gothbox and glided over to Sam and his brother. I touched Sam, and he smiled before opening his eyes.

Quietly, he woke James and we exited through the door farthest from where Michael lay sleeping. I didn't look back. There was nothing I wanted behind me. We quickly began our walk downtown and caught the Provo Express south.

I pointed to Bill and Mariah, who were slumped against one another in a back corner of the bus, their long brown hair flung over their faces. Sam puckered his lips to one side, shook his head, and waved any concern away. We each took a row near the back of the bus, stretching our legs out with our feet hanging in the aisle.

We were on the bus for a long time. James' eyes drooped and fluttered open at every bump in the road. Sam was kicked back in his seat, but his eyes scanned everyone who climbed onto the bus. My heart raced with every mile until we passed the prison at the point of the mountain. We were out of Salt Lake County.

I turned to Sam. "Where are we going?"

Bill and Mariah shifted at the sound of my voice.

"The Mojave Desert in Southern California. My dad lives there. From there, who knows? Maybe follow the Grateful Dead." He smiled, leaned his head back against the window, and closed his eyes. "You should sleep a little."

But I couldn't. In one night, my entire world had changed. I let out a deep breath and looked around the bus. A few people near the front were reading the *Salt Lake Tribune*. A young man in a grey-brown suit was reading the *Book of Mormon*. A dark-skinned gangster bounced and waved his hands to the music in his ears.

My eyes found Mariah's. She was awake, but I had no idea for how long.

She smiled. "You guys are going to follow the Dead?"

Sam opened the eye closest to her. "Yep."

She elbowed Bill. He snorted and tasted his own mouth.

"They're going to follow the Dead." She pointed to us and bounced in her seat. "Can we go with you?"

Sam shrugged. "Sure, why not?"

I didn't care where we were going, as long as it was far from Salt Lake City. Provo City was the end of the bus line, and the five of us stepped off the bus. I stood still for a few seconds and breathed. I was free.

Sam held out his hand. "Are you coming?"

The corners of my mouth twitched, and a smile spread across my face.

I placed my hand in his.

Nicole Lowe

the rising of the sun

Seventy-five percent of runaways are female.

chapter eleven

Judge Cruz turns to Carl, the guardian ad litem. "Mr. Johnson?"

Carl stands. "Good morning, Ms. Hardy. I just have a few questions for you."

She wipes tears from her cheeks with both hands. She nods her head and takes a sip of water.

"How many felony charges do you have pending?"

"One."

"If McCartni comes to live with you, where will she go if you go to jail or prison?"

Sabrina's eyes drop to her lap. "I'm sure one of my friends or family would take her."

Her answer doesn't really matter. It's the question itself that has the greatest impact. It's the fact that if she's convicted, she may be unavailable for her child for up to five years. Another loss for McCartni. Another placement failed.

"You have appointments to begin the services on your child and family plan, is that right?"

"Yes. I have a therapy appointment. I have an interview. I've been calling on drug treatment. Now I know I need to call about domestic violence treatment."

"I believe Ms. Lowe asked this, but your answer was vague. Why has it taken you nine months to make appointments so you can begin services?"

"I was depressed."

"How long do you think McCartni should wait for you to become the mother she needs?"

"I don't know."

———

Denny's was the first restaurant we came across. We slumped in our seats around a corner table.

"Coffee?" asked a young man with a smart haircut and a shirt stiff with too much starch.

"Yes," Mariah said.

"And cheese fries with ranch dressing on the side," I added.

The four of us were exhausted. My thoughts flowed like molasses dribbling down the trunk of a maple tree. Everything was in slow motion.

The smell of cheap coffee rose around us as the waiter flipped our mugs over and filled each one. They were the same cups as the ones at Dee's, cream colored with a brown lip and interior.

"We should find some place to crash," James said.

I was shaking my head before he finished the sentence. "I want to get out of the state, first."

I needed to be as far from Michael as I could get before he hunted me down—or before my desire for the safety of his arms overwhelmed me. Already, that desire tugged at the back of my mind like a kite on a string.

"And how do you propose we do that?" James asked, resting his forehead on the top of the table.

"Steal a car," I said.

James slowly lifted his head and stared at me open-mouthed.

"This is Utah County," I said. "Lots of Mormons. They trust in the goodness of everyone. There are a bunch of cars out there with the keys in them. You don't have to hot-wire anything. We'll just open the doors and check for keys in the most likely places until we find one."

James laughed.

Sam rested his hand on the table and drummed his fingers one after the other. He took a sip of his coffee and leaned forward. "She's right. It's our best chance to get out of here. It'll be dark in a few hours, and we can easily go through cars in an apartment complex."

I leaned in, lowering my voice. "Once we get out of state, we have to change the plate on the car to that state, and we should be fine as long as we follow all the traffic laws." Michael had told me about changing the plates.

The waiter came around and refilled our coffee.

"Can we get more creamer and sugar?" Mariah asked.

"We can go to my dad's for a few days and then drive up the coast and catch the Grateful Dead in San Francisco," Sam said.

James shook his head. "What about just hitching?"

Sam raised his eyebrows and looked at Mariah and Bill, then finally at me. "That's not going to work right now. We need something less noticeable."

A bowl of creamer and sugar slid onto our table. "Anything else?"

Five hands with dirt under their nails reached for the creamer.

"I'll bring more," the waiter said.

"Thanks," I said.

James pulled back the paper top of a creamer. "This is nuts, but whatever. I'm in. But we ditch the car in Frisco."

Sam ripped open five white packets of sugar. "Agreed."

Three hours later, James dropped a set of keys in the middle of the table. "You guys ready to go?"

Sam, Mariah, and I slid into the back seat of a VW Jetta. James and Bill took the front.

"The car was unlocked, keys in the ashtray, and a full tank of gas," Bill said, craning his head to see us. "And it's a VW, so it was like destiny. I know it's not a bus, but it's all good."

Bill and James were the only two with licenses, so they took turns driving through the night. It didn't take long for sleep to pull me down into its darkness.

"Where are we?" I mumbled through lingering sleep.

"Arizona," James said.

The morning sun cast its glow over the desert, which I had never seen before. It was as if the sun had set on the earth rather than rising in the sky. We continued south for two days until we reached Ridgecrest, California, in the Mojave Desert.

Rambler homes with yards of straw-colored grass and sagebrush sat on both sides of the asphalt road. The barren land was invaded by thriving sagebrush and desert mountains, steepling their sedimentary fingers toward the oceans of the sky.

The car pulled to a stop in front of a squat house and we all filed out. Sam walked to the front door and knocked three times.

We heard people moving around inside.

"Just a minute," a woman's voice called.

A few seconds later, the doorknob rattled and the door swung open. A tall man in his forties with grey hair stood before us, wide-eyed.

"Hi, Dad," Sam said with grin. He looked pleased at the surprise on his father's face. "Everybody, this is my dad, Peter. Dad, this is... everybody."

Peter waved us inside. "What are you doing here?" he asked, his eyes dancing between Sam and James.

James had the sense to look a little sheepish, but Sam's grin only broadened. "We just wanted to stay a few days and then we're headed up the coast to see the Grateful Dead."

Peter raised his eyebrows. His light-blue eyes sparkled. Both Sam and James resembled their dad—James more than Sam, but both sons shared their father's height, hair texture, and build. The sharp facial features, too.

"Well if you're staying here, you can help me dig out the vegetable garden." He introduced us to his wife, Helen, who welcomed us with hugs and offers of food.

Sam and I settled into a hammock in the back yard. The gentle breeze did little to cool us as we talked.

"Have you always been gothic?" Sam asked.

"Before I was goth, I hung out with rockers and gangbangers. We drank." I paused. "A lot."

"I used to drink too, but it was causing me a lot of problems with my friends and my mom. My baby brother's dad was a mean alcoholic. I don't want to be that. Promise me you won't drink anymore?"

"I promise."

The hammock swayed from side to side.

Being Michael's lover and the bearer of his children was not what I was meant to be. I was more than that. I wanted to embody the balance of the darkness and the light—to speak out against injustice, and to stand for those too weak to stand on their own. That was my true destiny.

Sam read to me from *The Tao of Pooh* every night. I fell in love with the simplicity of it, the playfulness, and its deceptive depth. We shared our fears and our dreams. Sam conversed with me instead of just telling me what to do and where to go. He wanted my opinions and ideas about things. We spent nights in each other's arms, and he sang to me quietly. We made love, melting into one another. It was vastly different from the manipulation and control that I was accustomed to.

The converging of Sam's world with mine ignited a spark. It was small, but bright. Like a moth attracted to a lamp, I refused to turn away from him. Salt Lake City and all the people there faded, obscured by the dense fog seeded by Sam's promise of becoming something more.

He tossed his hacky sack into the air and caught it as we walked down the scorching sidewalk. "The Order of the Silvermoon will show others the true reality, its parallel nature, and the give-and-take between life and death, which must reach a balance in order for life to continue. We all see the world from different perspectives and use different words to describe what we believe. But truly, it's all the same, coexisting within each other, entwined as the strands of a rope."

He stopped and turned to me. "I want you to be a member of the Order. Will you?"

I took a few more steps and then turned to face him. "I can't imagine devoting my life to anything but discovering who I am, and the nature of life and death, as well as helping others to do the same."

"Good." Sam took my hand in his and we continued down the street. "As we travel, we will gather elves, vampires, and others to prepare them for the War of the Races that will bring about the unveiling of the dual nature of the world. All members must be prepared, both spiritually and physically. Such unveiling was attempted during the two World Wars, but something went amiss and souls from the two parallel worlds became trapped in the wrong reality during the power exchange."

I nodded. "When is all of this going to happen?"

"The War of the Races is prophesied to occur in the next ten to fifteen years. It will change the dynamics of the world, and it will be another major exchange of power between this world and the world of the elves. The veil between the worlds will be ripped, possibly for good."

"Let's go," James called from the front porch.

Startled, my head sprang up. I hadn't even noticed we were already back to the house.

"I'll tell you more later," Sam said and squeezed my hand.

Bill and Mariah were already in the car. We were going to San Diego, where Sam's cousin, Josh, lived.

Nicole Lowe

Sam and I walked around San Diego, hand in hand. Palm trees were new to me, trunks with brown paper packaging. My fingers explored their rough bark as we passed them, one after another. We lounged on the grass in Balboa Park and strolled to the beach.

I had never seen the ocean before. The briny air caressed my face as I breathed it in, listening to the rolling waves and gentle splash as they reached the beach. I walked out into the water, wanting to feel it in my hands and not just on the wind. The water pulled each grain of sand from beneath my feet. My toes dug in and my thoughts washed over me.

We all depended upon so much to draw our next breath. Not only did we depend upon Mother Earth, but on one another. We were interconnected, and without one another we had no sense of who we were as individuals. Without each object and element, we did not exist.

Crouching down, I touched the water. It moved between my fingers, and I pressed them into the sand, smiling at the newness of it all. The sun hovered on the edge of the rippling horizon. The water reflected a fiery sunset. I refused to go until the cool blues of twilight descended.

We returned to Josh's apartment. He smoked everyone up with some Purple Haze buds. Green hues of pine and aspen knotted together with purple fuzz. We crashed there that night and left early the next morning.

We sped north along the highway. Bill was driving.

"Um, I think we have a problem," he said.

We were somewhere between Los Angeles and San Francisco. Bill looked over at James. "The gas gauge is dropping. Fast."

James leaned over to see. "Holy shit. Pull over."

Gravel flipped up into the wheel well as he pulled the car onto the shoulder of the highway.

"Do I smell gas?" Mariah asked.

"Everybody out," Sam said.

Sam, Mariah, and I leaned against the metal barrier on the edge of the road. I held onto my hair to stop it from whipping me in the eyes.

James got down on his stomach and peered under the car. "There's a hole in the fucking gas tank!"

"I bet it was that pothole we hit a ways back," Bill said, spitting his long hair out of his mouth.

James stood and kicked the tire. "What are we going to do?"

"Check the trunk for something to fix it," Sam yelled over the wind and whooshing of cars flying by at seventy-five miles an hour.

Bill reached through the driver's window and popped the trunk. James rummaged around in the trunk. He came out with a blue rubber stress ball and some duct tape. "Worth a try, I guess."

"Not much choice," Bill said.

James dropped down to the gravel again and wormed his way under the car. A few F-bombs later, he wormed his way back out and wiped his hands on his dirty jeans as he stood. "No more smoking in the car."

The smell of gasoline filled the car.

"Roll down the windows," Sam said from the back seat.

"We're never going to make it to Frisco," James said. "I need a god damn cigarette."

"We'll make it," Sam said. He wrapped his arm around my shoulders and pulled me close to keep me warm as the wind rushed in through the open windows.

There were no more stops, not even to use the bathroom. When we arrived in San Francisco, it was full night. I struggled to open my heavy eyelids. My stomach rolled as we cruised up and down hills lined with two-story houses, every one of them packed together like cigarettes.

"Find someplace to park for the night," James said.

"Where?" Bill asked.

"Anywhere."

Bill parked on an uphill. James jumped out of the car. I fought my need for sleep and pushed myself upright.

153

James' head came into view. "It's not leaking as bad. Just dripping. I think the hill and the tank being low must be helping."

"Nothing we can do about it tonight. Let's get some sleep," Sam said.

James climbed back into the front passenger's seat. "We'll have to ditch it tomorrow and figure something else out."

The next morning, we rolled down to Market Street to find a place to have coffee and work out our next move.

"I need to use the bathroom," I said.

"Me too," said Mariah.

James pulled the car to the curb. Mariah, Sam, and I climbed out of the back seat.

"We'll be back," Sam said.

"We'll keep circling the block until we find a parking spot," Bill said as he and James pulled away.

We found a McDonald's and went straight to the bathroom. I pulled on the handle to the stall. It didn't budge. I looked under the door. No feet. Then I saw it. The bathroom stalls required money for the door to open. I shook my head and looked at Mariah. She shrugged.

We'd left everything in the car, so we wandered in and out of various places looking for a free bathroom. No luck. We had to ask for spare change to get the money. Twenty minutes later, we all walked back to where Bill and James had dropped us off.

They weren't there. We waited. Thirty minutes passed.

"Where the hell are they?" Sam said, handing me the cigarette we'd bummed off a stranger on the street.

I pulled the nicotine into my lungs. "They'll be back."

We waited.

We asked another person for a cigarette and shared it between the three of us.

And we waited.

We asked for spare change in the hopes of buying coffee and fries once Bill and James returned.

Sam was pacing the small section of sidewalk we had occupied for the last hour and a half. "Where did they go? James wouldn't just leave." Sam plopped down next to me. My hand traced the bones of his spine through his shirt. There was nothing to be said.

We waited the rest of the day, not knowing what else to do. The sun began to dip below the horizon.

"We gotta find someplace to sleep," Sam said.

I stood and rubbed my hands over my butt. It was sore from sitting on the concrete all day.

"Is there a park nearby?" Mariah asked a kid with a skateboard.

He pointed up the hill. "Couple of blocks up."

"Thanks."

Sam scuffed his shoe on the sidewalk. "I just don't understand where they could have gone. Something must have happened. James wouldn't have left us."

All of our blankets and other belongings were in the car. Neither Mariah or I had shoes on. We huddled together under bushes in a park throughout the night, taking turns in the middle.

I watched the sun come up, blowing into my cupped hands and rubbing my bare feet. Mariah and Sam were still sleeping. I needed a cigarette, but we didn't have any. They were in the car.

I shook Sam. "I'm cold. Can we get into the sun?"

We went back to Market Street and sat in the same spot, not sure what we expected to find. Bill and James would not have left us here.

We walked up and down Market Street.

We walked up to Haight and Ashbury to see if we could find them.

Nothing.

We returned to Market Street and sat waiting.

A couple of old men lounged against the concrete foundation of a brick building, wearing the scent of urine and acidic vomit. Bottles protectively wrapped in brown paper bags were near at hand. We hadn't eaten since leaving San Diego and despite the smell around me, my stomach growled.

"I'm so hungry," I said.

Two women with dreadlocks and torn-up jeans stopped. The one with fiery hair said, "The Catholic church serves lunch for the homeless at the UN Plaza." She pointed down the way they had come. "Just straight down the street."

One of the old men rolled onto his elbow and pushed himself up, bathing us in a fresh wave of vomit and urine. "Come on, youngins." We followed him.

Lunch turned out to be peanut butter and jelly sandwiches and an apple. I sucked on each bite, savoring the taste. Scarcity brought a new appreciation to the ordinary. The volunteers serving lunch told us where the mission was and said we could get showers, food, and a bed if we needed. We also found out that, for five dollars, we could take a bus to Santa Rosa.

The sun was at its full height, its warmth gentle in early March. We walked back to our post on Market and Seventh and waited.

Sam picked me up and set me on a stone bench. He wrapped his arms around my waist and buried his head in my stomach. He looked up at me.

"I love you," he said.

I smiled. "I love you." I believed those words as they passed my lips. They held more truth than any words I had spoken to anyone in Salt Lake.

Hope is the belief that something you desire will come into being. Without hope, we are dead. To have hope, you must desire more than death. I found my desire. I desired a sense of belonging, a sense of safety, and acceptance. I found these things in Sam. I found my hope.

Mariah sat on the concrete sidewalk, leaning against the matching grey stone building. She pulled one of her legs beneath her and picked at the sidewalk with a stick, flinging pebbles beneath people's feet as they passed.

"What are we going to do now?" she said. "I don't think they're coming back."

"We'll continue to hang around Market for a couple more days," Sam said. "Then we'll leave, with or without James and Bill. Their disappearance doesn't make sense, but we need to keep moving north."

"Are we going to steal another car?" I asked.

Sam blew smoke out of his nose and pressed the cigarette butt into the ground. "We'll hitchhike."

"I'll just stay here," Mariah said, switching legs.

"If you want." Sam shrugged. "It will be easier to catch a ride out of Santa Rosa than San Francisco. We need twenty quarters each for the bus."

Asking for spare change never bothered me. People could tell me no if they wanted. I didn't care. Most of the time, they ignored me. I wondered if the people with earbuds actually had music playing, or if they just used them to have an excuse not to talk to people like me. It didn't take long for us to get the money we needed.

"And now we wait," Sam said after a pretty woman with dark hair handed him the last quarter.

The same old men who had led us to lunch sat against their building. They were wrapped in layers of coats smudged with the filth of the city streets. Their faces and hands were rugged from a hard life.

In desperation for an answer, Sam crossed the sidewalk. His shadow fell upon them and their yellowed eyes squinted up at him. "Any chance you two were here a few days ago?"

"Sure were," said the one with the grey beard, "got nowhere better to go."

"You see a blue-grey VW with four doors from Utah parked across the street yesterday?" he asked. The pleading of his last chance for understanding cracked his usual casual tone.

"I saw the cops bust a couple of guys in a car like that, not sure where it was from. We were sitting right here. A couple of cop cars came screeching around the corner, pulled up in front and behind this car, pulled out their shotguns, and told the two guys inside to come out with their hands up. They came out right away, with cops screaming at them to get on the ground with their hands behind their heads. They got handcuffed and shoved in the back of a police car. The cops towed the car." He waved his hand as if it were a normal, everyday event.

Our mouths dropped open. We hadn't even considered that possibility. Sam flashed a look to both Mariah and me. It had to be Bill and James.

"Do you remember what they looked like?" Mariah asked.

The old man snorted the snot from his nose to his throat and hocked a loogie. It splattered at his feet, which were wrapped with dirty cloth. "Nah. Brown hair, tall. One with long hair, one with short. That's it."

"Thanks, man," Sam said, and handed him a dollar.

I moved in close to Sam as we hastened down the street. "My ID was in the car, Sam."

"I know." He took me by the arm and guided me down the street. "We need to get out of here soon, and off this corner now."

Mariah followed a few steps behind.

We made our way back toward the UN Plaza and ate lunch.

Mariah asked, "Where are we going?"

Sam sighed. "I don't know yet. Something will come up."

At the edge of the square, a young black man in a backward Chicago Bulls cap stood with his hands in the pockets of his sagging pants. His eyes roamed the crowd. A group of skaters stepped off their boards and approached him. They spoke and exchanged something. Dealer. Sam let go of me and I fell back with Mariah, linking my arm in hers. We really didn't have the money for a sack.

"What's he doing?" I asked Mariah.

"Looks like he wants some weed. Can't say I blame him. It would be nice right about now."

Mariah and I stopped a few paces back. Sam stood beside the guy, looking out at the people in the square. "Hey man, we're new to Frisco and looking for place to crash for a few days and figure out what we're going to do."

The guy didn't look at Sam. "Where you from?"

"We just hitched in from San Diego. Thinking of following the Dead north to Seattle."

"You got money?"

Sam arched an eyebrow. "Man, if we had money, we wouldn't be here."

The guy laughed. "I want to help you and your girls out. You seem pretty cool to me. We can hang out, and you can tell me your story. You smoke weed?" He looked Sam up and down and laughed. "Yeah, you smoke weed."

Sam grinned.

"Name's Jack," the guy said.

Sam reached out to shake Jack's hand and got a fist bump instead.

"I'm Sam. This is Mariah and Nikki." Sam pointed at each of us in turn.

"There's a little get-together at my place tonight," Jack said. "You can get whatever you want: weed, acid, mushrooms, cocaine, and heroin. It don't matter. It'll be there."

We followed him to his blacked-out Escalade. It was a fifteen-minute drive to his house. The place looked the same as all the others on the street.

He opened the door and let us inside.

"Nice place," Sam said.

I ran my hand over the leather couch. A smoky glass-top table sat in the center of the living room next to a pool table and a foosball table. There were five bedrooms in the house and a hot tub out back.

"Yeah, it ain't too shabby," Jack said. "Come upstairs, man, I want to show you some stuff."

Sam waved for us to stay there. Mariah and I sat in the living room.

About ten minutes later, Sam came down. His eyebrows were drawn together and his shoulders were tensed. He didn't slow down as he hit the bottom step. He waved us toward the door. I grabbed Mariah's hand and moved.

Jack followed Sam down the stairs. "Oh man, don't be like that. I'm sure we can work out some type of split."

Sam shook his head and flung open the front door. "No, man. We can't."

We left quickly, not looking back.

"Jack thought I was your pimp. He wanted to pimp you two out at the party tonight and split the money."

Nicole Lowe

It was a long, silent walk back. We spent another night huddled together under bushes in the park.

It was barely light out when Sam rubbed my back to wake me.

"Ya know what we need?" he said.

"What?" I asked, rubbing the sleep from my eyes.

"Backpacks and a few blankets."

Mariah rolled over. "Where are we going to get those?"

Sam got to his feet and brushed the leaves and dirt from his pants. "The mission." He ran his eyes over me. "The police have your gothbox and they'll be looking for you as a goth. We need to change your look."

I nodded. "The mission will have clothes, right?"

With my gothbox in police hands, I didn't have any makeup anyway. I had lost some poetry, crystals, my Led Zeppelin tape, cigarettes, and whatever money I had. Gothic me was gone, along with the last remnants of my Salt Lake life. I wasn't sorry to see her go.

I dug through a donation box at the mission and picked out jeans, a t-shirt, a bra, and a pair of underwear. When I went into the bathroom to change, I looked at myself in the mirror. I was totally different. My smile was bright and my cheeks had color.

When I pulled my black leggings off, I found blood in my underwear. I closed my eyes and felt the chain tethering me to Michael release. I pulled on my new clothes and opened the door to my new life. I tossed my goth clothes into the dumpster behind the mission.

We spare-changed money to replace what we had used over the last twenty-four hours, plus a little extra for coffee and food once we arrived in Santa Rosa. We walked over to the UN Plaza, got lunch, and waited until it was time for the bus. Sam was trying to teach me how to play hacky sack.

"Sam!" someone called from behind us.

Sam's eyes sprung wide and his head whipped around.

James and Bill were running toward us.

"Oh my god, I thought we'd never see you again!" Sam said, locking forearms and then embracing them both.

Never Let Me Go

Mariah flung her arms around Bill and wrapped her legs around his waist.

James and Bill told us everything that had happened. It was just like the homeless guy on the street had described.

"Did they find my stuff?" I interjected.

"They asked about who you were," James said. "I told them we had just picked you up on the side of the road in Utah, and I didn't know anything about you."

Bill wiped the tears from Mariah's face. "I said something similar."

"How'd you get out?" Sam asked.

James smiled. "No charges filed. They were just happy to get the car back undamaged."

"I knew you didn't ditch us." Sam clasped Bill on the shoulder.

In Santa Rosa, we found an overpass to camp under for the night and made plans to hitch out in the morning. We stashed our things and went looking for chow. We rounded a corner and walked right into the arms of two police officers.

"Why aren't you kids in school?" the female officer asked.

"Because we're over eighteen," Bill said.

My heart hammered inside my chest. *Relax,* I told myself.

Sam didn't miss a beat. "We're here visiting friends."

"What are your names and dates of birth?" she asked. Her long blonde hair was pulled back into a tight bun.

Sam and I had planned for this, and he had given me an ex-girlfriend's name and birthday. I'd practiced the name and birth date until it flowed from my mouth as easily as my own. Sam didn't have this problem, since his mom never reported him as a runaway when he took off. James, Bill, and Mariah were all over eighteen.

I gave the fake name and date of birth.

"How long are you visiting?" she asked.

"We're leaving in the morning," Sam said.

The call over the radio came back as all clear, so they let us go on our way.

Sam wrapped his arm around me. "Have a good day," he called over his shoulder.

We found an IHOP, its bubble-blue letters shining like a lighthouse welcoming a ship into port. I took a deep breath. God, I didn't want to go back. I closed my eyes and took another deep breath. My lower lip quivered. Please, I couldn't go back.

"Not too hard, right?" Sam said, dropping his hand into mine. I was shaking. He gave my hand a gentle squeeze. "It gets easier."

Hitchhikers in California are more likely to be victims (71.7 percent) than perpetrators (28.3 percent) of major crimes. Eighty percent of the crimes against female hitchhikers are sexual in nature.

chapter twelve

Judge Cruz leans forward in his chair and nods to Sabrina's attorney. "Mr. Lundberg," he says, "your witness."

I flip to a clean sheet of paper and jot the following words across the top: *J.L. cross mom.*

Jake stands and buttons his suit coat, glancing down at the notes on the table before him. "Sabrina, have you been taking your drug tests?"

"Yes," she says. "I haven't missed any, besides when I was in jail."

"And what have the results been?"

"They've been clean for two weeks."

"Have you been able to contact the House of Hope for drug treatment?"

"Yes, and I'm on the wait list."

I scratch the letters *H-O-H* into the margin of my notes.

"Are you attending any groups?" Jake asks.

"Yes."

163

"Which groups?"

"The interim groups that my caseworker told me about."

"How long have you been going?"

"Three weeks."

Clarice, my caseworker, leans into me. Her chin is at my shoulder, and the smell of sweet strawberries fills the space between us as her hair falls forward. "She's never told me that," she whispers.

I make another note.

Jake looks down at his yellow notepad and checks off a line. "Have you completed a parenting class?"

"Yes. Love and Logic. I finished it last week."

"Have you filled out your housing applications?"

She smiles and scoots to the edge of her chair. "Yes, for Salt Lake City and County. I turned those in two weeks ago."

His questions are bringing out good points, but her hourglass has already run out. Carl is leaned back in his chair.

"What are you going to do for housing if McCartni comes to live with you before you're approved through the city or county?" Jake asks.

"I have a friend I've known since high school. They have a little girl too, and will rent their second bedroom to me for $250 a month."

"Will she help you with McCartni and the new baby?"

"Yes, she's going to watch them while I go to work."

"Do you have a job interview?"

"Tomorrow, with Maverik."

"Have you been taking your medication?"

"Yes."

"How do you feel on it?"

"So much better. My feelings don't go up and down. I can sleep better and I'm not as grouchy."

"Are there any warrants out for your arrest?"

"No, I've cleared them all."

Jake pauses reflectively. "Sabrina, do you love McCartni?"

"Oh my God, yes. With all my heart. I would do anything for her."

Sam and I stood on the freeway on-ramp with our thumbs out. The five of us had to split up to hitchhike; few drivers ever stopped for more than two people at a time. Bill and Mariah hitched together. James went off on his own. That left me and Sam—the imperfectly matched couple.

Sam was holding up a cardboard sign with the words *Eugene, Oregon* written in bold, black letters. He ran a hand through his mouse-brown hair and wiped the sweat from his forehead with the back of his hand. His hair was getting long, and sweeping his shoulders now.

"Shamanism uses peace pipes and ceremonial tobacco," he said. "To initiate and close ceremonies, the shaman blows the pipe smoke in each direction, thanking the spirit for blessing the tribe or person. Shamanism draws power from the four elements and the four corners of the world."

The sun warmed my back as the gravel jabbed into my bony butt. I sat cross-legged on the side of the road, scribbling down notes in my journal. Learning different practices of drawing energy toward myself and others was a central part of my training in the Order of the Silvermoon. He waited for me to finish marking up the page. I turned my face up and the sun lit up his blue eyes.

Sam continued. "Bushido uses candles, incense, the pentagram, circle of power, an altar, and a god figurine. They use chanting and mediation. Bushido also draws power from the four corners and elements."

A car slowed and pulled to the side of the freeway on-ramp. I closed my journal, ran my fingers over the soft crinkled cover, and tucked it under my arm. I slipped the pen into the back pocket of my ripped-up jeans and walked toward the car. The man who got out had bushy black hair and eyebrows. He made his way to the trunk of his car.

"Hey thanks, man," Sam called, jogging forward.

"I'm not going far," the driver said and opened the trunk.

"No worries. Do you mind if we throw our stuff in the back seat instead of the trunk?"

The driver shrugged his shoulders and closed the trunk. "That's fine."

"I'm Sam." He threw our bag into the back seat and held the door for me to get in. "And this is Nikki."

I smiled at the driver before slipping into the back seat. Sam shut my door and climbed into the front before the driver reached his door.

There were a few precautions we took when hitchhiking. We tried not to put our pack in a place where we couldn't get it out if we had to bail on the ride. And I didn't get in before Sam did, unless the driver wasn't in the car.

He dropped us off after passing a few off-ramps. It wasn't far, but it was something. Every time we caught such short rides, I wondered if we had missed out on scoring a longer one if we'd waited a few minutes more. The only reason to ever reject a ride was if your intuition flared up in warning.

Sam stood with our sign while I sat on the side of the road. I pulled my journal back out and he continued where he had left off.

"Paganism uses an altar with candles, drawing the power from the four winds: north, south, east, and west. Present in most Pagan rituals are a chalice, sword, a dagger, incense, pentagram, wood, or sprig. They use rune stones and Tarot cards. The robe worn by the priest depicts the forces being summoned. There is a circle of protection—either psychic or made with salt. The caster speaks the incantation in the language most power for the caster. Spells are the summoning of the forces of creation, which are then directed into the world in a certain manner."

Patrick had explained magic in similar ways. It reminded me of the black-and-white picture where some people see a maiden and others see a crone. The truth was tucked beneath the surface. We all looked at the world and saw things differently, even when we were staring at the same object at the same time. I taught Sam about the powers of crystals, rune reading, numerology, palmistry, and astrology.

We traveled day and night, making our way along Highway 101. Sam spoke with the Hispanic driver whose weathered hands held the steering wheel at ten and two. We were flying through the redwood trees at Big Sur in a white cargo truck. Sam played Sherlock Holmes, deducing the driver's interests based on items in the truck, the radio station they were tuned to, and the driver's words.

I stared out the window. I disappeared into my mind, where only the trees and I existed. The smell of pine and earth broke through the glass. I could feel the ridged hide of the redwoods. My feet sank into the mattress of pine needles and discarded branches. The trees in Saedric, my home, made these look like matchsticks. No one told the redwoods not to reach higher and higher toward the sun, because it was what they were born to become. The trees in Saedric spoke to me—not in words, but in my soul. It was as if I had a second heartbeat, a second breath inside of me. This world and this body felt dead.

Rocks kicking the inside of the wheel well scattered my thoughts. I slid out of the truck, dropping the last foot to the dirt. Sam swung our army-green backpack over his shoulder and laced his other arm through the strap.

Raindrops tumbled out of the night sky, cooling the ground and plunking into the puddles gathered at the edge of the road. I tilted my face toward the clouds and stared up at their blue afterglow. Spreading my arms out, I spun in a slow circle, letting the rain wash over me.

Sam laughed.

I wanted to cry. This human body was cold and silent.

A hundred feet off the road, Sam found a relatively dry place where the tree branches protected us from the rain. He laid out the tarp and our blankets, and we crawled inside.

I glimpsed the stars through the fluttering leaves and crooked fingers of the trees as the wind gently shifted. The scent of rain was heavy in the air, and the pattering of the drops as they touched gently down upon the earth surrounded us.

"I need to tell you something," Sam whispered into the dark.

"Okay."

"When we reach Montana, someone is waiting for me."

My heart froze.

"My soul mate," he said. "Arielle."

I wanted to eject the cassette tape he was playing and pull its glistening brown tape from its plastic casing, ripping it with my teeth as it cut into my gums. But I didn't move. I didn't talk. I willed the words to not mean what I thought they meant. I drew in a slow breath of damp air.

"Before I left Montana to fulfill my destiny, to gather more members for the Order of the Silvermoon, our souls were bound to one another. We knew for this journey to be successful, our paths would diverge for a time and we would be with whomever we were drawn to. Her path remained in Montana, and mine brought me to you."

Sam paused, rolled onto his side to look at me. "I do love you and I always will. I will teach you, protect you, and help you find your soul mate. Once we find him, as difficult as it will be, I will place your hands in his and allow you to follow your destiny."

I looked into his face, searching for the deception I craved. I found none. The angular cheekbones, narrow chin, and peaked eyebrows were sincere. Stray strands of hair slipped out of his high ponytail. He looked away from me and pushed the strands behind his ear. A stream of cold air blew between us through the opening in the blankets at Sam's waist. It twisted around my leg like a chain back to the darkness.

"I wanted you to know now, rather than springing this on you when we reach Montana. You will have more important things to focus on there. You will have your training to be thinking about, more than ever. I understand if you don't want to be with me any longer. If that's your choice, it will not change anything. I will continue to love you, teach you, and protect you. It is your choice."

He lay back and clasped his hands together across his stomach, waiting for my response.

I was quiet while I considered what this meant for me, for us. I squeezed my eyes tight. There was no *us*. There never had been. Returning to Salt Lake was not an option. Michael would convince Brenden I was not worth the trouble, and once I was dead, they could use Shelly to reunite the elves.

Out here, my strength and power would grow, and I was compelled to continue gathering my elves in preparation for the War of the Races. I decided there was nothing I could do about the situation. It did not change what I had come here to achieve: spiritual knowledge, physical strength, and my ultimate goal—to reunite my dark elven people.

The blossoming relationship with Sam had nothing to do with my choice to leave. I would continue along the path I had begun to walk. I would not share my whole self with him. I needed to guard parts of who I was. I found no harm in continuing as we were, for a time.

"We can continue as we are," I said, "but I will not share everything with you anymore. If I choose to keep my thoughts and feelings to myself, you must respect my choice." My words became ice crystals in the cold air.

He furrowed his brow. Nothing more was said. He wrapped me in his arms, and I lay there watching my breath turn to ice, listening to his breathing. Its warmth brushed the back of my neck.

Napalm stripped away my security, my happiness. I lay there with melted, blistering flesh slipping from my bones. After the liquid fire ceased to burn my soul, I rebuilt my walls stronger than before.

I slipped into sleep and the redwoods appeared in my mind. They were a blur to either side of me. My feet floated over the surface of the earth. A low growl emanated from all directions within the surrounding fog. I reached inside myself, searching for the earth's energy, but it was lost to me in this body. The wolf pursued, as it always did.

The cracking of a stick startled me into wakefulness. I sat bolt upright, searching the dark woods that surrounded us.

"What's wrong?" Sam asked.

"It's..." I stopped. "It's nothing."

I lay back down and spent the night listening to the creak and rumble of the forest.

———

The next morning, we continued on our journey. Various rides brought cigarettes and food along the way. One or two even kicked down a couple of dollars, but by the time we arrived in Eugene, we were out of money.

Our last ride had been a couple of hippies headed to Eugene in a pale-yellow VW bus with a white top and pink and orange flowers on the sides. When they picked us up, we found Bill and Mariah already on the bus. We shared our hitching stories as everyone passed two glass pipes packed with dark-green bud plucked from the driver's many mason jars, which were stocked to the lids.

My transformation from goth to hippie was complete by the time we walked into Eugene, Oregon, on February 24, 1995. The words and phrases I used, the way I held myself and moved, even my perspective on the world had changed. I was a ragdoll wanting to live, and to feel every breath enter and leave my body. I wanted to touch every flower, rock, and tree. I wanted to feel the sun warm my skin each morning.

The sun's kiss upon my skin was a sensation long missed. Back home, that wasn't possible in my vampire body—but in this body, I was able to enjoy that simple, forgotten delight.

We found James the following day. He was out asking for spare change, waiting for us to show up. It didn't take long to find a new place for coffee and cheese fries. We sat in an IHOP, all five of us, thinking of ways to drum up some funds.

Sam and I were thinking long-term. We needed funding for the Order of the Silvermoon. James thought the Order was a joke, but he needed money just the same. Sam hadn't talked to Bill and Mariah about the Order, and it wasn't my story to tell. Bill and Mariah were merely our traveling companions, but money was always a concern when traveling.

Asking for spare change supplied us with the money we used for coffee, food, and other small items. Sam, Mariah, and I were all decent thieves and acquired most of our belongings—journals, beads, crystals, pens, books, jewelry, and clothing—by way of the five-finger discount.

Sam tapped the ash off his cigarette. "We should sell acid."

"I don't know," Mariah said from across the ash-strewn table. "I could pick up some beads and hemp twine from a bead shop and make necklaces, bracelets, and anklets to sell."

"We could make stress balls, too, from balloons and sand from the park," Bill suggested.

"That's not going to generate enough money," Sam said.

"Acid?" James asked, lighting a cigarette and leaning back in the booth. "Not weed?"

I laughed and inhaled my coffee. "You guys'll smoke it all." I choked. "And *everyone* sells weed. We'll never make any money. Acid is the way to go."

Sam jumped in. "We could buy here and sell in Idaho and Montana, where it's three times as much. Then hitch back to buy more. Nikki's right about the competition with weed. I can use my money from Dad to get us started."

Sam's dad sent him a hundred dollars a month for child support. He sent it wherever Sam happened to be each month. The challenge was finding a place for him to wire or mail the money.

"The necklaces and stuff will give us a good front," I said.

"I don't know," James said. "We could get locked up for a long time. Trust me, you don't want that."

Bill nodded.

Sam looked around the table at the three naysayers. "We can buy a sheet and sell it here for three dollars a hit, then buy three sheets and take that back to Montana and sell it for five." Sam wrote out the calculations on a napkin. "We'll live off the money we make from selling necklaces and such. We'll come back here on the Greyhound and buy a ten pack, then go back to Montana to sell it for five bucks a hit."

I put my cigarette out in the ashtray, which was near to overflowing. "If you think you're going to get busted by the cops, eat everything you have."

"To everyone outside of us, we're here to go to Cougar Hot Springs. It's about fifty miles from here," Sam said.

"Whatever, man," James said. "I'm in."

We drank the dregs remaining in our cups and went to find a camp for the night.

We chose a spot in the woods alongside the Willamette River, which concealed us from view. It was beautiful, but lacked other requirements of a good base camp. Mainly, it was too far from where we needed to be each day.

We looked for places close to necessary resources, like coffeehouses, bookstores, farmers markets, and the local illicit drug zone. Every city had one. You just had to know what you were looking for.

We wanted a place inside the city where we would be hidden from view while sleeping. We could usually find small wooded areas, high grass, or bushes that worked. We also wanted a place that could shield us from rain and wind.

It took a week for us to get to know the city enough to establish our territory and find a more convenient base camp: an overpass with a bed of tangled ivy. Tall bushes were crowded on one side where we stored our gear during the day.

It was a chilly morning when we moved to the overpass base camp. We moved in a rush after we found our stuff scattered along the riverbank. Someone had found our bag and gone through everything.

Sam pulled on an extra shirt. "You look tired."

"I'm okay," I said.

Sleep evaded me most nights. My mind lay cluttered with loss and desire. I saw why Sam did not wait to tell me about Arielle. I should have been cherishing the remaining time I had with him, but I longed to find my soul mate. I sought him in everyone we met.

Sam dropped our bag into the ivy. "Do you have the lighter?"

I rubbed my hands over my pockets. "No, I thought you had it."

"Fuck. It's probably in the bag." Sam scowled.

We shoved everything in as we found it on the ground. Everything was jumbled together.

"I'll get some matches," I said.

I scampered over to a 7-Eleven a few blocks away. As my hand came up to push through the glass doors, I collided with a young man. He wasn't more than sixteen. As I stumbled back, he caught me by my outstretched arm.

"You alright?" he asked.

I looked up into his blue eyes. "Yes, I'm fine."

He smiled, showing his teeth.

I walked to the counter and asked for some matches. The cashier slid a pack across the counter.

"Thanks." I tucked them into the back pocket of my jeans and walked to the door.

The blue-eyed boy was waiting outside. "You have a cigarette?" he asked.

I pointed toward camp. "I do over there. I was just getting matches, actually. My name is Nikki."

"I'm Jacob."

"Well, Jacob, my cigarettes are two blocks that way. If you want one, you'll have to come along."

He smiled. "I have a lighter."

I led the way back to camp.

As Jacob and I approached, Sam looked up. He had a cigarette hanging out of his mouth and his eyebrows were raised in a "who's this?" expression.

"Sam, this is Jacob. We ran into each other at the 7-Eleven."

Sam stood, wiped his hand on his pants, and extended it. "Glad to meet you."

I handed Sam the book of matches. He tilted his head and closed his left eye to prevent smoke from irritating it as he lit the cigarette.

Jacob said, "Nikki tells me the two of you just got into town?"

"We hitched in from California," Sam said. "Heading to Cougar Hot Springs, hopefully. We're trying to figure out a way to get there and meet some cool cats here in town."

I stood slightly behind Jacob. Sam met my eyes and I mouthed the words, "Dark elf." He nodded.

"I'm going to meet up with my friend Tao and smoke up," Jacob said. "You two want to come?"

"That would be way cool," Sam said, abandoning his gear-organizing efforts.

Neither Tao nor Jacob knew of anyone headed to the Springs any time soon, but said they'd let us know if they heard anything.

Jacob's raven hair fell from behind his ear and he brushed it back each time. His smile started with a spark in his eyes and then spread to his lips. He wet the rolling paper with his tongue and rolled the joint with deft, nimble fingers. He handed it to Sam to light.

Sam took a hit and passed it to Jacob. Jacob took a hit and then tried to pass it to me. I waved my hand and shook my head.

I wondered if Jacob was my soul mate. The thought became a cyclone in my mind. I was drawn to him, but it could have been my own creation, my own desire for him to be Arcadio, my dark elven soul mate—and my desire not to be alone, to have someone who understood me. Sam would know.

It was dark as Sam and I walked back to camp, hand in hand. He hadn't said anything since we left Tao and Jacob.

Finally, he spoke. "It's not him, you know."

I sighed. "How can you be sure?"

"Arcadio has green eyes."

"You've seen him, then?" The pitch in my voice rose.

His words came out slow and deliberate. "Only once. Before I became a wood elf, I walked a very different road. A dark road. I was known as Necrolunarian. I turned from that path long ago. He is not Arcadio."

When we got back to camp, Bill and Mariah said they wanted to go find some dose. We walked to Thirteenth Avenue and found a guy selling five strips for seven dollars. We bought two and split up the hits among the four of us.

We walked the streets for hours, laughing until our stomachs hurt and our eyes watered. We found a Safeway grocery store during our wandering and decided the name was a sign that it was a safe place to pick up cigarettes and food. Inside the store, we split up.

The aisles were empty, other than employees restocking shelves. I looked around for a clock. Midnight. I walked up and down aisles, looking for anything that might be good. Hunger wasn't something you felt when you were on acid. It was more about being aware of the last time you ate.

Obviously, I didn't want anything that had to be cooked. I made my way to the cereal aisle, then the chips, and then the crackers and cookies. Ritz? Too dry. Oreos? Yuck. Chicken in a Biskit? Yes. I pulled the blue-and-white box from the shelf, shoved it down the front of my pants, and folded my arms. I continued to wander for a few minutes. Nothing else looked appetizing, so I left.

I found the others a little way down the street. Sam and Bill both came out with cigarettes. Mariah came out with Kudos bars. The Chicken in a Biskit was delicious. The Kudos, not so much.

Eventually, we ended up back at camp, no longer hallucinating. We were physically tired, but mentally wired. Sam and I lay in our blankets.

"Sorry about Jacob," he said.

I planted a quick kiss on his cheek. "No worries. Things happen in their own time."

I rolled away from him. I lay awake for a long time. He was awake too. We were each lost in our own thoughts. Would love forever elude me? Maybe I was right before, and it didn't exist.

No.

I've reclaimed my hold on hope and I refuse to surrender my dream.

The next morning, Sam and I picked up a box of food from the food bank and stored it at our camp. We pulled the ivy over it to conceal it.

We walked to the mission, took showers, and got some wool blankets. Afterward, we were hungry. The food box was for breakfasts before we had enough money from panhandling. We strolled toward our favorite pizza shop, Pizza Pipeline, and asked for spare change along the way. By the time we got there, we had enough for pizza now and coffee at IHOP later.

We got the pizza and called Sam's dad about wiring child support money. We considered getting a P.O. box since we planned to be in Eugene for a while, but decided it would be better for him just to wire the money. Things changed all the time; there was no telling where we would be in a month.

Once we received the money, we went to IHOP to wait for Bill and Mariah, who had gone off on their own after showering. Sam was frustrated with them and thought they were hiding something. They never showed up, but James did.

He slid into our booth. "I found someplace cool to stay."

Sam raised an eyebrow.

"I met these cats who have a green bus. Let's get your stuff and you two can move in."

Sam looked at me.

"Why not?"

He shrugged. "Let's do it."

We scurried over to base camp and Sam shouldered our pack. We left Bill and Mariah's stuff there. The green bus was parked near Jefferson Street. We arrived as the sun set.

On our first night in the green bus, I sat in the back, alone, writing in my journal. I finished reading the first book of the Dragonlance elven trilogy, *Firstborn*, which told the history of our people. Sam and James had gone for a walk. James said he needed to talk with him alone. Sam wasn't pleased, but I told him I needed some alone time anyway.

I closed the cover of my journal and tucked it away. I leaned back on our duffle bag. It weighed as much as I did.

The coven must be in chaos with me missing, I thought. Michael had probably flown into a rage when he woke up and found me gone. A pang of sadness came over me. I was my people's hope of being reunited, and had I left.

Brenden had wanted it as much as I did. Images of dancing at Confetti and Michael brushing the hair from my face tore into my mind, searing the air in my lungs. It seemed like a lifetime had passed. My fingers played with the rough crystal and smooth beads draped around my neck—gifts from Sam. Things were different now.

Sam's head poked through the door of the bus. "Nikki, will you come talk to me?"

I got to my feet and went to him. Rain sprinkled my bare skin. We walked for a few blocks in silence.

"James is worried about you," he said. "He thinks that you seriously believe in the Charade. That you honestly believe you are a vampire elf enclosed in a human's body."

My blood throbbed inside my skull. My internal organs became shards of glass. Chaos and confusion blurred my vision. I wanted to

177

scream, "Of course it's real!" but the sound only reverberated inside my throbbing head. I bit my tongue until I tasted metallic blood. Sam was looking at the ground and missed the avalanche of emotion.

"I told him you're not naïve and brainwashed," he said. "I told him you are able to sort out the spiritual part from the game." He looked at me, his eyes pleading for me to say I had known it was a game all along.

I looked at the sky, hoping that the gesture would pass for exasperation. The rain hit my face, washing my thoughts and feelings away.

"Of course I know it's a game," I managed to say. "While you guys were gone, I was sorting through things."

Sam smiled and wrapped me in his arms.

Pulling my arms to my chest, I rested my head against him. My heart collapsed. The whole time, I had been living in a beautiful world made of glass. Now it was shattered. Any step I took from here would leave me seeping blood from my soles.

Most teens with depression will suffer from more than one episode. Up to forty percent have more than one episode within two years, and seventy percent will have more than one episode before adulthood.

chapter thirteen

```
Jake studies his notes, paging through them, then
takes his seat.
    Judge Cruz sips from his glass of water. "Ms.
Lowe?"
    I slide a pen and notepad toward Clarice.
"Write down any questions or comments you have on
here."
    Clarice has worked for Child and Family
Services for four years. She no longer has that
doe-eyed look about her; she sits with her back
straight in a sleek, grey dress suit. She's
young, maybe twenty-six, but she's seen more
child suffering than most fifty-year-olds have —
at least in the United States.
    Child and Family Services has a habit of
hiring young women just finishing their
bachelor's degree when they're twenty-two or
twenty-three. It was the same for me. But the
life I led before was different from many others.
    Most of the new-hires believe the world is a
safe place, where they can grow into successful
mothers and wives. They believe they will be the
```

one who changes the direction of these families' lives by showing them compassion and understanding. They have dreams of a warm home in cool, painted colors, surrounded by a white picket fence — their imaginary toddlers splashing in the kiddy pool set in the center of a deep, green lawn. The caseworkers who come to the realization that reality is not the same as they once believed are the ones who continue the work. The others find jobs that breathe life back into their fading dreams.

The chair rolls back easily as I get to my feet.

"Thank you, Judge, just a few."

Sabrina is still glowing from the light Jake sprinkled onto her case with his cross-examination. My eyes meet hers. Not all twenty-two-year-olds believe in the green lawn and the picket fence.

"How long is the wait list for House of Hope?" I ask.

"Umm... I don't know."

Out of the corner of my eye, I see Clarice writing. I glance down. In her careful print are the words: *Three months without drug court.*

"Ms. Hardy, do you have a certificate of completion for the Love and Logic course you said you completed?"

"I had one, but then I had to move again, and I don't know where it is."

"When was that?"

She presses her lips into a thin line. She looks to Jake, who sits without expression at his table. His face remains impassive, unmoved by the questions she sends silently across the courtroom. She wants him to do something — to stop my questions.

"A month ago, I guess," Sabrina says.

"You're not sure?"

She exhales hard through her nose and turns away from me. "It was a month."

"Do you have a signature sheet showing the interim substance abuse groups you have attended?"

"I was in a rush to get here this morning. I couldn't find it. I thought being here was more important than a piece of paper." Color crawls onto her cheeks.

I am removing the bricks from the house she and Jake have begun to build for her and McCartni.

At this stage in the case, she is powerless to stop the destruction of the dream she carefully built — the dream that has fueled her last few weeks of success. She sees me as no better than anyone else who has victimized her. She still doesn't understand the choices have always been hers.

A cigarette rested between my lips. I held the flame to its end and pulled the air through the packed tobacco. Smoke filled my mouth, throat, and lungs. I released the thick cloud slowly, watching it rise and dissipate into thin air.

You could have said my eyes had been opened. I wished instead they'd been ripped out of my head. My world was burning again. The yellow, orange, and blue flames fed on my soul. For days, I struggled to put out the fire that surrounded me—trying to find purpose and meaning in the world. The *only* world.

"You alright?" Sam asked. "Where are you in there?"

I put on a mask. I was always good at that. "I'm fine."

The realization that the Charade was only a game had to come at some point. I'm not sure my reaction would have been different if it had come later. I was laid bare before the world. I was nothing, as I'd always been.

My spiritual and physical training went on as planned. Just not for the War of the Races. It would go on because it was all I had left. I wanted to know how to fight and protect myself. I wanted to learn about different types of magic and rituals. Religion was the ultimate bridge to making sense of what people feared and what people could not understand, a bridge to the gods. It gave them purpose and meaning. It was a guiding light. For some it provided superiority, and for others, sanctuary. Religion drew humans in because of their very nature, their insatiable curiosity, and need for answers. In that regard, I was no different from anyone else.

The Order of the Silvermoon still existed. It was just that its mission was different from what I'd originally understood it to be. The Order wanted to educate people about spirituality. The belief was that, through spirituality, we would save the world from those who sought to conquer, dominate, and destroy it. The Order believed all people should be protectors of the earth and the animals, not its rulers. The only way to accomplish this was to open people's minds—showing them that living in peace and oneness with nature was true survival.

I was sitting outside of Anatolia's restaurant, asking for spare change. Sam sat next to me. The concrete and brick still held the night's chill. Rough hemp twine passed back and forth between my fingers as I passed time weaving necklaces and bracelets. Natural oils from a person's skin softened the twine as it was worn. I laced glass, clay, and bone beads onto the twine with pendants of silver, glass, or stone.

A shadow came to a rest on me. I looked up into Jacob's face. His black hair brushed his chin; he pushed it back behind his ear. It fell forward again, and again he brushed it back. "What are you tying?"

"A necklace. I've already done some anklets and bracelets." I pointed to the straw-colored twine decorated with bright clay beads and silver fairy bells. He wasn't Arcadio. Arcadio had never existed.

"You got a bowl you can kick down?" Sam asked, getting to his feet.

Jacob pulled a dime bag from his pocket and tossed it to him.

Sam caught it in his hand. "Sweet. You have time for a bowl?"

They sat and passed the pipe between them.

"You know if anyone has dose on Thirteenth Avenue?" Sam asked, holding the smoke in his lungs.

Jacob nodded and took the lighter. "Yeah, but there's a lot of bunk dose out there, so be careful."

He hid the pipe in his cupped palm when people stopped to look at the necklaces. A woman bought a bracelet with bone beads and another with fairy bells for her daughter. The girl had on a baseball uniform. Her mother tied the bracelet around her wrist and the bells danced to their soft, high-pitched song.

My lips began to form the words, "Oh say can you see..." I could almost feel my father's warmth next to me. His arm held me tight to his side. Baseball had been our thing. We watched every game together and he came to every one of my softball games. I could throw the ball fast, but never straight. The Pink Panthers was my team. I played shortstop. We took second place. The trophy was in the bottom of my closet, covered with a mass of black clothes, surrounded by combat boots.

Sam tapped the bowl of the pipe on the sidewalk. "We've got to meet my brother at IHOP. You want to come and have coffee with us?"

"I've got homework that's due tomorrow," Jacob said. "Sorry, man. See you around."

"Thanks for the bud."

Bells jangled against glass as Sam and I pushed through the door at the used bookstore. The musty smell of aging stories made me smile. I stopped to breathe it in.

"You coming?" Sam said. "We need to hurry. James is waiting."

I clattered up the wooden stairs and slid the second and third books of the elven trilogy from the shelf. I needed to know how it ended. My fingers ruffled the soft pages and I tucked the books into the back of my pants, pulled my shirt over them, and strolled down the stairs.

Sam took my hand as we rounded the corner of the street and the IHOP came into view. The Charade was shattered, but the fragments of glass remained. The story and the dream lived on in my heart.

James was sitting at a table with Bill and Mariah. He stood and hugged us both. I sat and moved into the corner. Sam slid in next to me. James grabbed a chair and pulled it to the end of the table.

"Where have you two been?" Sam asked Bill and Mariah, not hiding his frustration.

"We've been taking care of a few things," Bill said. "Where did you guys move to?"

We talked and told them about our friends in the VW bus. James broke the news that he was going to hitchhike back to Missoula. He told us to find him when we got into town. No one asked why or protested his leaving. We just accepted it.

Sam said, "We were able to get hemp and beads today, and I know where we can get tie-dyed balloons to make the stress balls."

"We sold one necklace today," I said. "I think they'll be good for trading."

"That's true." Sam nodded his head in agreement.

"I heard there's a Saturday market that starts soon," James said.

Bill and Mariah silently followed the conversation with their eyes and ears. At the first break, Mariah jumped in. "I think I'm pregnant."

Three pairs of wide eyes fixed on her, trying to figure out the appropriate response based upon her expression, unable to discern much. We looked at Bill. He was grinning from ear to ear.

James was first to find his tongue. "Congratulations! What's your plan?"

Mariah took Bill's hand in hers and rested them on the table. "I want to go to the free clinic tomorrow to find out for sure. Will you come, Nikki?"

"Um, yeah. Of course," I said, shaking off the astonishment at last.

"We haven't decided what we'll do if I am pregnant," Maria said, "but we can't stay here. Maybe go back to Utah where my sister is."

Bill nodded his head.

They both seemed happy about the pregnancy. The whole time I thought I was pregnant, I felt suicidal; I wanted to end the pregnancy any way I could. I felt bad for her, but tried not to show it.

There was a huge line at the free clinic the next morning. The guys went to the food bank to eat and spare-change enough for everyone's coffee and an order of cheese fries. The plan was to meet up at IHOP or our usual panhandling spot in front of Anatolia's. After three and a half hours of waiting, we got the results. The test was positive. Mariah was thrilled.

"Bill will be a great dad and I've always loved little kids," she said. "I worked in a daycare once and just loved it. I always wanted to take the kids home with me."

"I'm happy for you," I lied.

We left and headed for the bead shop to pick up more beads, sewing needles, crystals, and pendants before meeting back up with the guys.

The cowbell on the front door clanged as we pushed our way in. A middle-aged woman with silver-streaked hair and mom jeans rolled up over her belly button sat on a stool behind the counter. She peered at us over her wide-rimmed glasses.

Mariah continued to chatter while I riffled through containers of beads. "I hope the baby is a girl."

A colorful clay bead slid down my sleeve.

Mariah stood to the side of me. Her hands were in constant motion as she spoke. "We'll have to stop smoking cigarettes."

A few more beads disappeared into my sleeve. I put my hand in my pocket and they dropped inside.

Mariah was not looking at the beads at all. I checked back into her chatter.

"And no more acid," she said.

I walked to the trays of crystals, saying nothing to her. My mind was a tornado of memories of Michael.

"I think the weed will help with morning sickness," she said.

I smiled and nodded as crystals slipped down my sleeve. I took a few steps sideways.

Mariah followed right beside me, picking up beads and letting them fall through her fingers. "We're going to have to get normal everyday jobs to take care of the baby."

The cowbell announced our departure.

Mariah and I turned down Willamette Street toward Anatolia's. Once we saw the guys sitting on the sidewalk, Mariah ran to Bill. She jumped into his arms and kissed him. I continued walking. Bill was just as excited as Mariah. I just didn't understand. Would I ever be excited to have a baby? I shook the thought from my mind.

We walked to Pizza Pipeline and got a pizza to share. After eating, I showed Sam the crystals I picked up. I'd grabbed two of each, as always.

I placed each stone in his palm as I told him what they did. "This is amber, which recharges energy, is warming, and emotionally balancing. This one is bloodstone. It clears away psychic blocks and boosts energy. Jade strengthens our connection to the earth. Malachite enhances vision and promotes inner peace, hope, and success."

Malachite, with its swirls of different shades of green, was my favorite. The swirls wove in and out of the stone, never ending. Sam eased them into the medicine pouch around his neck and kissed my forehead.

The guys went down to Thirteenth to find a sheet of acid. Mariah and I hung out at the overpass camp and made necklaces. She talked about her and Bill's plan to go back to Utah and live with her sister until they could get on their feet.

"Will you deliver some letters for me or make some phone calls when you get back to Utah?" I asked.

"Of course," she said, and without missing a beat, started throwing out baby names.

I wasn't listening. I was lost in my own thoughts about Sam and Arielle. I would be alone again when we reached Montana. I wanted him to be happy, and I knew he would be. She was his soul mate. My heart ached at the thought of being a solitary star again. I wouldn't be physically left behind, but once they were together, he would confide in her, teach her, and love her. I would be nothing.

The guys came back from their acid hunt emptyhanded. I wanted to get high. The world was a better place with acid in my veins.

It was dark out, and Mariah wanted to go to sleep. Her parents had purchased bus tickets for her and Bill to return to Utah the next morning. Sam and I went back to the IHOP while the others stayed at camp.

Sam sat across the table from me and sipped at his coffee. "Magic is a state of mind. It is control of the consciousness. Your will can control the fibers that connect us to each other and every other object in the world. In order to use magic, you must imagine what it is you desire—you must believe it to be so, with your complete mind and will. If you're able to do this, your will does the rest. It reaches into the fabric of life and weaves together the path that you desire."

"We used different words for things when I was goth," I told him, "but the concepts were the same. Tell me about astral projection and the astral body."

Nicole Lowe

He blew smoke out of his nose and continued. Tendrils of smoke escaped his lips as he spoke. "It's much the same. First, you must be able to be present and aware while in the astral state, which is the most difficult part. After that, it's the same."

"How do you do that?"

"In the beginning, the easiest time to tap into your astral consciousness is as you're falling asleep. It's there, in the space between the conscious and unconscious mind, that you can feel your astral body. Without coming into wakefulness, you focus on the feeling of your astral body. Once you're able to sense it, you can direct it to places and in actions. Any amount of fear or doubt will prevent you from obtaining control. Having achieved control from that space, you will begin to feel it at other times, and then soon you will feel it always and can use it at any time."

That night, I dreamed I was back in Salt Lake. Michael was waiting for me when I stepped off the Greyhound. He grabbed me around the throat and threw me to the ground. The street was full of people, but no one stopped. No one even looked my way. He kicked me and I awoke, breathless. I was in and out of consciousness the rest of the night. I tried to work on astral projection, but Michael was always there, waiting for me.

We ate raw ramen noodles while we packed up our bed as the sun rose. Sam and I were still staying in the bus, but we always had to be ready to move. We headed over to Thirteenth and spare-changed, all the while trying to find someone who had a sheet or at least a good connection.

"I'm going to give Mariah some letters for my family and friends in Salt Lake," I said.

"You need to forget about Salt Lake before you want to go back there."

"I know, but I want them to know I'm alright." The soles of my feet brushed the ground and I fell a few steps behind him.

We strolled Thirteenth all day and all we found was six hits, which we split between the two of us. I closed my eyes as I placed the paper on the center of my tongue. I wanted to feel it until it dissolved. Acid was my happy place.

Never Let Me Go

Tucked into the corner of a booth at IHOP, we smoked and watched people. We were lost in our own discombobulated thoughts. We stared at random objects, watching them morph as the hallucinations intensified.

People, in general, fell into three categories: stick people, marionettes, and ragdolls. Stick people were rigid, stiff, and unbendable. They had meltdowns when the world and people wouldn't conform to their ideals. Marionettes were puppets. They personified what the world expected them to be, rather than being true to who they were. Ragdolls followed their own path. They moved with the world, not against it. They were free from the weight of what the world thought of them.

Sam's pen danced across the page, creating people and worlds from my dreams of the Charade. The creatures got up off the page and moved about our table, as if on a stage. Life was a big production where everyone played a different role. When you were on acid, you stepped out of your role. More accurately, you became acutely aware of the various roles people played and the stage they all shared. The trick, when you were tripping, was to continue in your assigned role in the presence of anyone who was not tripping. You couldn't let the world know you'd seen backstage, because most of them weren't aware there was a backstage or a stage crew.

After we started coming down, Sam pulled my journal to his side of the table, turned to a fresh page, and began writing.

Nikki,
I know that when I go back to Montana it means that I will have to leave you. All I can give is now, and I hope it's enough. I want you to know that even though we won't be together, I always will be with you. I love you, and you should always remember that I always will, in some way. May your path be green and golden.
P.S. You are beautiful.
Sam

Green and golden. My path had never been green and golden. I spent another night running from Michael, only this time the wolf

189

was right behind him. I jerked awake twice, and each time Sam asked what was wrong. I just rolled over.

Before the sun came up, we walked across town in the chill air. It was time for Bill and Mariah to leave. The four of us shared a table and coffee for the last time. We walked to the Greyhound station. I watched Bill and Mariah climb inside with their backpacks slung over their shoulders. Mariah turned back and waved. The bus pulled away from the building. Its exhaust, like smoke burning the remains of a house, rose into the ashen morning. The taillights became pinpricks and then disappeared from sight. No tears. Never tears.

James was gone. Bill and Mariah were gone, and Sam was scheduled to leave too. In the end, it always came back to this. Maybe this was all there was, and it wasn't just at the end of life that we were alone, but from the beginning. My thoughts and experiences were mine alone. My perception of the world was mine alone. Clinging to people, ideas, places, and things only caused pain. Time devoured them all.

After the bus disappeared in the distance, we shuffled over to Thirteenth and scored a sheet of acid. We each took five hits and waited an hour. Nothing. Not even a tingle. It was bunk. We hustled back to Thirteenth and found the dealer. He was surprised when we told him it was bunk. He gave Sam his money back. We found another dealer.

"I'm Duck. What are you looking for?"

Duck was a large man. It wasn't hard to figure out why he was called Duck.

"Dose," Sam said.

Duck waddled a little closer. "How much?"

"A sheet."

"Ooh, I don't got that tonight. All I have is six."

"We'll take them, and if we like it, can you have a sheet tomorrow?"

"No problem," Duck said. "I'll be right here."

We dropped three hits and waited. We wandered up and down the streets.

Sam was blowing smoke rings. "I feel bad about the situation between you and me. I don't want to hurt you."

"You won't. I won't let it hurt me, so stop worrying about it."

You can't make me cry. It was what I'd said as a child, and it was still true.

We were sitting outside the Hult Center admiring the frog statues when the acid kicked in. The frogs were stacked one on top of the other, each of them as tall as me. The knees and elbows of the frogs began to crack and crumble. They blinked fragments of rock from their eyes. Their eyes ground in their stone sockets as they rolled around, loosening up. The frogs wanted to be free; not even stone could hold them. An olive-green frog pulled a top hat from behind his back and bowed, extending his hand to me. I placed my hand in his and we danced.

All sense of self was lost in the acid trip. The world became what your mind made of it. You built a world from pieces of memory and experience, combined with your physical surroundings. A fearful person created a nightmare. A selfish person became a paranoid conspiracy theorist. A joyful person created beauty. A ragdoll flowed in and out of all creations, because they were all of these things and none of them.

We slept most of the next day away. I awoke with a rumbling stomach. Sam and I stumbled from the bus, blinking against the sun's rays. A yellow clamp was locked on the rear tire. We stood there shaking our heads at the lock, passing our last cigarette back and forth. We got back on the bus, collected our belongings, and rolled up our blankets. Sam packed it all snug into our pack and hoisted it onto his back. Time to move on.

We went in search of Duck. The dose had been decent. Not great, but good enough to sell and not feel like we were ripping people off. Our plan was to leave Eugene once we had the sheet. We sparechanged enough money for a final pizza, then sat drinking coffee at IHOP for a few hours, writing, drawing, and reading our books. The dealers wouldn't be slinging acid until after dark.

Sam again brought up him having to break up with me. I believed the topic cluttered his mind as much as it did mine.

Nicole Lowe

A grin pulled at the corners of his mouth. "You should break up with *me*."

I laughed. "I'm not the one with the soul mate."

"True," he said, stretching the vowels. "I will be the one to break up with you on three conditions. First, you have to keep me warm at night. Second, you have to hold my hand when we're somewhere people might think I'm pimping you off. And third, you can't hit on other guys around me. If you don't keep these conditions, you have to break up with me."

Smiling and shaking my head, I agreed to his conditions. We finished our coffee and cleaned up our stuff.

Thirteenth Avenue was deserted.

"We can never get a break," he said.

"What do you want to do?"

"We're going north."

Three rides got us to a little town called Wilsonville and then one more to Salem, Oregon, where we slept under an overpass.

Sam stared up at the concrete overhead. "We need money."

"I could call someone in Utah?" I said.

"I hate that idea, but it's all we have."

We could have waited for Sam's child support money, but that was still a month away. We could have spare-changed enough money for a sheet over a few weeks, but we tried not to spend that money on dose or weed. Even street urchins had values.

The next morning, we caught a ride to Portland. We connected with some gutter punks playing hacky sack at Pioneer Square. Sam jumped into their circle, catching the sack and popping it up over his head. They shared a bowl with him.

Afterward, we lounged on the red-brick stadium steps of the square, watching people come and go. We decided to continue heading north and prepare for the cold trip east through the mountains to Montana.

"When do you want me to call Utah?" I asked.

He stared at me defeatedly. "Whenever."

I called Melanie's house collect. Nick picked up the phone.

"Still hanging out at Melanie's, huh?" I said.

He ignored my question and immediately asked where I was. When I refused to tell him, his voice took on a note of anger. I said I needed money. He said he wouldn't send me a dime unless I called my mother first to let her know I was still alive. Apparently, she'd come around Melanie's numerous times looking for me.

Raindrops pattered against the plastic shell of the payphone booth as my fingers dialed the familiar number instinctively. My mother started crying as soon as she heard my voice.

"Where are you?" she asked.

"I just wanted to let you know that I'm alright," I said.

"I love you. Please come home. It's different."

"Mom—" I whispered into the receiver.

"You won't be in trouble. No one will ask you questions. We just want you home. I just want you to see a therapist."

"I can't—"

"I want you to be warm and fed. Patrick is home. He stays home most of the time now."

The yellow streetlight bounced off a black-and-white police car as it glided around the corner. Sam's eyes screamed at me that it was time to go.

"The state authorities have been accusing me of abandoning you and neglecting you because you're not attending school," she said.

I was beside myself with this nugget of information. She had never abandoned or neglected me. I had abandoned *her*.

"Your friend Abigail gave Michael a hundred dollars to find you in San Francisco, and he snorted it up his nose. We put up posters of you all over in Salt Lake, California, and Oregon. Your dad was in a plane crash, but he's okay. Your rat chewed holes in your waterbed, but he's okay too. I promise things are better. Please, Nikki, come home. We'll buy a bus ticket for you."

The line fell silent.

"I was so scared when the police called from San Francisco saying they had your purse," she finally said.

"I'm fine, Mom. I love you."

"Please, Nikki."

I returned the phone to its receiver. I turned my head slowly toward Sam, surprised at the words that fell from my mouth and sank into the quicksand of my brain.

"I'm going home," I whispered.

One in seven young people between the ages of ten and eighteen will run away from home.

chapter fourteen

Judge Cruz peers over his thick-rimmed glasses. "Mr. Johnson?"

Carl doesn't look up from his laptop. "I don't have any questions, Your Honor."

Judge Cruz turns to me. "Next witness, Ms. Lowe."

"Your Honor, the state calls Clarice Anderson."

Clarice stands and smooths the back of her skirt. She walks to the court clerk's desk and raises her right hand.

The clerk gets to her feet. Her back is bent, her eyes attentive as she delivers the oath with ease. "Do you swear to tell the truth, the whole truth, and nothing but the truth?"

"Yes," Clarice says.

The judge makes a note on his bench blotter. I assume he's jotting down my caseworker's name. "Ms. Anderson, please take a seat on the witness stand."

Clarice climbs the two steps to the witness stand, sits, and pours herself a cup of water from the carafe within arm's reach.

I wait until her eyes meet mine.

"Ms. Anderson, where do you work?" I ask.

"The Division of Child and Family Services."

"How long have you worked there?"

"Four years."

Most caseworkers don't make it more than twelve to eighteen months in child welfare. Many go back to school, and the rest discover they are not emotionally built for this line of work. Four years shows fortitude and compassion. It's the belief that if you can save one life, it's worth everything. That's what gets you through the tough days.

"Are you assigned to McCartni Hardy's case?"

"Yes. I've been assigned since the beginning."

It's common for caseworkers to be changed out a few times during a child's case. In some cases, the judge is the only person involved from start to finish. Even the change of a caseworker causes stress for a child, particularly for older children who understand the caseworker's role in their life. When that happens, it hits them like another loss — one more person who has left.

"How long has McCartni been in state's custody?"

"Just over twelve months."

"Is she placed in a potential adoptive home?"

"Yes. And they have signed the intent to adopt."

Not all foster homes want to adopt the children who are placed with them. Even if they're licensed to adopt, some decide they cannot meet the child's needs long-term due to their need for supportive services, which end at adoption. These children don't change placements, but have significant medical or mental health needs that cause them to remain in state's custody until they turn twenty-one.

"How long has McCartni been placed with her foster family?"

"Since she was placed into state's custody."

I slide my fingers down my yellow notepad, keeping track of where I am in my line of questioning.

"At the beginning of this case, what was the goal?"

"To return McCartni to her mother."

"What did Ms. Hardy need to do to have McCartni returned?"

Clarice slides forward to the edge of her chair and rests her clasped hands on the bar before her. "We created a child and family plan which outlined the steps Ms. Hardy needed to take to have McCartni come home. She needed to have random drug tests and test clean. She needed to have a substance abuse evaluation and a domestic violence assessment. Once those were done, she would need to follow through with the recommendations. She also needed to have a safe home and enough income to take care of McCartni and herself."

I set my pen on the legal pad. "Let's take each one of those, one at a time."

Clarice sips her water and nods her head. Her green eyes aren't smiling. She has spent the last year trying to help Sabrina. She has watched her hold and snuggle McCartni while they read story after story in the visiting room. She's driven Sabrina to detox in the middle of the night, only to find out the next morning that she left within ten minutes. You don't spend a year of your life advocating for someone and not hurt when they don't reach their goal.

On the night of March 16, 1995, I boarded the 10:45 bus to Salt Lake City. I rethought my decision with each step. Sam stood on the curb, wiping tears from his face. I took a seat by a window so I could see him for as long as possible.

We planned to communicate by leaving messages with Arielle. Sam and I agreed I would stay in Utah until mid-April, then I would meet up with him in Missoula.

I made six promises to Sam before I got on the bus. One, I wouldn't flirt with other guys while he was around. Two, I wouldn't wear makeup. Three, I wouldn't get tied down. Four, I wouldn't drink alcohol. Five, I wouldn't get married unless I was in love. And six, I wouldn't forget him.

I wasn't sure if he believed I would ever come back, but I believed I would. I didn't know how, but if I willed it, it would come into being.

The bus slugged along the road and I rode with it, leaving behind a trail of tears and snot. I didn't sleep; I didn't feel tired. I was nervous about going back. The bus stopped in Boise for a break and I got off to smoke. I missed Sam. I hoped he would be happy with Arielle. I hoped she would be good to him and give him everything he deserved—all that I would have given him, and more.

I considered walking away from the bus. Returning was a mistake. I didn't want to go back to Utah anymore. I flicked my cigarette and turned to face the bus. Everyone was getting back on. The bus driver stopped at the door and looked around for anyone missing. Hitching alone was dangerous, so I dragged my feet back onto the bus.

When I arrived in Salt Lake, I felt entirely incompatible with my surroundings. My heart beat against my ribcage. Worms squirmed in my stomach. I was not the same person who left.

My mom hardly recognized me as I approached her. The knowledge that I would be leaving again in a few weeks gave me minimal comfort. I didn't know what to say to her. There was an awkward silence, and she sucked me in for a suffocating hug. I choked and then relaxed into her embrace.

I didn't have an explanation, and she didn't ask for one. I didn't want to be around anyone. I didn't want to become attached. I was hoping I could convince Patrick to return with me, but I wasn't sure if I could trust him anymore.

"Your dad stopped flying after the crash," my mom said, trying to make conversation on the drive back. "He's taken a job with Kennecott."

I stared out the window of the car. It was dark outside. Any emotion I felt about the incident was miniscule compared to the ache in my soul with Sam so far away.

The house looked the same from the outside, but inside it I felt out of place. I sat on the floor of Patrick's bedroom. He hadn't changed.

"I wasn't worried about you," he said. "I've always known you were safe and would come back. Where have you been?"

"A lot of places," I said.

"Are you leaving again?"

I looked away.

"I thought as much," he said.

"I want you to meet Sam and join the Order of the Silvermoon. The Order is going to bring true enlightenment to people, revealing the interconnectedness and teaching balance between life and death. I want you to be a part of it. The Charade, it's not real."

"I know the Charade is not entirely real, but the magic is."

I could feel his eyes watching me.

"I've learned so much." I showed him the drawings and notes in my journals.

"I need a few days to decide," he finally said.

I went to the kitchen and made some ramen noodles. It had been a long time since I'd eaten them cooked.

My mom knew about some of what had happened before I left. I wasn't sure who told her, or how much she knew. I wasn't going to talk to her or anyone. She made me an appointment for me to see a psychiatrist in a few weeks. She called the school to re-register me. I didn't want to go back there. This was more complicated than I had anticipated.

My thoughts and feelings were scrambled. I wanted to scream and pull my hair. I felt trapped.

I promised Sam I would return, and I promised not to break that promise. I just wanted to go to sleep. I walked into my bedroom. The darkness there was preserved. Images of Brenden and Michael danced through my head. My fingers brushed the velvet blazers hanging in my closet. Once again, the razor split my skin and crimson dropped snakelike across my pale flesh. It was dark, and I was alone. I was always alone.

...I can't breathe. He's on top of me again. His blond hair is in my face and his teeth tear at my throat. No! Stop! I push him away with all my strength. I can't move. I'm going to be sick...

I woke up shaking, soaked in sweat. I lay in the blackness of my room. I saw the wolf's face in the dark shadows. I squeezed my eyes closed and his face was still there, burned into my eyelids. I shouldn't have been drinking with someone I didn't know. I wanted to forget. Why did it keep coming back? I fought off sleep until the sun broke free of the night.

I sat at the kitchen table across from Patrick. He slid the box of Fruity Pebbles toward me, then the milk. My parents were at work. My little sister was at school.

"If you plan to return to the Order of the Silvermoon, you better stay away from downtown Salt Lake. Michael and Brenden are out for your blood. Michael said he would only take you back if you came back on your hands and knees. Your leaving caused a divide in the Black Hand. Only Brenden can help get things back to normal, if you want to return to the coven. I can arrange for you to talk with him alone."

I did not want to deal with this situation. "I've broken free from my bondage to the Black Hand, and I will not knowingly put myself back into its cage."

He smiled and nodded his head. "In that case, Spider and Ogre want to speak with you. They've been in New Orleans and are very interested in what you've been doing."

Spider and Ogre were more loyal to Patrick than to Brenden. It was always that way, but still I hesitated. The darkness was still inside of me somewhere. I could feel it. If I came too close to that old life, I feared it would consume me once again. It was so familiar to me. I could descend into that world before I was aware of what I had done.

I shook my head. "I don't know."

My mom gave me a few days to adjust before insisting that I go back to school. They assigned me a new locker and gave me a new class schedule. I hung out in the student services office most of the day, not feeling up to walking into a classroom. No one questioned my presence. No one asked if I needed any help.

I was fighting the urge to fall back into my old ways, the person I was before. The internal isolation was pulling me back into a life of death and the walking dead. When I was out walking around, I could feel it sneaking up on me, but when I turned around it melted into the shadows. It pressed down on me when I lay in my bed at night, thoughts running uncontrolled through my head. My joy and happiness began to decay. I missed Sam.

I sat in my bedroom and forced a safety pin through my belly button. It took a while because the pin was dull. The pain reminded me I was alive. It felt good. I needed to get high. I wished Sam was with me. I was alone again, always alone. The cadence of death's voice rose and fell on the breeze, rocking me gently.

```
                        i wish

                  i feel your heart beat
                     i feel the pain
         i wish i was walking with you in the rain
        i love you in a way i don't quite understand
         i wish we were together in never-never land
                    you're in my dreams
                    you're on my mind
         your voice i hear like you're right beside me
                  but i am here in bed alone
            god, i wish i wouldn't have come home.
```

    I was being torn apart between thoughts of Sam, Michael, and my mom. Each wanted different things of me, and I wanted to be those things for them.

    I threw myself at school like a starving child at a buffet. It was the end of the term, and I was failing everything. I wanted to get straight A's, and I knew they were within reach. I decided to postpone my visit to Montana until spring break so I wouldn't miss any more school.

    My parents were not asking questions. It was better that way. They wouldn't understand my answers, anyway. They were not being intrusive or restrictive. My mom said she wanted me to stay home and go to school. In turn, I was allowed to hang out with my friends and have sleepovers.

    The thought of walking away from my mom left my insides raw. I decided I could complete my physical and spiritual training with Patrick, and take martial arts classes. Sam could send me books, and we could talk on the phone.

    I knew that going into Salt Lake would bring my undoing. Its pull on me was relentless, and gaining strength. I wasn't sure I would be able to prevent myself from tumbling back into the Black Hand, and back into Michael's arms. Some nights, I lay awake and he called to me. I longed to go to him. I reached out, and our fingertips brushed. I wanted the comfort of my old rhythms and the safety of the shadows, but none of it was real. The Charade had been revealed.

I was remaking myself from broken pieces. Nothing was left whole or untouched. I was forcing two completely different puzzles together. What would remain in the end would be a patchwork of all I had been. The emptiness stood before me, deeper than ever before. One step in its direction and I would have been home, and the despondent incompleteness would end.

I tried to use astral projection to reach Sam. I sat in the corner of my room, leaning against the wall to remain slightly alert. When I entered that semi-conscious state, I couldn't focus my mind, and I wound up falling asleep.

I wondered if my dreams were Sam trying to contact me. Only he would understand the emptiness growing within. I hoped he was happy with Arielle. She had everything I craved.

I woke up the next morning with a renewed commitment to leave for Montana. I decided to tell my mom the reasons for my leaving—why my journey was so important to me, and how it could never end until the world had achieved a true understanding of spirituality. Only then could the Order of the Silvermoon rest.

When I told Patrick everything, he agreed to come with me. Whether or not he truly believed in the cause wasn't as important as his support for what he saw as something deeply important to me. I hoped my mom would have the same ability to understand. But even if she didn't, I was still determined to leave.

I planned to tell her on our way to the appointment with the psychiatrist, but that day never came. On March 31, 1995, Patrick and I left the house as if we were going to school. Instead, we walked past the school and got on the bus.

I told him that we needed to avoid all of our old haunts, at all costs. The last thing I wanted was to deal with the drama of the Black Hand and the Charade. I didn't want to be sucked back in. Patrick agreed.

When I asked him where we were going, he said, "My friend Anna's. I have two other friends staying there, Luna and Olga. They were going to California, but I want them to come to Montana with us."

"Where are they from?"

"Connecticut. They ran away from home."

On our way to Anna's house, an old friend hooked us up with some LSD.

Anna's was a deep-rooted house with wood siding and peeling, dark-blue paint. There was a ground-level porch at the front of the house. The roof had a steep pitch. The floors were hardwood, and the appliances in the home were timeworn. Wooden window frames and short, narrow stairs characteristic of the early 1900s filled the house.

Anna was Wiccan. The scent of sage and patchouli floated through the warm home. A tapestry of the moon and stars hung on a wall in the living room. A circular rug on the floor resembled the sun. The floors creaked like old bones when you walked. Candles of various colors stood guard around the room and across the fireplace mantle, along with bundles of sage.

Luna and Olga had been staying with Anna for a week. Luna had an internal fire about her, which was probably what drew Patrick to her. She was frail, with long, fine red hair and green eyes. Olga had long, blonde hair. Her blue eyes lacked the fire in Luna's. Both girls wanted to go to Montana with us.

"We don't have a lot of travel options," I said to Patrick. "I can think of only one: hitchhiking. I can take Olga with me, and you and Luna can go together. We will meet up on a regular basis to make sure everyone's alright."

"There's no way I'm being separated from Luna," Olga said.

"Look," I said, "we don't have any money to ride the bus. We don't know anyone who can take us there, and we don't have any money for gas, anyway. Asking for spare change for gas will take a month."

Olga shook her head and clutched Luna's hand, turning it white.

"I've hitched before, we'll be fine. We can take the bus to Brigham City and then start making our way north. It should only take a few days."

I was getting nowhere with them. "Okay," I said, rolling my eyes. "We could steal a car." I wanted to get on the road and away from downtown.

"No way!" Luna said, ending that possibility.

Patrick raised both his hands for us to stop arguing. "If it's meant to be, something will present itself."

Once the sun streaked the sky with rays of orange and pink, we each dropped two hits of acid. I hadn't tripped without Sam since we met. My breath caught in my throat and I fought back the ache in my chest. I needed this high.

"Let's go somewhere for coffee," I said.

"What about money?" Luna asked.

Patrick and I looked at each other and laughed. We knew where to get some coinage.

Salt Lake City was the headquarters of the LDS Church. They owned a large piece of property downtown called Temple Square. It had beautiful gardens, historic buildings, hotels, and a distinctly phallic business tower.

We walked to the gardens. A large fountain had been erected in the center, with man-made white granite rivers running down both sides of the garden. There were stone walkways and beautifully-groomed flowerbeds throughout. Patrick and I took our shoes off, rolled up our pant legs, and jumped into the fountain. It was less than two feet deep. We collected some of the money from the bottom of the fountain, enough for fries and coffees for everyone. We skedaddled before we were caught on the security cameras and the guards showed up.

I wondered if the wishes tied to the coins still came true if the coin was removed from the fountain. I assumed the LDS Church gathered up the money every so often and donated it to charity, or put it in their own welfare programs. I was in need of charity, and didn't have any problems taking what I needed. Olga and Luna were aghast at our behavior. *Give them two months on the street and see what they'll be willing to do for food,* I thought.

We sat at Dee's on North Temple, drinking coffee and eating cheese fries, waiting for the dose to kick in. If the Charade had been real, Luna would have been an elf and Olga would have been a human. Luna flowed with the world around her; Olga had an underlying paranoia of others. I still held onto the dream of the Charade, safe inside the locket of my heart.

We walked the city streets, our eyes pulled along by the tracers behind cars. The *be-boop* of the crosswalk signal tugged me back to so many acid trips and touched the darkness still in my heart.

We arrived at Anna's house around midnight.

"I can see things," Olga said. Her dull blue eyes stared past everyone.

Laughing, Luna said, "Well yeah, you're tripping."

Olga shook her head lazily. "No, I see dark shapes with red eyes." She began to cry. "They've come for me! They've come for me!" The cadence and pitch of her voice rose with each reiteration. Wringing her hands, she continued. "They say I'm a whore and a bitch. They're here to kill me."

"It's not real," I told her. "Look at me." I tried to turn her head, but she was screaming.

Luna ran to her, grabbed her hands, and tried to calm her. "Shhh, Olga. It's okay, it's not real, nothing is there. I promise. Nothing is there." Luna's voice was shaking, and her lower lip quivered.

Olga turned on Luna, trying to claw at her face and screaming unintelligible words. Her voice wasn't her own. Patrick hauled her away from Olga. Luna was sobbing.

"It's the acid, Olga. Nothing is there. You're hallucinating," I told her. She fell to the floor, writhing and thrashing.

Then Luna began to scream. She sounded like a woman who'd just lost her child.

Patrick grabbed me by the arm. "Get Luna out of here, now."

I grabbed Luna and pushed her from the room. Once we were downstairs in the living room, I got her to calm down by asking her to tell me her and Olga's story.

"Olga and I have been best friends since elementary school," she said. "She came to me a few weeks ago and asked me to run away with her."

"Why did she want to run away?" I asked.

"Olga was afraid of someone. She had been dating a guy at their school. I didn't like him. Olga stopped hanging out with me. Then one day she called, asking me to leave with her."

Luna was finally calming down.

"I'll be right back," I told her. "Do you want some tea?"

She nodded. "Please."

I went back upstairs to check on Patrick and Olga.

Patrick and Anna had placed Olga in the center of the room and surrounded her with a circle of salt. She was screaming and clawing at her own face. An orange candle had been placed in the center of the circle to cleanse negative attitudes, situations, and places. Anna lit candles at the four corners—two white candles for truth and purity, and two gold candles for enlightenment and protection. Patrick held a lighter to a stick of sandalwood incense.

I stood in the doorway and watched.

"She's fighting a spiritual attack," Patrick said, leaning in against my ear. "Anna says there are ghosts in the house, but nothing demonic. Sometimes the ghosts turn lights on and off, and sometimes you can hear them walking around."

Olga's screaming eventually stopped. Soon after, she became calm and fell asleep. I turned to the sound of footsteps on the stairs and saw Luna rounding the corner.

"I want to see her," she said.

Patrick blocked her path. "You can't. You'll break the circle of protection."

Luna sank to the floor. I tried to pull her up, but she wouldn't move.

Patrick crouched down and put his hand on her shoulder. He brushed her hair out of her face. "I'll watch her and come get you when it's safe."

Luna and I went back downstairs and played with the tracers in the firelight while Enigma played on the stereo.

We slept late into the next day. Once we tumbled out of bed, we sat slumped on the couches, drinking coffee. Olga didn't remember anything from the night before.

Montana remained tacked to the front of my mind and I kept explaining the only way we were getting there was by hitchhiking or finding a ride from someone. Since none of us knew anyone heading north in the next week, we only had one option.

Luna and Olga started whispering to each other. I stopped, looked at Patrick, and raised my eyebrows.

He shrugged.

We waited.

Finally, Luna said, "We have money to buy bus tickets to Montana." She looked at the floor. "We didn't tell you before, because we weren't sure we could trust you."

"Seriously?" I said.

"After last night..." She cast a quick glance at Olga. "We want to help."

Olga was smiling and nodding in agreement.

Patrick laughed.

Luna told us that when she and Olga left Connecticut, they took all the money they could find in her house. It was about eight hundred dollars. With that problem out of the way, we went to spare-change money for food. On our way into the city, we stopped at the Greyhound station. It was one hundred dollars for each ticket. Luna bought four. We were leaving at eight in the morning.

I never spoke with my mom about leaving. She would be hurt and disappointed. She thought things had been going well, and they were. She wouldn't understand that death hunted me in Salt Lake, but Montana was where my sense of belonging, safety, and acceptance awaited.

I was exhausted when we got back to Anna's, but I lay awake for a long time, a million thoughts careening into one another inside my head. Would Sam be surprised to see me? Would he be happy to see me? What would he think of Luna, Olga, and Patrick? How would I handle being around Arielle? What if I didn't like her? Would I be able to focus and learn what I needed? Would I even be able to find Sam once we were in Missoula? What was I going to tell my mom? I let out a deep breath and eventually drifted off to sleep.

Nicole Lowe

Forty percent of African-American youth and thirty-six percent of Caucasian youth who live on the streets sell drugs, primarily marijuana, for money.

chapter fifteen

I clear my throat and commence my line of questioning. "Ms. Anderson, to your knowledge, what has Ms. Hardy done to obtain safe housing for herself and McCartni?"

"She is currently living with some friends."

Not the answer I want, but I know it's hard for caseworkers to go from advocate to adversary.

"When did she move in?"

"A few weeks ago."

"When did she tell you about her housing?"

"Today."

"Where was she living before?"

Clarice hesitates, but not because she doesn't know the answer. She knows it all too well — and she knows the impact it will have here.

"She was homeless."

"Is this the first time she's had a place to stay over the last twelve months?"

"Well, she has stayed a few days here and there, but this is the first time she has had a consistent place for more than three days, with her own room."

"What about employment?"

"She's never provided any verification of employment."

"How many drug tests has she completed?"

"About seventy-five."

"Has she missed any?"

"When she was in jail, and a few here and there, but mostly she's been taking them."

"Has she been clean?"

"For the last two weeks, she has."

"Did she complete her substance abuse assessment?"

"Yes," Clarice says.

"What was the recommendation?"

"Residential, at House of Hope."

"How long does residential treatment take?"

"Six to eight months, and then they go to outpatient."

Parents have twelve months to complete enough services to make it safe to place the child back in their custody. If they are unable to do this, the state files a petition to terminate their parental rights, which is where we are with Sabrina and McCartni.

I wonder if I could have done it. If I could have finished all of the services the state would have asked of me. I'm not sure I could have. I'm not even sure fifty percent of people could manage what we ask these parents to do.

"To your knowledge," I say, "has Ms. Hardy completed a substance abuse program within the last twelve months?"

"No, she hasn't."

"Has she completed a domestic violence assessment?"

"Not that I know of."

"What have you done to help Ms. Hardy complete services?"

"I've helped her set up appointments for her evaluations. The state pays for the drug testing and would pay for her evaluations. I have provided her with housing applications and offered to help fill them out. I've supervised visitation between her and her daughter. I've given her bus passes so she can get to her appointments. I've held child and family team meetings once a month to help keep her on track, and I've taken her to detox twice."

"What happens after you take her to detox?"

"She leaves."

The next question is harder. Clarice knows it's coming; we went through all questions yesterday.

"What are your concerns if McCartni is returned to her mother?"

The blink of Clarice's eyes lasts longer than normal as she takes a deep breath. "Sabrina has not addressed any of the reasons McCartni came into custody. She has a long history of drug use, homelessness, and returning to a domestic violence perpetrator. There is nothing to support her contention that she will complete the services she started three weeks ago, when she has done nothing for eleven months. McCartni is not safe with Sabrina."

"Do you believe adoption is in the best interests of McCartni?"

"Yes."

"Why?"

"Because Sab… Ms. Hardy hasn't done any services, and McCartni is bonded to her foster family. She has all of her needs met. She loves them, and is comfortable and safe in their home."

We reached Missoula on April 6, 1995. I was able to contact Arielle during the bus ride to get a message to Sam about our arrival. Hopefully, he would be at the bus station. My heart skipped a beat when I saw him. He was leaning against the grey brick wall, smoking as our bus slowed to a stop.

He tucked a stray hair behind his ear. His smile widened with each step I took toward him. My steps quickened into a run. I dropped my bag and reached for him. He took me into his arms and spun me around. The others followed more slowly. We went to coffee at Finnegan's restaurant to catch up.

"After you left," Sam said, "I caught a ride with a trucker most of the way here. It only took me two rides. Hitching alone is much quicker." He told me that since then, he had been hanging around, waiting for me to get there.

"I never doubted that you would come," he said. "I've been sleeping by the railroad tracks that go through town. A friend,

Brock, has a VW bus parked close by. Brock and James have been staying there."

"How is James?" I asked.

"He's well."

I avoided the topic of Arielle. Sam hesitated sometimes, as if he couldn't find the right words. I called my mom, but there was no answer. I left a message telling her that Patrick and I were together and safe.

My heart had grown familiar to the ache of loss. It had forgotten the joy and lightness of love. When I saw Sam, it remembered. And I hurt more than ever for what was no longer mine.

I watched him in utter fascination—every motion of his body, and every changing expression on his face. My body screamed out to touch him. I caught myself reaching for him before my mind had a chance to prevent it from satisfying the craving for his warmth.

Sam pulled his hand beneath the table when my fingers brushed his.

"Sorry," I whispered.

Until now, I had not realized how much he had captured my heart and my soul. My heart was lost to him, forever, even if we never touched again.

"We need to celebrate your arrival," he said. "I know where we can get some dose." His smile made his cheeks pop up and his eyes squint.

Not wanting to wait until nightfall, we all dropped together. Olga had another bad trip. She thought bugs and snakes were crawling under her skin. We tried to get her to calm down, but it was a lost cause. Luna stayed with her in Brock's van while Sam, Patrick, and I walked around the city, enjoying the high.

Sam started laughing. "Watch this." His smile brightened even the sunny day.

He placed his hands against the side of a building and pushed. The entire building swayed as if it were made of rubber. Patrick and I were hijacked by laughter. We caught our breath and then resumed laughing as we followed Sam down the street.

Sam stopped in front of a gas station. "They have indestructible spoons here. You can chew on them and they don't break."

I recalled the soreness of my jaw and the empty packs of cigarettes that followed a night of hard tripping. Every trip, I'd clench my jaw tight. The only time I'd stop was to smoke.

The spoons were made of soft plastic. We each picked a different pastel color and left. They were fantastic. We could bend and twist them all day, and they didn't split or crack.

We continued our tour of Missoula. As we walked along the Clark Fork River, I reached out and touched the trees, letting their leaves brush against my skin. I could smell the damp earth and the water. We laughed and chased each other through the trees and across the logs that stretched across the river. I felt the wind against my face and it tugged at my hair.

At three in the morning, Sam laid out all the blankets we had always used, as if nothing had changed. Patrick retreated a few feet away. Sam and I lay together, coming down off the acid and gazing at the stars. Once we were inside the blankets and warm, he wrapped his arms around me and let out a deep sigh.

"I've missed you so much." His warm breath caressed my neck just below my ear.

"I've missed you too."

"Since your return, I've been so uncertain about what to do," he said. "But now it all seems clear. Will you marry me?"

I lay still until he rolled up onto one elbow and looked down at me. A smile suddenly stretched across my face. I felt that if I held it back any longer, I would explode. I pulled him down to me. "Of course I will. I love you with all that I am. I always have. I always will."

"At Stonehenge, in a Wiccan ceremony?" he whispered.

"Perfect."

Sam kissed me.

"Can we stay in Europe awhile?" I asked.

"If you want, we can. There's no reason the Order can't teach people there."

We decided not to tell anyone about the wedding besides Patrick, until Sam had a chance to break things off with Arielle. It was going to take some time to find the right moment. He wanted it to be an amiable conclusion. He needed her to get his money from his dad, as well.

In the morning, we went to Finnegan's for coffee. Luna and Olga decided to go back to Connecticut. Luna believed Olga's struggles were a result of leaving the way that they did. They had already called home. Patrick was distraught by this loss. He had been sure their path and ours were united. There was nothing to say. They had made up their minds.

We told them we would see them off safely. When they left to get their belongings from Brock's van, we stayed behind and wrote goodbye letters to them. We never got the chance to deliver them. We never saw them again.

Despite the loss of more friends, the three of us—Patrick, Sam, and I—started concocting a plan.

"We should go back to Eugene," Sam said.

We were sitting across from Patrick and James at Finnegan's. Cheese fries, creamer, sugar, and coffee crowded our table.

"It's the best place to get a sheet of dose," I explained to Patrick. He nodded.

"We can wait until my child support comes. It should be here soon," Sam said, pouring two creamers and three packets of sugar into his coffee.

James stuffed some fries into his mouth, leaving a trail of cheese to the plate. "You can't hitch with three," he said around the fries.

I looked to Sam.

"Hitching with three is nearly impossible," he said. "It would be better if Patrick stays with James."

"But I've just gotten him back," I said. "I want him to come with us."

"I would rather go with you guys," Patrick said. "I know it will take longer. There's no real rush, is there?"

Sam shrugged. "We can try, I suppose."

James shook his head and got up to leave. The bell jangled as he passed through the door. When he was gone, we told Patrick about our marriage plans.

"With the way Nikki talks about you, I'm not surprised," Patrick said. "Welcome to our family, Sam."

"We're getting married at Stonehenge," I blurted out.

"And how are we getting to Europe?" asked Patrick.

Sam began to write out the plan on a napkin: Once we got the sheet in Eugene, we'd travel back and forth, selling in Missoula. With a ten-pack, we'd start making our way east, selling as we went. By the time we hit the eastern seashore, we'd have sold out of acid and would have enough money to get plane tickets for the three of us.

I called my mom. She cried and was upset I had taken Patrick with me. I told her I was sorry, but that this was something we had to do. I hoped one day she would understand. I told her this was bigger than my family or me. I didn't give her the details because I knew she would probably never understand. I promised her I would call weekly and let her know both Patrick and I were alright. I didn't tell her where we were.

She told me she had gone to the doctor to run some tests and that they were concerned she had something serious. She said she would get the results the following Monday. I promised her I would call Monday evening. When we finished talking, Patrick got on the phone with her. We had agreed before calling not to tell her any details and not to tell her our location.

That afternoon, we walked to Hellgate High School so Sam could talk to Arielle about having his dad send his money to her house. Patrick, James, and I waited across the street under the shade of a maple tree.

Arielle was beautiful. She had long, auburn hair, porcelain skin, and full, rose-tinted lips. She was taller than me, but not as tall as Sam. She hugged and kissed him. He pointed to us and led Arielle over by the hand. He introduced us and told her he had invited us over to her friend Liz's house to watch movies that night. This was going to be awkward. I smiled and told her how happy I was to meet her.

"You were wonderful with Arielle," Sam said when we were alone. "Thank you. I know going over tonight will be difficult, but we need to go. I need to act as if nothing has changed, at least for now."

"I understand," I said, trying to sound nonchalant, even with the torrent of conflicting emotions filling me.

"I'll try to find a chance to tell her, to break up with her soon. But until then, I must act as if you and I are not eternally bound to one another."

"My love for you will make this easy. I know you love me," I said, forcing a smile.

At Liz's house, we all sat on the downstairs couches, eating popcorn, watching *Natural Born Killers* and *Excalibur*. Sam and Arielle were cozy together, holding hands. He whispered to her and kissed her. They laughed about inside jokes.

I sat with Patrick and tried to ignore them. I knew this would be uncomfortable, but Sam was not attempting to put any space between them. I felt entirely inadequate to be with Sam. Arielle was beautiful and intelligent. She had things Sam needed. Like a house, money, and resources. All of which I didn't have, and probably never would.

We left at one in the morning.

I didn't walk beside Sam as we made our way back to camp. Instead, I hung back with Patrick. I watched my feet move over the asphalt and told myself the situation was unavoidable and would be over soon.

James pushed Sam's shoulder from behind. "You're an asshole. I can't believe you made Nikki sit there and watch the two of you."

My head sprang up and Patrick caught my arm before I could move to defend Sam.

"You're playing a dangerous game, man," James said, then pointed to me. "I can't believe she is even willing to stay with you when you treat her like that!"

"She knows this is how it needs to be," Sam said in a composed tone. "We've discussed this. Nikki knows I love her, and we will be together."

We hadn't told James that we were back together, but he figured it out quickly. He stormed off, scandalized and dumbfounded. I knew I had to be more careful to prevent Arielle from finding out.

I stayed in my own space that night. I needed to be able to pretend Sam was just a friend. I needed to start right away. Arielle couldn't know. I didn't want to fail Sam.

A few days later, the four of us were sitting in Finnegan's drinking coffee and eating more cheese fries. Sam had received the money from his dad the day before, and we were putting the final plan in place to leave for Oregon.

James would stay behind in Montana with Brock and be a contact if we needed anything. Sam and I would buy a sheet and mail it to James to sell. It was faster than traveling back and forth. We would package the sheets in peanut butter or coffee to prevent any drug dogs from finding it. We would use Arielle to send and receive messages. Patrick would come with Sam and me to Eugene.

We were leaving that afternoon, on foot. A five-mile walk would take us to the highway. From there, we could hitchhike the distance to Eugene in five days. With the plan established, we went back to Brock's van and packed our stuff.

We didn't walk far before the crunching of tires on gravel signaled someone pulling up behind us. I turned to see who was stopping. At the same moment my eyes laid upon the police car, its siren let out a *whoop-whoop*.

My heart raced. I closed my eyes. I knew my mom must have listed Patrick and me as runaways. I was lucky to have gotten to Montana the first time—how in the world would I pull it off a second time?

The officer radioed in our names and hauled the three of us to the police station. Patrick and I played it smooth. We told the police we were in contact with our mom weekly and gave them her contact information. Sam gave them his mom's number. On the street, you acted as if you were supposed to be where you were and doing whatever it was you were doing. People tended not to notice you if you looked like you belonged.

The officer went into another room. Sometime later, he returned. We were released. I didn't know what happened, and I didn't really care.

We headed back toward the highway and stopped at a Taco Bell on the edge of town. It was close to closing time. We considered dumpster diving after they took out the trash and turned off the light—the closers would always throw away any food that was still in the warmer, wrapped and unspoiled.

Instead, Sam went inside and talked them into giving us what they were going to throw away for the night, which saved me from having to jump into the dumpster. As the smallest, I would have been volunteered. We munched on seven-layer burritos and mexi-nuggets while we sat at the freeway on-ramp, cars whooshing by.

A police car came to a slow stop.

"Not again," I whispered.

"You three can't hitchhike here," the gruff voice called out. "It's dangerous, especially in this weather."

The three of us looked up. Storm clouds were gathering overhead.

Sam waved at him. "Thanks, we'll move."

We got up, relief washing over us, and moved away from the road. It was late, anyway. Too late to get a ride.

"Let's get out of here," Sam said and swung our pack over his shoulder.

We found a place off the side of the road where the ground was sunken in, which would keep us out of sight. It also kept us sheltered from the wind that was starting to whip up dirt, leaves, and branches. We rolled out our beds and pulled the tarp over our heads, shielding us from the looming rainstorm.

The next morning, we stood at the on-ramp for hours, moving from one foot to the other, rubbing our hands together to stay warm. The day came and went with not a single offer for a ride.

"I'm going back," Patrick said. "I'll stay with James."

"Are you sure?" I asked. "We can make this work. It will just take longer."

"Sam's right. We're never going to get picked up with three of us. I'll crash here tonight and walk back to town in the morning. You guys go, there's really no other way." His teeth chattered as he spoke.

I agreed, but didn't want to leave him there. Sam didn't say anything during the exchange. He knew this was how it had to be. He had always known. Patrick would call our mom on a weekly basis and let her know we were alright. I hugged him for a long time, reluctant to let him go.

"We'll hurry back," I said. "And with any luck, we'll be reunited in a few weeks."

"I'm sure of it." He offered a weak smile and we parted ways.

After about twenty steps, I turned around and saw Patrick walking into the brush to set up camp for the night. He turned around and I waved. He waved back and then continued down the road. I watched him go.

Sam waited, without a word. His breath was as thick as the smoke rising from his cigarette.

We walked until we reached a 4B's restaurant and truck stop. We went in and ordered coffee. The counter was full of middle-aged, grizzled men with long-sleeved flannel shirts.

"Do you think one of them will give us a ride?" I asked.

Sam shrugged. "Worth a try."

He got up and went to talk to some of the truckers, trying to find us a ride. I pulled my journal out of our pack and opened it to the first clean page.

Sam came back after a few minutes and pointed to a bearded lumberjack-looking man.

"He's going to Osborn, Idaho. He says he'll take us when he finishes eating and gets a shower."

I took a sip of my coffee, added more sugar, and lit a cigarette.

"I don't like getting dropped off in Idaho," Sam said. "It can be difficult to get a ride out of the small towns spread across the state, but if he drops us off at another truck stop, we should be okay."

I nodded. Sam pulled out his journal and began to draw.

Once our ride was ready to leave, we headed out. I scurried into the sleeping quarters of the diesel and Sam sat up front with the driver. Sam talked about traveling and music, and the driver talked about his family. Sam made up some story about where we were going and why. I only half-listened. I couldn't see out of the truck and I was getting motion sickness, so I laid down, closed my eyes, and fell asleep. Sam shook me awake when we reached Osborn.

Our next ride took us to Kellogg, Idaho. The driver even kicked down five dollars. He hardly spoke a word of English, so it was a quiet ride. Our third ride was two college girls who took us as far as Coeur d'Alene. They also gave us five dollars, with a bonus pack of cigarettes. The fourth ride got us to Post Falls, about six miles from the Washington border.

We sat in Andy's Family Restaurant for a few hours, drinking coffee, writing in our journals, and reading. Then we made camp for the night, hopeful Eugene was only one more day away.

The wings of a raven beat the morning air as we shuffled alongside the highway with our thumbs thrust out. As we walked, Sam sang the theme song from *The Lion King*, Janice Joplin's rendition of "Me and My Bobby McGee," Peter Seeger's "Where Have all the Flowers Gone?" and Bob Marley's "No Woman, No Cry." I couldn't carry a tune to save my life, so I just listened and continued putting one foot in front of the other.

Fifteen horizontal green signs told us we've walked fifteen miles. No one stopped, not even a honk. Nothing.

I ran into the pack on Sam's back. "Sorry."

He laughed. "Let's camp here."

We were in the middle of the desert. There were no city lights ahead of us or behind us. Sam rolled out our blankets in a depression a hundred steps from the road. Despite not getting a ride all day, we were in good spirits. The night was warm, the stars were out, and the moon shone bright.

The lack of city lights and the flatness of the desert revealed even the faintest stars, as if someone had unloaded a dump truck filled with glitter in a solar breeze. We lay awake for a long time, talking and contemplating our own thoughts. Mine drifted between our future and our present situation.

The Order's mission was going to be difficult. I was not sure if going to Europe would make it easier or more difficult. It was possible, I supposed—people there would probably be more open to the truth. Everyone, the world over, was staring blindly ahead, walking down a path of extinction.

The next morning, we got a ride quickly. The driver was pleasant and had a fatherly feel about him. I slid into the back and read my book on astrology. Sam hit it off with the driver and they talked about a variety of subjects for hours. He dropped us off in Spokane, and we caught another ride in less than twenty minutes.

The second guy was just as friendly. He was a young guy, a college student, with shaggy hair and a stubbly face. He told us he was studying English and history. He and Sam talked the whole time about books I had never heard of. Sometimes, I felt like I had missed a whole piece of life somewhere. He kicked down some cigarettes before dropping us off in the middle of nowhere.

You got an idea of the person behind the wheel the moment a car pulled to the side of the road. Usually, it was the car they were driving, whether it was clean and whether the tires were in good condition. Did they screech to a halt, or come to a slow stop? Did they cruise past, then stop and back up as if they'd had second thoughts? Did they get out and help you put your stuff in, shake your hand, and introduce themselves? Or did they just pop the trunk? Sometimes, they gave us money or food. Other times, I felt claustrophobic in the car. Occasionally, they did something strange, like drop us off sooner then they said they would... or ask for money or sex.

We walked ten miles before another driver picked us up. Almost immediately, the guy gave me the creeps. His constant twitching was similar to how Michael used to twitch when he was using crack. He kept wiping at his nose, as if it was on constant run. Michael did that too. His twitching made me twitch. I wanted out of the car.

"You got any money?" he asked.

Sam raised his eyebrows. "Um, no."

"If you did have money, I would drive you all the way to Eugene." His words tripped over each other as they tumbled out of his mouth.

"All we have is ten dollars," Sam said.

"That's cool, man. I need to make a quick stop. Real quick, like fast." The twitching was spreading down his body as he drove us into the Tri-Cities. He wound his way through a neighborhood of old houses and stopped the car in front of a run-down house with a yellow lawn. He asked for the ten dollars. Sam gave it to him. He ran into the house.

"I don't like this guy," I said. "I have a bad feeling about this."

Sam nodded in agreement.

After a few minutes, the driver returned to the car. "You guys don't mind if I smoke a little, do you?" he asked, pulling a spoon from his pocket.

"Actually," Sam said, "we do. Can you just take us to the nearest gas station?"

"I can get you to Eugene, no problem. Just let me hit this rock and then we'll go." The guy was getting irritated.

Sam got out of the car. He opened my door and I climbed out, dragging our pack with me.

The car peeled out, fishtailing down the road.

Sam took the pack from me and hoisted it onto his back. He kicked rocks and garbage along the side of the road as we walked. "I can't believe I didn't see it when we first got in the car. Crystal addicts are all the same."

Once we were back on a main road, we found a gas station. Sam asked a couple of people for a ride to the nearest freeway on-ramp. Two women wearing straw hats said they'd give us a ride. We sat in the bed of their beat-up truck with our hair whipping in the wind like the branches of willow trees in a hurricane.

After they dropped us off, we waited at the on-ramp, hoping for a ride. After about half an hour, we started walking. We figured if it were us doing the driving, we would be more likely to pick up someone who was willing to put in some effort into getting where they needed to go.

Sam had to yell over the sound of the cars speeding past. "Where do you want to go when we get to Europe?"

"Paris, Venice, Rome, London, and Edinburgh," I said, imagining we were in each of them rather than walking down the hot asphalt. Talking made it easier. "How are we going to get our message across to people?"

"Well, there are a few options. We could use a straightforward way, stories, or in the shroud of the Charade."

"The Charade only focuses on a narrow group. Why would we use it?"

The loss of the Charade still stung. It was the death of myself. I never told Sam I had believed, and I never would.

"Just an option."

"I think we should go to colleges and university areas to find people willing to listen," I said. "It's where we've had the most success at connecting to others."

Besides, I wanted to see the libraries and coffee shops that were sure to be near.

Sam agreed.

A station wagon pulled to the side of the road. I was surprised to see children in the back when we reached it. A man got out and stood next to the driver's door.

"Hello," he said. "Happy Easter. Can we give you a lift into the city?" He looked like he had just left church.

Sam and I looked at one another, stunned. We hadn't realized it was Easter Sunday. We didn't even know it was a Sunday. None of that mattered when you were hitching.

"Um. Yeah, that would be cool," Sam said.

The driver was tall and slender, and looked the part of an outstanding, churchgoing citizen. He opened the station wagon's hatchback and Sam tossed our pack inside.

The man reached out his hand. "I'm Mark. That's my wife Mary in the car, and our children, Matthew, Noah, and Marie. One of you will have to ride in the back."

Sam shook his hand. "I'm Sam and this is Nikki. Thanks for picking us up. We've been walking forever."

Sam climbed in through the hatchback and Mark closed it. I opened a rear door and three little cherub faces looked up at me. I squished in with the kids.

"We were just talking about acts of service when we saw the two of you walking," Mark said. "Noah said he didn't think you had water or food. He thought we should do an act of service by stopping and helping you two out."

"Thanks, Noah," I whispered to the boy next to me. He was probably six years old. He nodded his head vigorously.

"We actually exited the freeway and then got back on to pick you up," Mary said. "We're not going far, but it's faster than walking."

They dropped us off in Kennewick. Mark wished us luck and gave us ten dollars before pulling away.

Next, an old hippy with a salt-and-pepper beard to the center of his chest picked us up. A green bandana kept the sun off his head and the long hair out of his sunbaked face. He smoked Sam up as we drove, and gave him enough weed to roll a joint later. He pulled into a McDonald's, bought us lunch, and kicked down fifteen dollars.

Our next ride was with another college kid who talked about wanting to get out and get away. He wanted to ride his bike around Europe and stay at all the hostels. Sam asked about the hostels. The kid explained that usually they were free or charged very little. You could stay the night in a room and move on the next morning. I sat in the back, wondering why there were not hostels in the United States. It would have been nice to have a dry, warm place to sleep every once in a while.

He dropped us off in some town in the middle of nowhere. Our next ride took us through Salem, and then finally into beautiful Eugene.

It was night when we finally arrived. It felt good to be back. I knew where everything I needed was, and it was all within walking distance of our overpass base camp.

Tomorrow, we would go to Thirteenth Avenue and find a sheet, setting our plan in motion.

"It's our house without walls," Sam said when we approached our old spot under the overpass.

It was like returning home after a long vacation. The smells, sights, and memories wrapped me in their warmth.

"Who would want it any other way?" I asked, smiling.

He swung our pack off his shoulder and set up our bed in the ivy.

Seventy-one percent of homeless youth meet the criteria for an alcohol or drug abuse disorder, or both. The longer young people remain homeless, the more likely they are to have a substance abuse disorder.

chapter sixteen

Judge Cruz glances up. "Mr. Johnson, your witness."

Carl stands and buttons his suit jacket. "Ms. Anderson are there any additional services you could have offered to Ms. Hardy?"

"There are other services," Clarice says, "but the problem was she wasn't following through with the evaluations. It was hard to know what she needed. And she needed to address the biggest and most difficult issues first."

"What do you believe her biggest and most difficult issues are?"

"Her drug use."

"Why is that the biggest issue?"

"Because it prevents her from being able to internalize any other skills she would learn from other services, and it prevents her from stabilizing to make other changes, like housing and employment."

Carl sits down.

Judge Cruz doesn't look up from his desk. "Mr. Lundberg?"

Jake combs his fingers through his hair and adjusts his glasses. "Ms. Anderson, have you supervised all of the visits between Ms. Hardy and McCartni?"

"Yes. They have been weekly, at my office."

"How long are the visits?"

"One hour."

One hour a week. That's standard visitation when your child is in the custody of the state. Caseworkers are assigned so many cases that they don't have enough time to schedule more visits. Family members can also supervise visits, as long as they can pass a background check and don't have a history of child abuse or neglect. They also have to be willing.

"Has she missed any visits?"

"No."

"Will you describe the visits for the court?"

"Ms. Hardy plays on the floor with McCartni and helps her take care of a baby doll by brushing her hair and pushing her around the hallways in a little stroller. She holds her and reads to her."

"Does McCartni seem to be afraid of Ms. Hardy?"

"No. She runs to her when she sees her."

"Does she appear to enjoy her time with her mom?"

"Very much."

Nicole Lowe

```
"No further questions, Your Honor."
    Clarice steps down from the witness box and
returns to her seat at my side.
    "Sorry," she whispers.
    I shake my head back and forth, press the mute
button on the microphone, and whisper back, "It's
the truth. The judge needs to make the best
decision. You have to present the facts as they
are, even if you think they could hurt our
position."
```

In Salt Lake, I was dangling from the end of a noose, twitching and jerking as the rope cut into my throat and suffocated me. In Eugene, I was free to breathe. We lounged on the grass in the center of the Saturday market, enjoying the warmth of the sun and the sounds of steel drums.

We strolled through white tents filled with jewelry, clothing, and art. Some had local produce, herbs, and bonsai trees. Still others had breads and traditional foods from countries as far as India, Taiwan, and Greece. We talked to other hippies and cats who came through. No one had any LSD, especially not in the amount we wanted. The only advice we got was to check Thirteenth Avenue after dark.

Our sunburned skin welcomed the coolness of the evening and the disappearance of the sun as we shuffled over to Thirteenth. The streetlights cast their pale yellow glow onto the sidewalk.

A dealer we'd bought acid from in the past sold us what he had left—sixty-two hits for fifty dollars. Sam and I each dropped six hits, leaving an even fifty, then walked over to our faithful Pizza Pipeline. Halfway through our cheesy-gooey pie, the familiar electricity of the dose waved through my veins. We gave the rest of the pizza to the first person on the street who wanted it.

Our desire to be free of the city led us to the forested trails surrounding the Willamette River. I stood on a bridge, listening to the sounds of the city and the sounds of the forest collide, reverberating around me. The spray from the churning water landed gently on my face. The waves came up out of the river. There were animals and faces in the water. The faces were laughing and screaming into the emptiness between us. I smiled and reached out for the water, but my fingers grasped only air. Every once in a while, someone on a bike would whiz past, the tracers clinging to my eyes for a long time after they moved beyond my sight.

Sam was laughing somewhere down the trail. I turned to the sound of his feet and found him walking toward me in his ragdoll way.

"We should hitch to Portland tonight to sell this." His eyes shone bright in the lamplight, pupils big enough to swallow the whole world.

```
                          trippin'

      the bridge sways in, the bridge sways out
         you're hallucinating, without a doubt
         drink the orange juice, drink it down
      you could walk right out of this stupid town
       everything's a picture smeared by your hand
        hey, look, you're no longer on the land
          the water has faces that talk to you
    you look over and see they are talking to me, too
       the sounds of the stone forest seem to bounce
       there's a lot more water than just an ounce
    the sounds of a tree-filled forest bounce as well
         you feel like you're under a hypnotic spell.
```

We never hitched while high. It was one of our rules. Too risky. We made a sign and sat by the freeway on-ramp, safely away from the road.

I was drawing in the dirt with my finger and suddenly got to my feet. "I need to use the bathroom."

There was a gas station across the street. It had one of those around-the-back bathrooms I hated, but I had to go. Sometimes when I was high, I didn't realize how bad I had to go—like a toddler so busy playing that they wet their pants. This was one of those times.

I raced around the back of the gas station. It took an eternity to get the key into the stupid lock. Once inside, I dropped the key and pushed the door closed. I had two layers of clothes on: my tie-dyed thermals and ripped-up jeans. I fought with my pants, trying not to trip out on myself in the mirror or the patterns in the floor. I finally got them down, but the toilet lid was closed. I wasn't going to make it. I jumped onto the sink just in time. It was better than the floor.

Holy shit! The sink broke free from the wall and I landed with my bare ass on the cold floor, pants around my knees. I struggled to my feet and pulled my pants back on. The porcelain sink hung from the tiled wall by its pipes. I stood staring at it before picking up the key and walking out the door, hands unwashed.

After I returned the key, I found Sam sitting on the curb in front of the gas station, both arms hung between his legs, apelike. A cigarette dangled between his fingers.

"I think it's a bad time to be hitching," he said with a grin. "It's like midnight."

We both burst into laughter.

We walked to the IHOP and burrowed into the corners of the booth, smoking up a storm and drawing feverishly. Sam drew random shapes that fit together at their edges and curves, but he left a small space between each one. It was like a puzzle, where each piece was repelled from the other by a low-level magnetic field. I attempted to mimic it, but mine was not nearly as creative or beautiful.

We watched the way people's bodies moved as they came in and out. Some people had a certain flow about them; others were more puppet-like. We found faces in the walls and in the ashtray. It was always faces.

The waitress didn't talk to us beyond asking if we were doing alright or needed anything else. She came around and filled our coffee and creamer dish. I looked up at her. She had dark circles under her eyes. She wanted her shift to be over so she could go home.

Sam counted the cigarette butts in the ashtray. It was how we counted the passage of time, because neither of us had a watch. He decided we'd been there long enough. Normally, we each smoked one cigarette an hour. There were about ten cigarette butts in the ashtray. We smoked more when we were tripping.

Sam stood and shouldered our pack. "The sun is coming up and we should probably sleep this trip off."

Portland still seemed like the place to go the next day, and it only took a few rides to get there. We arrived with enough time to spare-change money for hamburgers before the sun set. It didn't take us long to realize we hated Portland and shouldn't have come. It was too big and too busy. It had big-city paranoia. We dropped two and a half hits each and started walking out of town. We made a sign that read *Eugene*.

Our first ride took us to Salem. The second got us to Albany, and the third was a trucker who kicked down five bucks and two packs of cigarettes. He dropped us off at a truck stop right outside of Eugene. We found a restaurant and ate fries, drank coffee, and wrote in our journals. I was exhausted, and we still had to get to camp. Sam pulled my journal toward him and wrote on an empty page:

Stars begin to dot the midnight-blue sky. A raven's call can be heard in the receding light. Awareness and awakening, a new consciousness arises with the night. I wake to see you lying there, so peaceful yet distraught, living in a waking dream, awaken, blink, feel your body alive and now refreshed. Walk with me to the meadow of life, and be at peace with the simplicity of oneness and the great nothing. –Sam

We walked the rest of the way into Eugene and got back to camp around ten. I was so tired. Molten rock ran down the back of my throat, causing me to wince in pain each time I swallowed.

Sam touched my forehead. "You have a fever."

"I need to see a doctor, I think," I said.

The next morning, I went to the free clinic where Mariah and I had gone when she found out she was pregnant. They diagnosed me with strep throat and gave me a ten-day supply of penicillin. Sam and I walked toward Thirteenth to sell a five-strip so I could eat more than fries. I kept falling asleep while we walked.

"You need to go back to camp and sleep," Sam said.

"What if the cops see me there?"

"What if they see you falling asleep on your feet? You look like you're on heroin."

My eyes flew open at the word. "Good point," I said. I wondered where Hunter was.

Sam woke me in the afternoon and we ordered real food: pancakes and sausage at IHOP.

It took three days for me to start feeling better. We were spending all of the money we were making off the dose on food, which was not good because we needed money for another sheet. We went to the food bank and got a box of food. The food didn't need to be cooked or refrigerated—ramen noodles, fruit, bread, peanut butter, and cans of chili. We hid it in the ivy around our camp.

We dropped two and a half hits each and waited. Nothing. Neither of us knew if a person could build up a tolerance to LSD the way they could with other drugs, but we knew this dose was good. A tolerance was the only explanation. We had forty hits left to sell, and we needed to score another sheet with the money we made on them.

We each placed a five-strip on our tongue the following night and again got nothing. Twenty hits remained of the sixty-two we'd bought. By our calculation, we should have had thirty. We figured we must have counted or cut the sheet wrong.

The shortage required a reconstruction of our plan. We decided to mail the dose to Montana for James and Patrick to sell for five dollars a hit. In turn, they'd send the one hundred dollars back. With that, we'd buy another sheet and start over.

It rained hard all night. A web of lightning stretched across the sky and waves of thunder rattled the world. I loved the rain. The way it smelled, sounded, felt, and the how the air seemed clean and crisp after a storm. The fresh morning air was full of birds chirping and twittering.

Everything we had was soaked. With nothing to wear, I picked up a new tie-dyed dress from a local shop by way of the five-finger discount. We spare-changed until we had ten dollars, and then walked to a laundromat to dry our stuff.

It rained frequently in Eugene. Usually, we could keep our stuff dry, but not always. After the laundromat, we went to the post office and mailed the twenty-strip to Arielle's house, with instructions for Patrick and James.

Back at camp, Sam pulled our pack out of the bushes. The food box was gone. We wouldn't be able to get another one for a week. As frustrating as it was, we assumed whoever took the box needed it more.

We always managed to get food. It was just nice to not have to panhandle every day. People got sick of seeing you out there all the time. They'd say things like, "Get a job." We couldn't get jobs. We were underage, had no address, and no identification. Sam occasionally picked up yardwork or landscaping work for the day, and we also made and sold things for money.

We could have made a large profit asking for spare change every day, but we didn't. If you never took more than what you needed from your environment, it would continue to provide for your needs. People who sucked the life out of the earth by taking more than they required were the ones who caused the problems. They never had enough to satisfy their desires.

We spent most of the day lounging in the sun in the forest around the river. It saturated my bones and infused my heart with brightness and warmth. With every breath, I thanked the earth for my life and vowed to never lose sight of the great gifts I'd been given: freedom and love. I needed nothing more than Sam at my side and the strength of my body to move. With these two things, I was alive, and I was everything.

On our way to camp for the night, we cut across the road, jumped over the cement barrier at the off-ramp, and plunged into the ivy. I felt a sharp, searing pain in my right shin, then warmth.

"Sam," I called out. "I'm bleeding."

He picked me up and set me on the concrete barrier in the light of the streetlamp. My shin was split wide open, exposing multiple layers of tissue. Rivulets of bright crimson poured from the three-inch gash.

"How the fuck did you do that?" Sam asked, looking around for something to stop the bleeding.

"I ran into something."

He looked through the ivy and found a tall sprinkler head just below the leaves. "You need stitches."

"Yeah, probably."

"Wait here. I'm going to get some help."

A burger place half a block up the street still had its lights on when we passed. Sam took off running toward it.

The cut didn't really hurt. The blood looked like black webbing down my leg. I peered inside, pulling open the gash. It was deep. Footsteps beat the asphalt, and I looked up to see Sam trotting toward me. He picked me up and jogged me back to the restaurant. A tall guy in a white t-shirt, jeans, and black apron held the glass door open. Sam set me down on the table of a booth.

"This is Cameron," Sam said and pulled a chair over. He sat on it backward. Cameron, a part-time paramedic who was closing the burger shop, set a first-aid kit on the table and gently lifted my leg. He wiped the blood away and turned my leg back and forth.

He pointed at the gash. "I'm pretty sure that's your bone. You need stitches."

"Can you give us a ride to the hospital?" Sam asked.

"All I have is my bike."

"Just wrap it," I said. "I can walk."

"You really shouldn't walk on it," Cameron said. "You'll lose a lot of blood. Do you have a friend or family you can call?"

Sam and I shook our heads in the negative. There was no one.

Cameron called an ambulance. My mom was going to love this. I forgot to call her about the strep throat, too.

The doctors in the emergency room called my mom and put eleven stitches in my leg. Cameron was right. It was sliced to the bone.

A nurse in pink scrubs handed me the phone. "Your mom wants to talk to you."

"Hi, Mom."

"Why aren't you and Patrick together?"

"Did you talk with him?" I asked.

"Last week. He's fine. You need to come home. You keep getting sick and hurt. Please come home, Nikki."

"I was going to call about the strep throat, but I forgot."

"I had a gun shoved in my face last week while I was paying on a loan." Her voice shook.

"Are you alright?"

"I'm not dead. I didn't have any money. He just left."

"I'm sorry, Mom. I'll call you tomorrow at 6:30 and let you know how I'm doing."

She started to cry. "Nikki, please come home."

"I can't. I love you."

I set the phone on the receiver and took a deep breath. It was hard to talk to her.

Seventy-five percent of homeless or runaway youth have dropped out or will drop out of school.

chapter seventeen

I get to my feet. "The state calls the foster mother, Linda, as its next witness."

Maxwell holds the double doors open as Linda enters the courtroom. She is a middle-aged woman. Silver strands bunch at her temples and run along the part in her auburn hair. She sets her purse on the benches at the back of the courtroom.

"Your Honor," I say, "I would request that we use only Linda's first name."

"No objection," says Jake.

It's echoed by Carl.

Judge Cruz waves Linda into the courtroom. "That's fine, Ms. Lowe. Linda, will you come forward and be sworn in, please?"

Linda has a slight wobble to her stride. She carries a few extra pounds, which speaks to her enjoyment of life.

She takes her oath and the judge motions to the witness box. "Please take a seat." He flips to a clean sheet of paper in his notepad. "Ms. Lowe?"

I begin. "Linda, what is your role in McCartni's case?"

She flicks her gaze in Sabrina's direction and then back to me. I smile and raise my eyebrows. She was concerned about testifying in front of McCartni's mother, but it can't be helped. Sabrina has the right to cross-examine the state's witnesses, and Linda is critical to showing the judge what is in the child's best interests.

"I'm her foster mother."

"How long has McCartni been living with you?"

"It'll be twelve months in just a few days."

"How many children do you have?"

"My husband and I have two biological children who are adults, and four adopted children."

"How old are your adopted children?"

"Seven, ten, thirteen, and seventeen."

"Did you adopt them through the state?"

"Yes, when they were much younger. The older three are full siblings. We adopted our youngest about a year ago."

"Are you currently licensed to adopt?"

"Yes, we are."

"When McCartni was first placed in your home, did she exhibit any behaviors which caused you concern?"

Linda purses her lips and pulls her eyebrows down in a juvenile fashion. "When we first got her, she would only eat chicken nuggets and macaroni and cheese. We had to slowly introduce vegetables and fruit into her diet. It took about six months, but now she eats everything."

"Did she have any other concerning behavior regarding food?"

"Well, it's not uncommon for foster children to hoard food, and our seven-year-old did for a time. McCartni had the same fear of not having enough to eat. She would hide food under her bed and pillow. Sometimes, I still find it in her drawers, but not very often now."

"How did you help her resolve the hoarding?"

"I put a basket of snacks in the kitchen just for her. She was able to get them whenever she needed something. The only rule was they needed to stay in the basket and not hidden in her room."

"How was her sleep when she came to live with you?"

She pauses and bows her head. When she looks up, her eyes are red and glossy with tears. "She would scream in the middle of the night for hours. She would hit and kick and just scream."

Maxwell holds the box of tissues out to her and Linda tugs one from the box. I take a sip of my water. I want the emotion and the words to hang in the room. I want everyone to have an image of two-year-old McCartni screaming in the middle of the night.

The tap of my water bottle on the table resounds in the silent courtroom. "Would she say anything when she was screaming?"

Linda nods. "Don't hurt Mommy. Don't hurt Cartni. Bad Daddy."

"How long did she have the nighttime screaming?"

Linda takes a deep breath and clears her throat. "For about six months."

"How was her behavior during the day?"

"Most of the time, she was very sweet and loved to help, but if you told her no, she would kick and hit and scream swear words at the top of her lungs."

"Does she still do that?"

"Only after visits with her mom."

"Does she do anything else concerning after visits?"

"She will wet her pants."

"Did McCartni have any medical issues when she came to live with you?"

"She needed a few immunizations and she needed a lot of dental work. She had five cavities, and two of her baby teeth had to be removed because they were infected."

"Linda, do you love McCartni?"

"Absolutely."

"Do you believe there is a bond between your family and McCartni?"

"I know there is."

"How do you know?"

Linda's smile fills her hazel eyes and perks up her cheeks.

"In the mornings, McCartni runs laughing through the house, in and out of every room, making sure everyone is home. She calls out their names as she finds them. She sings while she colors at the table. When she finishes a picture, she puts it on the fridge and then leads each person by the hand to see it. She dances with her brothers and sisters whenever there is music. She hugs and kisses the whole family. Before bed time, she snuggles with my husband on the couch and reads three stories."

Again, I let each image of McCartni's freedom and joy come to life in the minds of everyone in the courtroom.

"Are you and your husband willing and able to adopt McCartni if she is freed for adoption by the court?"

"She's our little girl," Linda says. "Of course. We want to adopt her."

The sky was flawless. Not even a wisp of clouds marred its surface as we asked for spare change. We didn't have much luck, and were relieved when Jacob showed up with some dank green, a strain of weed that carried a heavy smell and stuck to the inside of your nostrils. He smoked Sam up, distracting us from our plight. He kicked down some liquid LSD, but it didn't do anything to us. We called Arielle, Bill, and Sam's dad, but there was no answer.

We had to rethink our plan, yet again. This was becoming a theme. Our new plan was to get the money from the twenty-strip we'd sent to James and Patrick, buy another sheet, and send it to Arielle. She'd sell it and send us the money. We'd live off Sam's child support until we got the money from Arielle and returned to Montana with six sheets.

Nothing was working out very well, but things would come around. They always did. It was the way of the world. The ups and downs generated momentum for the world's energy to continue.

Later that night, we finally got in contact with Sam's dad. He wired us the child support and we found good dose. Not great, but good enough. We tripped all night and crashed the next morning.

The sun was heading back toward the western horizon when we woke up. We trucked it over to the bead shop and picked up various types of beads to make necklaces for everyone in Montana. We headed over to the mission, washed our clothes, and took a warm shower. I let the water run over my body for a long time. People took many things for granted that others often had to do without. After our showers, we called Arielle to find out what was going on.

"Did you get the package I sent?" Sam asked her.

"Of course I did. What the hell were you thinking?" Arielle screamed.

I could hear her yell as I stood next to Sam, smoking.

"I could have been arrested!" she shouted. "My parents' house could have been searched. It's a federal crime to send that through the mail!"

Sam covered the mouthpiece. "She's a little angry."

My laugh made me choke on the smoke escaping my lungs.

"Did they sell all twenty?"

"There wasn't twenty. It was only sixteen."

"Arielle, I'm positive it was twenty."

"Well it wasn't when it got here," she said.

"Where is James?"

"He and Patrick left to meet you in Eugene. They should be there any day."

Sam paused and rubbed his forehead with his thumb and forefinger. "Do they have the money?"

"Yes. When will you be back?"

I never wanted to go back there, but I knew that was unrealistic.

"I don't know," Sam said. "A few weeks, maybe."

After talking to Arielle, we questioned our plan to send another sheet for her to sell. There was no telling how much we would get back if we sent a full sheet. She couldn't cut up a twenty. Time for a fresh plan. We'd get the money from Arielle, buy a sheet, and take it back to Montana to sell ourselves. Sam would return to Eugene alone and pick up six sheets. He would be able to travel faster alone, and it would be cheaper with only one mouth to feed.

Once he returned to Montana with the six sheets, we'd sell those and take the Greyhound back to Eugene to pick up a twenty-pack and make ten thousand dollars. With that, we would buy a book (one hundred sheets) for five thousand dollars. We would sell that in Montana, Utah, and anywhere else we decided to go on our way to Europe, while living off the other five grand.

```
                      ode to my love

   so much within your mind that which you do not
                           show
    you hold within your person something i'll never
                           know
     dreams and thoughts and visions twist themselves
                         into you
     but i sometimes have the feeling that the ones you
                     share are few.
       thinking deeply, i realize you give me all you
                           can.
     your love, your faith, your companionship; it's
                  enough for me, a mere man.
      in my heart, i hold a place that you alone can
    touch, and i know it's not your thoughts, but your
                  love that gives so much.
                    sam (april 28, 1995)
```

"You guys need to wake up." The voice was a deep rumble. A flashlight's beam in my face and a not-so-gentle nudge by a steel-toed boot pulled me the rest of the way out of sleep. A broad-shouldered officer with a flashlight stood over us. A pudgy cop with a crooked nose stood just behind him. His hand was resting on his belt.

Sam and I wiggled out of our blankets and got to our feet.

"What are your names and dates of birth?" Shoulders asked.

Sam gave them his information and I gave them the false information I had learned before. Crooked Nose walked ten feet away to call it in on the radio.

Shoulders asked more routine questions. "Where are you from?"

Sam gave him the rehearsed answers. "We're just heading back to Montana from California."

"What are you doing here?"

"We've been traveling around."

"Do you have anywhere to go?"

"We'll be leaving today or tomorrow."

Crooked Nose walked back over and said we were all clear.

They watched, arms folded across their chests, as we packed our stuff.

The remnants of sleep stayed wrapped around us as we dragged ourselves to the IHOP for coffee. We hung out until eight in the morning and then found some trees to sleep under. Once we woke up, it was two in the afternoon. My stomach growled. Sam raised his eyebrows and I shrugged my shoulders.

"Guess we should get some money," Sam said.

I spotted Patrick first, as he and James came around the corner of the brick buildings. Patrick's smile wrinkled his eyes and dimpled his cheeks.

My feet got all tangled with one another as I rushed to get up.

"Arielle wasn't happy about you sending the dose to her," James said.

Sam rolled his eyes. "How was hitching?"

"It was way easier than I thought it would be," Patrick said.

I wrapped my arm around my big brother's shoulders. "Let's show them the city and track down some dose."

We spent the night tripping out along the river and ended up coming down at the IHOP. The sun was just cresting the horizon and spilling its light through the large windows.

"I'm going back to Salt Lake," Patrick said.

"What?" I said. "Why? You just got here. You can't leave."

Sam rested his hand on my thigh under the table.

"Seeing the two of you so happy made me realize I love Sandi, and I'm going back to get her. I'm not leaving forever. I'm just going back to get her and then we'll meet you in Missoula," Patrick said.

I didn't know how they would get back or if he really would come back. I couldn't stop him from leaving, and I knew how much it hurt to be away from the one you love. I fought back tears and just nodded my head.

"I'm leaving too," James said. "Going to Seattle and then back to Missoula. I'll meet up with you guys there and help sling the dose."

On May 3, 1995, Sam and I finally got the money. We found a sheet and dropped a couple of hits to make sure it was good. We spent the night in giggle-fits, billowing clouds of smoke and walking all over town. It was good.

I called my mom to check in before we left Eugene.

"You need to come home and get your braces off your teeth," she said.

"I know, Mom." I had popped off all of the brackets besides the ones on my molars.

"The Division of Child and Family Services came to the house, and they're considering abandonment charges against your dad and me."

"How can they do that, Mom? You don't have any control over what I do or where I go."

"Just come home and get emancipated."

"I don't know when I can get to Utah."

At one point back during my gothic days, I'd asked her to have me emancipated. Of course, she had refused. Interesting how things came full circle. Ups and downs. It was what made the world go around.

I was in desperate need of a new pair of shoes and we did a lot of walking. We went into a chain supercenter. I browsed the shoes while Sam scouted out the cigarette section. I tried on a few pairs until I found ones I liked. I set my old shoes in the box and tore the tags off the new ones. Sam and I met back up a couple of blocks down the road.

We stuck our thumbs out on the freeway on-ramp and made it to Salem in two rides. We decided to crash there for the night. The next afternoon, we ate breakfast at Denny's and stuck out our thumbs at the freeway on-ramp again. An older man picked us up and gave us a ride to some little unmapped town. Our next ride took us to Seattle.

We dropped a couple of hits of acid and tripped around the city. We heard there were services for runaways and street kids where we could get food, showers, and wash our clothes. There was no way we were going to risk getting caught by the police again, so we steered clear of those places. The Grateful Dead show was a few days away, and there would be cheap sheets of acid. We couch-surfed with a few people we met around town.

It was Mother's Day.

I called my mom. There was no answer, so I left her a message wishing her a happy Mother's Day. Some part of me thought that was cruel, but I really did mean it. She was a great mom. I was a horrible kid.

Over the next few days, we sold the rest of the sheet we had. We called Sam's dad and convinced him to send more child support so we could get tickets to the Grateful Dead show. Sam's dad came through and sent the money, but the show was sold out.

We went to the venue anyway, hoping to pick up four sheets in the Lot. The Lot was what everyone called the little village made up of VW buses and tents where Deadheads gathered before and during concerts. After the show, we were going to Kalispell, Montana, to visit Sam's family. From there, we'd head to Salt Lake, arriving between June first and fifteenth. I'd get the state off my mom's ass and then we'd be off to Taos, New Mexico, for the Rainbow Gathering. The Gathering was from the fifteenth through the twentieth of June. We hoped to pick up a twenty-pack of acid while we were there.

The Lot was incredible. The little city had sprung to life in a matter of hours. The *boom-tec-a-tec-boom* of drums started at sunset, followed by the deep call of a didgeridoo. It all resonated in the spaces between buses. The sounds of harmonicas swam through the air. Bonfires blazed. Women and children with bells on their hips and ankles danced. Laughter fluttered across the blooming meadow of people.

Sam held my hand and guided me along as I turned my head to see everything. I didn't want to miss anything, and I didn't want to forget.

A family invited us to their fire to share bread and stew. Sitting between Sam's legs, I laid my head back on his chest and we listened to the music of the Grateful Dead from outside the stadium walls. I wished we could be inside. I wanted to feel the vibrations of the music and the hum of the crowd.

Before the night was over, we scored a sheet of acid with Grateful Dead suns printed on each hit. It broke my heart to have to rip it to pieces.

We were back on the road late the next morning with the family we'd had dinner with the night before. One day and three rides later, we made it into Spokane.

"How long do you think it will take us to get to Kalispell from here?" I shouted over the freight train thundering by. Spokane was a major railroad hub for the northwest. Trains came in and out, all day and night.

"Depends. I say we jump on that train."

I pushed my lips together and out. "Hmm, alright." It would be faster if we figured it out. We made our way into the train yard.

"How do we know which train to get on?" I asked. A swarm of bees coalesced in my stomach.

"I'm not sure it matters, as long as it's going the way we need to go," Sam said. He pointed to a train. "That one is going east. Let's try to catch it."

We ran alongside the train. It was going faster than it appeared at first glance. Sam was running behind me, waiting for me to grab hold and pull myself on. I reached for the ladder, but my fingers slipped off the rung and I stumbled.

I ran faster and grabbed the next ladder with my left hand. My right hand reached and missed. The train was dragging me. I pulled hard with my left arm and my right got hold of the rung. I swung my legs up and scooted back so Sam could throw the bag up and jump on. But he didn't.

I scooted out to the edge and peered back. Sam was hanging onto the ladder of the car behind mine. He pulled himself up, poked his head out to see me, and smiled. He gave me a thumbs-up. Relieved, I leaned back and brushed my blackened hands off on my pants, leaving streaks of grime from my hips to my knees.

I kept checking to see if I could see Sam. I was worried he would jump off and I wouldn't know. The train began to slow down. I looked back and saw Sam poke his head out. He raised his hands and shook his head no. He didn't know what was going on.

The train continued to slow down. I checked again for Sam. I saw our bag fly off the train car. Sam climbed out on the ladder and was getting ready to jump. I climbed out on the ladder too, my heart pounding in my chest. Sam jumped away from the train and rolled.

I let my feet hang off until they scraped along the ground. It was going too fast for me to just let go, and I didn't want to get caught on something. I pulled my feet back up and got ready to jump and roll. I pushed off with a twist so that I'd be facing away from the train when I landed.

My feet hit the ground and I tried to run out of the fall, but couldn't. Pulling my arms and head in, I rolled forward through the rock and dirt.

Sam was standing over me when I came to a stop.

"I think we got on at the wrong end of the train yard," he said.

I sat sprawled on the ground as the dust cloud dissipated. "I think we should stick to hitching."

It didn't take long to hitchhike to Kalispell. Sam's mom's house was ten miles south of town. His younger brother, Joseph, lived with her. He was just a little younger than I was. Sam's aunt, cousin, and her husband also lived there.

We stayed for two nights and sold some dose in town. Sam's mom loaded us up with peanut butter and jelly sandwiches, granola bars, and cookies. Then she gave us a ride to the edge of town. We made good time to Missoula.

The first night there, we set up camp near the river. We bought chocolate Yoo-hoos at the gas station on our way to the diner and ate french fries sprinkled with ranch dressing powder. In the morning, we moved our camp by the railroad tracks and went to Finnegan's for coffee.

"We have seventy-nine hits left, right?" Sam asked.

We had taken a few between Spokane and Kalispell.

"I think so."

"Let me see it," he said.

"You have it."

"No, I don't."

We slammed the rest of our coffee down, dropped three dollars on the table, and ran out the door. We dumped everything out of our backpack onto the tarp. We unfolded and refolded everything, thinking it might be caught inside of something.

"Maybe we left it in Kalispell?" I said.

Sam called Joseph and had him look around for his rune stone drawstring sack, where he kept the acid. Joseph couldn't find it anywhere. He told Sam he'd call Arielle if he found it. We wanted to just go back and look for it ourselves, but we had to wait for Patrick and James.

It had to be there. It just had to be. We couldn't start over again.

Patrick returned to Missoula driving a van. Sandi was with him, and another girl named Valerie that I didn't know. Valerie was the opposite of Sandi—thick, chin-length hair, tall, and wiry. I never warmed up to Valerie, but James did. Not long after her arrival, the two hit it off.

We drove to Kalispell. Every few miles, the van stalled. It took us twelve hours to drive one hundred and fifty miles. We searched the house and couldn't find the sheet of acid. I'd had the rune stones tied to my jeans, so it was my fault for losing it. Every time we got good acid, something went wrong. We could never seem to get things rolling. We went back to Missoula, downtrodden.

The loss of the sheet and no money from Sam's dad for another month caused no change in our ultimate strategy. We were returning to Salt Lake, and then headed to the Rainbow Gathering in New Mexico. Taos would be our next chance to pick up a sheet of acid.

Back in Missoula, we stayed at our friend Autumn's apartment. Autumn, James, and Valerie worked on the van, trying to get it ready for the trip back to Salt Lake. It took a week to stop the van from constantly stalling. It still stalled, just not as much. James and Valerie took turns driving. They were the only ones with driver's licenses.

We arrived in Salt Lake City on June 9, 1995.

Nicole Lowe

By the eighth grade, twenty-eight percent of adolescents have consumed alcohol, fifteen percent have smoked cigarettes, and 16.5 percent have used marijuana.

chapter eighteen

"Mr. Johnson?" says Judge Cruz.

"No questions."

The judge next addresses the mother's table. "Mr. Lundberg?"

Jake turns to Sabrina, who wipes her nose with the back of her hand and shakes her head. Jake stands halfway, his hands habitually moving toward the button of his jacket. "Nothing, Your Honor."

"Next witness, Ms. Lowe."

I stand. "The state rests."

"You're free to go, Linda. Thank you." Judge Cruz flips the pages of his legal pad back to the beginning. "Why don't we take a ten-minute break."

He stands and smooths the arms and length of his black robe. We all stand and remain silent until the judge and Sabrina leave the courtroom.

I swivel my chair to face the guardian ad litem. "Carl, are you going to give a closing argument?"

```
He shrugs off his jacket and hangs it on the
back of his chair. "I don't think it's
necessary."

    Closing argument isn't evidence. It's mostly
used to sum up the case and to streamline it for
the judge, particularly when you can't present
your witnesses in any chronological order.

    In truth, there's no need to go through the
facts of this trail again. It's almost cruel to
stand here and read Sabrina a litany of reasons
why she is unfit to be McCartni's mother. She's
already heard it once. And she will hear it again
before the day is out.
```

I stopped at the bottom of the steps. Then slowly, I took them one at a time. One. Two. Three. The white steel door stared at me. Corralled by the black iron railing to my right and left, I knocked on my parents' door. I hadn't seen their house as my home in a long time. I couldn't walk in as if I lived there. The road and the streets were my home. Everyone else stood behind me on the lawn, including Patrick. I cast a quick glance back and he smiled.

The doorknob turned. I watched the space between the door and the frame grow by each fraction of an inch.

The screen door stood between my father and me.

I wasn't sure what one said under such circumstances.

"Hi, Dad." I struggled to get more words out. "These are my friends, Sam, James, Valerie, and Sandi."

Fury colored my father's neck and cheeks.

"Get the hell off my property!" He pointed at Sam and James. "Step one foot on my lawn again and I'll shoot you both." He slammed the door.

Welcome home.

Nicole Lowe

We drove to Dee's on North Temple and sat drinking coffee, eating cheese fries, and trying to figure out what to do next. No money, no dose, no place to stay, and more mouths to feed than ever before. The consensus was to get jobs and work until our first paychecks, then hightail it out to the Rainbow Gathering in Taos.

James and Valerie were both over eighteen and had state-issued ID, so they had jobs within a few days. The rest of us were sixteen and younger, and without identification. Getting an interview without an address or phone number was problematic. If we did get an interview, we had no way of providing proof of our age.

James and Valerie grew sick of being the providers and decided they were leaving.

"You guys just get high and sit around all day doing nothing," James fumed.

Sam lit a joint and let out a puff of smoke. We were sitting in a circle on the lawn in Memory Grove.

Laughing, Sam said, "Yeah, man, what do you want me to do? No one is hiring me." He looked up at James through slitted, bloodshot eyes.

"You're a dick and a lazy ass, you know that?" James said. "You're not even taking care of your family, man."

Sam waved his hand at James. "If you want to leave, leave."

James and Valerie stayed for a few more weeks, but once they got their paychecks, they left together for Montana. Patrick stayed with my parents, and Sandi returned to her mother's house. Sam and I lived in Memory Grove. I went to my parents' to wash clothes and see my mom, but the tension in the house was as thick as green Jell-O.

Europe drifted further away, into the dense fog that was settling around us in Salt Lake. There was no possible way we'd be able to finance the Order of the Silvermoon working for minimum wage. Dealing dose was the only way we were going to be able to make it work.

Sam received money for his birthday, and his child support. He was leaving to visit family before the winter snows closed the pass. He left two hundred and eight dollars with Patrick and me to buy a sheet or two and start slinging dose. I returned to my parents' house while Sam was gone.

It took one night for the wolf to catch my scent again.

...I can't breathe. It's so dark. I can't even see what is in front of my face. I feel his hot breath on my thighs, and then his teeth. I try to kick him away from me, but my legs won't move. My scream is choked off as his hand shoves a cloth into my mouth. It's so dark...

I jerked awake. My breathing was ragged and heavy. I went to the window and slid it open. The warm summer air calmed me. I watched the stars and the moon and wondered how far Sam had made it and where he was sleeping tonight.

The day after Sam left, Patrick and I found a sheet for a hundred dollars. We sold a few hits that night. We sold to those who came searching for an escape from reality. We had signals to alert one another if we got a bad vibe about a person we were selling to, or if we saw cops coming down the street. Both of us had agreed that if the cops ever came up on us during a deal, we would eat everything. The word on the street was they charged you for each hit of acid, which got you five years in lock-up. It was better to risk psychosis, or what trippers called perma-fry, than to risk getting locked up.

That Friday, we set up at a corner in the center of the city to deal. Concrete benches lined the sidewalk. There were some of the old goths hanging around, and the gutter punks sat on the sidewalk. A couple of gangbangers slid into view. They ticked their heads upward toward Patrick and me.

"You guys know anyone looking for some crack?" the one in the red wife-beater asked.

"Nah, man, I don't," I told them. "We got some dose, if you want any?"

Wife-beater reversed his hat and shook his head. "Nah, we don't mess with that shit, it'll make you crazy."

Two street kids on skateboards rolled up behind me. "How much per hit?"

"Four dollars a hit, or fifteen for a five-strip."

The kid probed his pocket as I pulled the cellophane holding the dose out and sat on one of the concrete benches. I pinched the ten-strip wrapped in foil between my fingernails and laid it on my knee. I was unwrapping it to cut two hits off when I heard the sound of a revving engine and squealing tires.

My head popped up, scanning left and right.

Red and blue lights were flashing.

Everyone scattered in different directions.

I grabbed hold of Patrick's arm. Our eyes locked and I pushed him away. "Run, and don't look back! Meet me in the Grove."

He didn't move.

We stared at one another for what seemed like forever but was only a second. He pivoted on his toe, but looked back again.

"Go!" I commanded.

He went.

The cops opened their car doors. Black handguns appeared and slid into the V between the door and the car's frame. I turned my head, my eyes moving over my surroundings. The gangbangers, their hands raised, were going to the ground. The officers were focused on them.

I took off at a full sprint in the opposite direction Patrick had gone.

"Get on the ground!" I heard them yell.

I kept running.

My feet slid out from under me as I rounded a corner, and then another. I ducked into a crowd inside the ZCMI center.

I caught up with Patrick in the Temple gardens. We chilled for a few hours, waiting for our heart rates to come down.

―――

On Saturday afternoon, two people we'd sold to on Thursday found us.

"What are you playing at?" one of the guys said. "Your dose was bunk. We want our money back."

"It's not bunk," I said. "We've seen other people we sold to, and they didn't say anything, so I know it's good."

"We want our money back," he said again.

"That's a risk you take," I said. "But I'll tell you what. I'll drop a couple of hits, and if it doesn't take effect within an hour, I'll give you your money back."

We didn't need enemies all over Salt Lake.

I dropped a couple of hits and waited. Nothing happened. I gave them their twelve dollars back. Patrick dropped a couple of hits. Again, nothing. Bunk. Patrick and I didn't sell another hit.

I kept the sheet in the cellophane and a plastic baggie until Sam returned later in the week. He took a couple of hits and got nothing. He was pissed we were bunked. He bought another sheet with the remaining money.

It was bunk too.

Things were not going well.

Bandaloops had become the new hangout for what was left of the goths, gutter punks, hippies, and skaters in downtown Salt Lake City. There were pool tables, video games, and a food counter inside. The painted yellow-and-white brick building was on the corner of West Temple and 200 South.

The goth scene had transformed. Gone was the Charade and the magic of the gothic world. All that remained was the black clothing, dark makeup, and drugs. Lots of drugs. Not just LSD and a little crystal, but cocaine, heroin, and angel dust.

I looked at the remainders of my friends. They didn't need to wear pale makeup; their flesh was thin and grey. Their skin hung on their bones like cloth draped over broken branches. Even the new faces were gaunt and starved of life. And yet, I sold them more.

We had two dealers who kept us supplied with sheets for selling and personal use: Torry and Zippy. They weren't actual sheets anymore. Like all things, acid had evolved too. Usually it was a vial or a bag of Smarties candy. Zippy lived near my parents' but hung out downtown. Torry was a couch-surfer, like most of our friends. It was safer than having a place of your own. Between Zippy and Torry, Sam and I had an ongoing supply of acid.

Soon, we realized we had no way of getting more money aside from getting legit jobs. Sam got a job first, at McDonald's. Two weeks later, I got a job at Arby's. Not long after, Sam got hired on

Nicole Lowe

with me. Patrick worked at Arctic Circle and lived between my parents' and Sandi's. Jobs seemed reasonable, since our other "business" was not proving to be very profitable. Our dream of going to Europe was becoming more dreamlike and less reality with every passing day.

Sometimes, old "friends" would come in and remind me where I'd come from, who I was before. Michael was the most frequent visitor. He would sit and stare at me from across the food court. I had to work the counter because I was too young to use the slicer, putting me in his direct line of sight. He would pace the length of the wall opposite Arby's. When he came to order food, Sam would come up front and take his order.

Whenever Michael was near, my throat would close off and I couldn't talk above a whisper. The first time he came to the counter, I ended up dry-heaving over the toilet for thirty minutes. I had nightmares for a week. It got easier as time went by, but the flood of adrenaline never stopped. I didn't know what Michael wanted. The coven and the Charade had fallen apart.

Sam and I didn't want anything to do with my past life and tried to avoid areas where most of the goths hung out. Many had become so strung out they didn't recognize me, anyway.

We weren't dealing anymore, but we used every chance we had. Sam, Patrick, and I were tripping hard and laughing until tears streaked our faces and our stomachs hurt. We were laughing about trying to act normal as we walked through downtown Salt Lake to Memory Grove at midnight.

The traffic light changed: red, green, yellow, red, green, yellow.

I stood there, not moving.

The streetlamp's white light separated into a waving rainbow. It attached itself to my fingers and hair. I strung it between my fingers and tied it in beautiful knots.

The walk signal beeped: *be-boop, be-boop, be-boop.*

All at once, we turned to one another and stopped what we were doing. We realized that we must have looked high as hell, standing there staring at the lights. This caused another fit of laughter. Luckily, no cops drove by.

We chugged our way to the Grove and up to the meditation chapel, a place where people could sit in silent contemplation of those who had been lost in wars. As soon as we arrived, I realized my bladder was not going to hold much more. Tripping always made me forget about bodily functions. I didn't know if I was wet or dry. I didn't get hungry. I didn't know if I had to use the bathroom until it was an urgent need. I didn't know if I was cold or hot. The energy in my brain, which generally went into these senses, was diverted to amplifying the sensations of sight and sound.

Bursting, I jogged around to the other side of the building and crashed into the trees. There was no way I was going to make it to the bathroom across the river. I pushed through the trees a little ways, more out of habit than out of any desire for privacy. I unbuckled the bib of my overalls, folded it over, dropped them below my knees, and squatted.

When I finished, I stood and buckled up the bib. I looked down and saw my cigarettes sitting in a puddle of urine. *Damn it!* I picked them up with the tips of my fingers and wiped them on my pants. I opened the box, hoping the cellophane wrapper had kept them dry. Two were done for, but the rest of them were alright, for the most part. No one ever died from a little pee, right?

I stuck the cigarettes in my pocket and walked back over to Sam and Patrick. We smoked them throughout the night. No one said anything, and I never said a word about the pee.

The next afternoon, Sam and I were sitting on the park strip on the side of Bandaloops, delirious with exhaustion. We hadn't slept after our night of tripping. We sat watching the drifting clouds and people.

Sam began to cry. He took my hand in his. "I don't want us to ever just come together, exchange words, and then separate."

At that moment, it became clear to me that all life came into being, did its thing, and separated. Dissipated. It did not matter what it was, what joined it together, or what precipitating event caused its separation. Everything separated.

I held Sam's hands in my own. "We will travel our path together until it ends."

Nicole Lowe

There was nothing more to say.

After the moon rose, we trudged toward the canyon and the Grove to sleep.

Memory Grove had always been my sanctuary. After we had returned to Utah, I gravitated back to its loving branches and cool canyon breezes. Sam and I hid our pack within the underbrush by day and curled up there during the night.

We moved camp frequently, hoping to keep our stuff hidden from all the others who also found the Grove their home. Each morning, I awoke to birds singing and branches rustling with the wind as it caressed the mountainside on its course through the canyon. I lay awake, listening and reflecting. *How could anyone want more than this? What more could there be to life?* Then my bubble would burst as I realized that eventually, I too had to succumb.

It was chilly and I didn't want to move from Sam's arms, but I had to go to the bathroom. I grumbled and flipped the blanket back like tearing a band-aid off. I squatted in the bushes and saw clumpy blood. I rarely had my period on a regular basis. Whenever it decided to show up, I acquired a box of tampons. I didn't want to say anything to Sam. It was weird, and probably not normal, but I pushed it out of my mind.

When I got back to our bed, Sam was digging through our pack for "cleaner" clothes than what we had on. We dressed, rolled up the bed, and shoved it into our pack. He stashed it among the bushes, pulling fallen branches over it to conceal it from inquisitive eyes. We walked the two miles into the city to work.

Sam and I had become borderline productive members of society. After work, we went to the bank. We were standing in line to cash our paychecks when my legs buckled and I slumped to the green-and-black marble floor, unconscious. I woke up on a couch in the lobby.

"Nikki?" Sam was rubbing my hand.

I opened my eyes and he smiled.

"Are you alright?"

"I feel okay." I pushed myself up into a sitting position. "I don't know what happened. I was just really dizzy and then my eyes began to close."

A man in a green vest asked me if I'd had any food that day. I shook my head.

"Take her to get something to eat," he told Sam.

We went to Dee's on North Temple. Patrick met us there. I ordered french toast. Halfway through the meal, I started to experience sharp, knife-twisting pain in my stomach. I went into the bathroom and the pain grew worse, until I could barely move. I clenched my teeth together. I pressed the heel of my palm into my lower abdomen to make it stop, but it didn't. I lay on the cold floor in the handicap stall, curled into a ball. The intense pain passed after fifteen minutes. I stumbled out of the bathroom and told Sam what was happening.

"You need to call Mom," Patrick said.

I called her from the payphone in the lobby.

"Mom, something is wrong. I'm having stabbing pains and it won't stop."

She came and took me to LDS Hospital. Patrick and Sam waited in the lobby while my mom and I were taken back.

We sat waiting in the exam room. Neither one of us spoke a word to the other. I stared at my filthy shoes most of the time. The paper on the exam table crinkled every time I shifted position. The nurse came in and asked a bunch of questions and I answered them.

"Could you be pregnant?" she asked, looking from me to my mom.

"She's fifteen," my mom said.

"It's possible," I whispered.

The nurse gave me a clear plastic cup and told me to fill it in the bathroom.

My mom and I sat in silence, waiting again, until the nurse came back into the room.

"The pregnancy test is faintly positive," she said.

"What does that mean?" my mom asked.

"She is either pregnant or just miscarried."

My mom closed her eyes. Her breathing was even and deep. I watched her in silence. What could I say? I had destroyed the little girl she loved. And now, I had destroyed another life.

"She will need to be tested again in a few weeks," the nurse said.

They sent me home with my mom. But Sam was not welcome there, and I refused to be without him, so she dropped Sam, Patrick, and me off at Torry's house.

I lay awake, eyes gently closed, on the carpeted floor. I didn't feel like talking. I listened to Sam, Patrick, and Torry talk in lowered voices. I watched them through a slit between my eyelids.

My feelings about being pregnant were tangled knots sitting in my throat. The thought that my body might have killed something Sam and I had created was ripping me apart. Tears slipped from the corner of my eye to the carpet. I was also terrified of something depending on me for its life. But at the same time, I was excited about the two of us creating a beautiful child. My chin quivered and I bit my lip. It was the first time in my life I had ever had any desire to be a mother.

"It will destroy everything we were trying to do," Sam said, pressing his cigarette into the ashtray, causing it to grind across the dirty table.

"It totally will," Torry said, pushing the ashtray back to the center of the table. "It would be really bad, but you guys could get an abortion."

Patrick didn't say anything other than it would drastically change our plans. I rolled over. I was hurt and betrayed by what Sam had said.

I went back to the doctor two weeks later and found out I had miscarried. My emotions continued to soar and plummet, throwing me into a dizzying confusion.

Sam's feelings were clear. In celebration, Torry smoked up Patrick and Sam, and Sam bought a ten-strip and split it with me.

Sometime after, my sixteenth birthday came and went. The day could have been stunning, or it could have been drab. It didn't matter, because it was just another day.

Never Let Me Go

Leaves were turning to the reds, golds, oranges, and browns of autumn and the birds were riding the currents south to their winter homes. The first frost of winter came into the Salt Lake Valley with an early vengeance.

With the autumn came the beginning of another school year. Police hauled Sam and me in for truancy. We sat in a classroom while they called my mom. She came and had us released. It was the third time.

My mom took me to the school district to officially drop out of school. They gave me a card, the proof of my ignorance. It said I was not legally required to attend school and could be out during school hours. It was a license for the uneducated. It was a relief to both my mom and me.

Some nights, I lay awake watching the gauzy clouds weave themselves among the stars and a deep sadness would arise within me, bringing tears to my eyes. I blinked, and they glided down my face. The chasm separating who I was and who I should have been stood before me. I quaked with a longing for that life, but only for a moment. Then it was gone. Life was too short to spend time chasing a future that would never arrive, or to dwell on the past, which would never change.

Nicole Lowe

Twenty-five percent of children in the United States live below poverty level. Forty-five percent of children in the United States live in a low-income family.

chapter nineteen

Judge Cruz enters the courtroom and slips his robe back on. Jake is scrolling through his notes on his laptop.

I follow the judge's progression to the bench and then continue my scan of the courtroom. This room has become comfortable to me, which strikes me as an unsettling thought. This place, where the relationship between parent and child can be severed forever, has become something of a second home to me.

I bow my head and remind myself: those relationships can also be repaired. That is always the goal. It is the choice every parent faces when they stand before a juvenile court judge. Death of the parent-child relationship is always the last resort when seeking to provide the child with safety and permanency.

Those two things are paramount to a child's physical, emotional, and psychological well-being. It was that belief that drove me to the decision to sever one of the most significant relationships of my life. From that day forward, the course of my life had been altered completely.

I look over at Sabrina. Her blonde hair has fallen around her face. Her hands rest clasped together in her lap. She made the opposite decision.

And here we sit, at opposing tables, with the guillotine waiting in the center of the room. The overhead lights sharp on the blade. Our minds clouded with images of our journey here, and the choice we made at that critical crossroads.

Judge Cruz's voice interrupts the flow of memories. "Witnesses, Mr. Lundberg?"

"Sabrina Hardy, Your Honor."

Sabrina raises her head, shaking the hair out of her face. She stands, holding her shoulders back and her chin high. She's not going down without a fight.

My chest tightens. I hate this.

Jake smiles at her as she settles on the stand. His fist question is the one she's been waiting to answer all morning.

"Ms. Hardy, why should the judge give you another chance?"

Sabrina turns to the judge. "I've learned a lot and grown up. I was just a teenager when my first two children were born. I want to be a mother now. I love McCartni so much. She is my whole world."

She begins to cry and takes the last tissue from the cardboard box. "I'll do anything. Please, give me another chance. I can do this. I know I can." Sabrina's voice fades to a whisper. "I love her."

I watch the judge's jaw loosen and his lips shift. Compassion moves across his face. He wants to respond, but he can't.

Sabrina lowers her gaze.

"Does McCartni love you?" Jake asks.

"I know she does."

"How do you know?"

"When I see her at visits. She smiles so big. She runs to me and gives me a big hug around my neck. She tells me she loves me."

"What do you do on visits?"

"I help her build with blocks and take care of her baby doll, Annie. I read to her. I sing to her."

"Have you ever missed a visit?"

Sabrina rubs her fingers together. "Only when I was in jail."

"Did you contact the caseworker as soon as you were released?"

"I was released at three in the morning. I called her at eight in the morning."

"Tell us about your housing."

"I have a room at my friend's. It has my bed, and a bed for McCartni all ready. I have a dresser and some toys for her, like a cradle for her baby doll and a stroller."

"What's the most important thing to you?"

"McCartni, hands down. She is my everything. I live and breathe for her. I need her in my life."

It was October 6, 1995, when we stepped off the Greyhound bus into four inches of snow sparkling like diamonds in the Montana moonlight. Our feet slid in the slush. We had not arrived with winter in mind.

Goosebumps puckered our skin and shivers coursed through our bodies, nearly knocking us off balance. Sam and I grabbed our bags. It was 11:00 p.m. The wind-chill easily dropped the temperature below zero. We stood there in hoodies and sneakers, trying to get our bearings.

When I told my mom we were leaving for Montana, she wasn't happy. But what could she do?

We made our way to a diner about a quarter mile away. We had about fifty dollars to our names, and it had to last until we could get jobs. We ordered coffee and cheese fries—the usual. We hung out for a few hours reading, watching the snow blow around outside, and drawing until the diner was locking up for the night.

We went back out into the frigid air and biting wind.

"We need to find somewhere to keep warm," Sam said. He walked toward the back of the diner.

My teeth were chattering as I followed. Sam found a dishwasher-size cardboard box in the back by the dumpster and we carried it back into the bushes and trees. Sam spread out our blankets and we climbed inside. The cardboard cocoon was warm. I laughed because we had never slept in a box before. Sam smiled and we snuggled in for the night.

Around four in the morning, Sam shook me awake.

"I'm freezing," he chattered. "We need to move."

I crawled on hands and knees from the box. Pain zipped through me with every bending joint. We needed to move around to keep the blood moving or we were not going to wake up when the sun finally came out.

We shuffled our feet along the frozen ground until the sun sent out daggers of light from behind the glacier-packed mountains. Sam spread our cocoon out on the side of a hill to insulate us from the treacherous cold that seeped up from the earth. The hill shielded us from the sweeping wind and allowed the sun to warm our bodies. We lay there for a few more hours.

At eight in the morning, we walked back to the diner and Sam called his mom. She picked us up two hours later. We'd come to Montana because she said she would help us get on our feet, and told us there were jobs in Kalispell.

Sam and I slept in the basement on the family room floor. We rolled out our bed just like when we were out hitching, and each morning we rolled it back up. Sam's mom, Angela, told us we could stay until we got jobs, saved money, and got our own place. She said we had to look for jobs every day, which was fine by us.

Angela gave us warm coats and gloves to wear while we were walking around job hunting. Each morning, she took us into town when she took Joseph to school. We spare-changed for food and coffee. We put in job applications and hung out with people Sam had known when he was growing up. At night, we found a ride or hitchhiked back to Angela's house.

Sam's weed radar allowed him to find people to smoke him up nearly every day. Occasionally, when we could spare-change enough money, we got some dose and tripped, staying out all night. It took a month for Angela to tell us we had to move out.

"We had a family meeting, and everyone thinks you're not doing enough to get jobs," she said.

"We weren't invited to the meeting?" Sam asked.

"I'll take you into town in the morning, and then you're on your own."

Sam was angry and felt betrayed. His mom was kicking him out of her house, again, and there was nothing we could do.

He borrowed a tent from a friend and we found a place outside of town to set up camp. We were close enough to walk into town each day. After a few weeks of living in the tent, Sam was hired at McDonald's. Amanda, the manager, was a college student who Sam hooked up with weed whenever she asked. We moved into an extended-stay motel at the edge of town called Big Chief's with Sam's second paycheck.

We lived in a cabin. Each cabin had two rooms. The rooms had a queen-size bed, a sink, and a small counter with storage space underneath. There was a mini-fridge and hotplate for cooking. The bathroom was so small that I could pee and wash my hands at the same time. There was about two feet of space around each object in the room.

Amanda drove us to the food bank each week. I tried to use everything we got from there. We mixed rice or beans with nearly everything. We invested in a toaster oven to make bagels with cream cheese. Bagels were a special treat, because we had to buy them at the store.

Living at the motel gave us an address. An address seemed like such a simple yet important thing; knowing where you belong, and having a place to call home. A place where you could drop your role, step off the stage, and be who you were.

It became more of a sanctuary the more we were incorporated into what most would call "real life" or being "productive members of society." A society that required you to be something more. More than a traveler, more than a nomad, and more than a hunter-gatherer. No wonder so many people wanted to escape. Who has the endurance to continually achieve more?

I was true to my word and called my mom every week. She wanted me to come home for Christmas, but it would cost too much. We talked about everyday things. I told her how things were going for Sam and me, how beautiful it was in Montana, about the friends we were making, and how hard it was to find a job.

Our lives had become directionless; our dreams lost among all those that had been cast aside by others under the pressure of society to obtain status and material security. The eternal question of "Who am I?" burned at the center of us all. When our search for the answer was thwarted at every turn, we began to define ourselves by the possessions we gathered, rather than our commitment to our dreams and beliefs. It was the greatest death of all. How did Sam and I get caught in society's self-serving, materialistic security?

I lay on the floor of our home with my eyes closed, rummaging through the memories of the past year of my life. Of all the faces that stared back at me, my own revealed the most. My terror, hatred, and loneliness stared into the eyes of my joy, compassion, and strength. Would they ever become one and end this feeling of duality within me? The two had battled since I could remember, and I expected them to continue until the end.

One afternoon, the sun was shining and I was sitting on the sidewalk outside of the McDonald's where Sam worked, smoking. I relished the sun's warmth on my skin, especially in winter. I had spent such a long time hiding from its touch, covered in shadow and cloth, feeding the ice that grew within me. It would take ages to melt it all away.

There was a man on the corner with a litter of puppies in a rainbow-colored toddler playpen. I walked over to look. There were three balls of fur, growling and biting one another.

"How much are you selling them for?" I asked.

"I'm giving them away, actually," he said. "We can't afford to feed them all."

I picked one up and pressed its tiny nose against mine. "What type of dogs are they?"

"Half Border Collie and half Chow Chow."

"They're beautiful."

I ran back to McDonald's and asked Sam if we could take one home.

"I'll come look at them on my break," he said, smiling and shaking his head.

He came over while I was sitting on the sidewalk, snuggling the fuzzy pups. We picked out a female and named her Dusky Rune. She looked like a Siberian Husky. She had black, white, and brown fur. She was beautiful. We bought some dog food, a leash, and a collar from Walmart, foregoing bagels for a few weeks. We were a family and I needed a job.

Not long after, a new Perkins restaurant opened up down the street from Big Chief's. It was closer than McDonald's. They hired me to bus tables.

The work sucked. My job was to stand around, waiting for people to finish eating better food than I could afford. No one talked to me.

The waitresses and waiters were all preppy kids in their little cliques, just like in junior high school. I cleared dishes, wiped down the tables and the seats, and swept the floor under and around the tables. I took full tubs of dishes to the dishwashers. Again and again, all day long. Every few hours, I went out for a smoke break. Sometimes, Sam came in at the end of my shift and we would sit in the restaurant and drink coffee.

We bought psychedelic mushrooms to celebrate. Eating mushrooms was like chewing on a sponge that had dried after sitting in a puddle of river mud. We decided to brew it into a tea. Drinking warm, muddy water was slightly better than chewing it, but not by much.

Shroom trips were different from dose. They made your nerves hypersensitive, rather than messing with your vision and your mind. We talked about the Order and our dreams of Europe—topics that had vanished from our thoughts and aspirations. We had become focused on survival more than we ever had been on the road. And all the while, our reliance on society to meet our needs caused a specter of uncertainty to arise.

We spent the entire trip touching different things in our house: smooth, fuzzy, and rough textures. We saw tracers as each of us moved around. On shrooms, all of the imperfections I saw in others were gone. The world was beautiful. I was sucked into the land of Care Bears and My Little Pony. Despite it all, acid remained my drug of choice. I liked the intense hallucinations and mind-bending, chaotic thoughts. Shrooms were too mellow.

It was springtime. The sun was shining, and life was good. There was only one part of life I didn't enjoy: work. I stopped showing up for my shift. A few weeks later, Sam was fired from McDonald's for the same thing. It was time to go back to Utah. I called my mom and told her I was coming home.

"What can I do to help?" she asked.

"Can you pick us up in Butte?"

"Yes, of course. When?"

"In two days."

Nicole Lowe

We hauled our army-green pack from underneath our bed. We rolled up all of our clothes and signed out of Big Chief's. We had one last dinner with Sam's family before leaving. Joseph was upset we were going, but Angela thought it was best since we hadn't been able to get on our feet and jobs were hard to come by. We said goodbye to the few friends we had.

We used the last of our money to pay for gas for Amanda to drive us to Butte. My mom and Patrick were there waiting for us. The three of us—Sam, Dusky Rune, and me—sat in the back seat while Patrick caught us up on what had been happening in Salt Lake. I was returning to a place that hadn't felt like home since I was a child. Again.

A high school dropout will earn $200,000 less than a high school graduate over his lifetime, and almost a million dollars less than a college graduate.

chapter twenty

"Any cross, Ms. Lowe?" Judge Cruz peers over his silver frames.

I stand and straighten my skirt. "No questions, Your Honor."

None are necessary. We all knew what her testimony would be, and it doesn't change anything this late in the case.

"Mr. Johnson?"

"A few. Ms. Hardy, what are you going to do with McCartni if you go to jail or prison on those felony charges you have outstanding?"

"My attorney says I won't go to jail."

"What if you do?"

"I… I don't know."

Carl writes something on his notepad. "Why has it taken you nine months to start complying with services?"

"I couldn't get my medication. I was very depressed, couldn't get out of bed, and cried all the time. All I could do was drug test and visit."

Nicole Lowe

```
Carl sits down.

The judge looks next to Jake. "Redirect, Mr.
Lundberg?"

Jake stands for his final question. "Ms.
Hardy, do you love McCartni?"

It's a repeated question, and technically
objectionable. But no one is going to object.

"More than anything."

"And you're willing to do whatever it takes to
get her back?"

"Anything."

"Nothing further, Your Honor."
```

It was March, 1996. Our lives began to fall into routine. Sam and I were allowed to live in my parents' house. Patrick and my younger sister, Kara, lived there as well. Kara was twelve and finishing seventh grade. Seventh grade seemed so long ago for me. She was closing in on the age I was when I'd first left home: thirteen.

Kara looked like me. Her hair color, body build, even facial features were similar. But she still had a childlike appearance and naivety I'd lost by her age, when the darkness had unpacked and made itself at home inside my head.

The purple and black curtains in my bedroom window had to come down. I wanted the sun to light up my room. I left the masks and mime statue up. It seemed appropriate to do so; life still felt like a theatrical production of a tragicomedy. I stuffed all of my old goth clothes into white garbage bags for donation. I was never going back to that life.

Although my parents allowed Sam to live under their roof, they still refused to allow us to share a room. *Whatever,* I thought. At least we had a place to stay together. Patrick was kind enough to let Sam share his room.

We eventually found work. Patrick had quit Arctic Circle and had moved on to a job with McDonald's just a few blocks from my parents' house. Sam and I applied there too, and within a few weeks, we were both hired.

Fast food service was not what I would have called a rewarding job, but I eventually came to the belief that everyone should put in their time at a fast food joint at some point. It gave you perspective. You learned to treat people behind the counter as real people, after having been on the receiving end of some asshole's rant about having mustard on his kid's cheeseburger. He couldn't say, "Can I get one without mustard? Mustard was put on this one by mistake." That would have been too easy. Instead, Mr. Ass Hole—yes, Ass was his first name and Hole was his last—would throw the cheeseburger across the counter at you and ask for *your* manager, even if you just worked the counter and didn't make the fucking burger in the first place. People like that must have truly led horrible lives. Mustard never pissed me off like that.

We didn't go into downtown Salt Lake. Ever. Because of that, our ability to buy mushrooms or acid was seriously hampered. Weed, on the other hand, was everywhere, and Sam was like a bloodhound when it came to finding it.

The tension in my parents' house was palpable. My father and I never spoke. Sam and I stayed out of the house as much as possible. When we were home, we retreated to Patrick's room. Neither one of my parents liked Sam, but they were torn over kicking him out. They knew that if he went, I did too. No hesitation and no questions.

In June of 1996, we moved into our own place. It was a two-bedroom basement apartment in a red-brick fourplex. There was a fully fenced, shared back yard for Dusky Rune to run and play in. Both sides of the street were lined with old trees, three stories tall. We hung up our tie-dyed tapestries and bead door, and decorated the walls with posters of Bob Marley, the Grateful Dead dancing bears, and a marijuana leaf. My grandma gave us her old blue couch. We rented a washer and dryer from a rent-to-own center. We celebrated by getting some dose and tripping. It was the best way to become familiar with all the nooks and crannies of a new home.

James moved in with us in August. Sam told him he could stay as long as he got a job and contributed to the expenses. The bedrooms were full, so James slept on the couch.

For the first few weeks, James was great to have around. He helped with cleaning and cooking, and went job-hunting each day. But eventually, he rekindled the pursuit of dealing dose to get ahead in the money game and get to Europe. Sam was also willing to give it another try. We began contributing money when James found a connection with a gangbanger kid named Tyler.

Tyler was a short, rail-thin guy with a shaved head and a constantly-backward baseball cap. He wore his basketball shorts so low that his boxers were would hang out. The way he used his hands to talk, you'd think he needed them to keep his mouth going.

He had a pager.

He was definitely not a ragdoll.

He had sores on his face and arms, but they weren't track marks.

James said Tyler was cool, but Sam didn't trust him and turned down offers to smoke up with them. James began to hang out with Tyler more and more. One day, James left and didn't come back for days. When we came home from work, we found him sleeping on the couch.

Sam kicked James' foot. "What's up with you?"

He opened one eye. "Man, I'm sleeping," he said, and rolled over and buried his face in the couch cushions.

James was no longer the ragdoll we knew and loved. His mannerisms were jagged. He bit off his words just as his tongue forced them beyond his teeth.

Tyler wasn't the awesome connection he was supposed to be, either. There was no sheet of acid. James kept saying he would get it. He just needed more time.

Around sunset, James got up and left. He didn't say where he was going. Sam and I were asleep in our room when James stumbled into the house around one in the morning. He crashed into our bedroom door, pushed into our room, and threw the light on.

"Tyler just got his brains blown out!" he shouted.

Sam sprang to his feet. "What are you talking about? Calm down."

I sat up and rubbed my eyes against the blinding light.

"It was a bad deal and they just shot him! He's dead, man, he's dead. Fuck!" He punched the wall.

Sam led James out of the room and closed the door. I pulled on some sweats and shuffled to the kitchen to make coffee. Coffee was my comfort at all hours of the day or night.

James slept for two days after that and didn't leave the house for a week.

"You've got to get a job, dude," Sam said one afternoon. "We're trying to save up to get to Europe and we can't be supporting your ass."

"Whatever, man. I'm trying to get a job."

"No, you're sitting on our couch, eating our food, and using our stuff. I hate to be like this, man, but if you don't have a job in two months you have to get out of here."

James sat upright from his perch on the couch. "That's fucked up, I'm your fucking brother! I've done so much for your ass. Hitching all up the West Coast so you could be with Arielle and hanging out in Montana waiting for you while you're off partying with Nikki. This is bullshit! I've saved your ass so many times."

"Look bro, I know it's hard, but you've got to get a job."

James sighed. "I know."

Nicole Lowe

Eight out of ten teen fathers don't marry the mother of their child. Eighty percent of unmarried teen mothers end up on welfare.

chapter twenty-one

Judge Cruz leans back in his chair and rests his interlaced fingers on his stomach. "Closing?"

"The state waives, Your Honor."

"I'll waive as well," says Carl.

The judge turns in his chair to Sabrina's table. "Mr. Lundberg?"

Jake stands. "Briefly, Your Honor." He buttons his jacket, puts his hands in his pockets, then takes them out.

"Ms. Hardy loves her daughter, and her daughter loves her," he says. "She has visited McCartni throughout this case. She has drug tested throughout this case, even when she knew she would be dirty and could be held in contempt of court. She has gotten off to a slow start, but is committed and has made progress on all aspects of the child and family plan. She is moving forward. Ms. Hardy is very young, twenty-two, and didn't have any frame of reference for what makes an appropriate parent."

Jake looks down at his notes, scanning the page with his finger. It stops at the bottom. He takes a few more seconds to gather his thoughts. He looks up.

"She's pregnant now, Judge, and needs these services."

It's the unspoken part of this argument that has the most impact — not only on the judge, but on all of us.

In eight months, she will be back with another baby.

It was November, 1996. I was pregnant. I knew before then, somewhere in my mind. I just didn't want to acknowledge it. I had turned seventeen two months earlier.

I was afraid. Afraid I'd lose the baby again, afraid I would be a bad mother, afraid my mom would hate me, afraid my father would hate me more than he already did, and afraid that Sam would leave. I hadn't forgotten his response to the possibility of a child before. Nevertheless, I never questioned whether I would keep the baby. I knew I would.

I took a pregnancy test I bought from the drug store. It was positive.

Sam and I had talked about quitting smoking many times in the past because it was too expensive. We had tried to quit twice before, without much luck. He would always start back up again and I figured what's the point, if I'm around it all the time. But I found that for me, quitting was easy. It just took the right motivation.

I knew the baby hadn't been directly exposed to LSD. I hadn't used since June. Yet I had no idea whether my prior use would hurt the baby or not. I was too afraid to tell anyone. *Maybe after Thanksgiving,* I thought. I didn't want to ruin anyone's holiday.

On Thanksgiving morning, I rolled out of bed at five-thirty and put our nineteen-pound turkey into the oven. I lay on the couch, trying to sleep a little longer before I had to start everything else. I couldn't sleep.

What would I do if Sam left me? Tears trickled from my closed eyes. My chest tightened, and I took a few quick, shallow breaths. I hid my tear-streaked face. I got in the shower and was overcome with sobs. I sank to my knees. I already knew what it was like to lose Sam once. I had nearly lost him forever to Arielle. I was terrified to lose him again.

I cooked yams in the microwave and cut them up with brown sugar and butter. Dusky darted under my feet as a nugget of yam dropped to the floor. Sam, Patrick, and James busied themselves playing a round of *Magic: The Gathering* card game before moving on to *Final Fantasy* on Nintendo. I made a Waldorf salad, stuffing, a plate of relish, and a pasta salad.

Sam came into the kitchen and swiped a deviled egg from the platter. His smile made me believe he would not leave me when I told him about the baby. I spread the food out on the kitchen counter and we stuffed ourselves. Even Dusky got a plate.

I tried to push my fears out of my mind, but I moved about in a fog all day, distracted by my mental struggle. *When should I tell him? And will he leave me to raise the baby on my own?*

"Are you alright?" Sam asked.

The bedroom was dark, and I was making my way back to bed. I was getting up nearly every night use the bathroom. Between that, the frequent heartburn, and random crying spats, I was only sleeping a few hours a night.

"I'm fine. I'm just having a hard time sleeping." It wasn't a lie. But it wasn't the total truth.

"How come?" he asked.

I slipped between the blankets and he wrapped me in his arms.

"Just thinking about our future plans." Also, not really a lie.

December brought a torrent of icy rain. Sam and I were sitting at coffee with a plate of cheese fries between us, going over our finances. We wanted to be out on the road again in June. We wanted to have a VW bus or a Bug, but Sam thought we would have to forego that idea due to the maintenance and gas costs. It was the VW that finally pushed me into telling him. To me, having a baby would make owning a car absolutely necessary.

"I think that we need to have a car," I said.
"Why?"
I picked at the grime under my fingernails. "Because I'm pregnant." I lifted my eyes to his, but kept my head down.
He raised an eyebrow. "Yes," he said, then paused.
My throat constricted.
He smiled. "That would mean we need a car."
I took his hands in mine and stretched across the table to kiss him. From that day forward, the baby was a part of our plans. Sam told his parents that we were pregnant. We still planned to get married at Stonehenge when we got to Europe.

The morning sickness arrived in late December. It was the worst when I was at work and cooking over the grill. The food smelled so delicious that it made me extremely hungry. I would take my break and scarf down a sausage and egg McMuffin, then run to the bathroom and throw it right back up. It happened every time. You would think I would have stopped eating the damn things, but I couldn't resist them. Each time, I'd tell myself, *I won't throw it up, I won't.* But within five minutes, it always came back up.

When I was six months pregnant, I wrote my mom a letter and mailed it to her. *Can't get much more chicken than that,* I told myself. I assumed she must have been disappointed and angry, but if she was, she never showed it.

She hugged me, told me that she loved me, and helped me get ready to welcome the baby into our lives. She drove Sam and me to the prenatal appointments. She bought everything we needed for the baby: crib, clothing, diapers, stroller, and swing. She even bought us a car seat, even though we didn't have a car or driver's licenses. One of the last things she bought us was a wooden rocking chair, which creaked a little with each rock.

The ultrasound said the baby was a boy. Even before he was born, I sat in the chair and rocked him. Sam would lay on the couch with Dusky curled up at his feet, reading out loud for hours from the Dragonlance book series while we listened and rocked. On my days off, I read a book Sam's dad had sent us, *What to Expect When You're Expecting.* The book was interesting and had a lot of information in it, but it scared the hell out of me. There was so much that could go wrong, so many things I needed to know. I thought it was a miracle that any child and mother survived labor and delivery.

Once the baby was born, we were going to save up enough money to get a VW bus. A school bus would be ideal, but we would have to work our way up in the world. Our plan was to wait until the baby was about six months old, then hit the road again. We would homeschool him, which would be better. That way he wouldn't have to deal with all the mean kids in school and could go at a pace that worked for him. We could get a camp stove and coolers for the bus, and live free again.

Sam and I talked about names for the baby. We wanted his name to be meaningful and different from everyone else's, but something that couldn't be used to tease him easily. We wanted his name to be a compass for his life.

"What about naming him after you?" I asked.

"No way. And no one in my family." Sam didn't look away from the video game.

"I think he should have two middle names. You pick one and I'll pick one."

"That's fine," Sam said, throwing me a glance. "What names are you thinking?"

"Freedom."

The inspiration had come from the movie *Braveheart*. I wanted my son to fight for what he believed in, to fight for others when they couldn't fight for themselves. I wanted him to know what freedom meant and felt like. Freedom was the ability to choose, to dream, to act, and to believe.

I rubbed my hands over my swollen belly and whispered, "Freedom." I turned to Sam. "What about you?"

"Orion."

"After the constellation?"

Orion had been a comfort to us while we were on the road. It was always there, and we could always find it. Orion was a great hunter, and the son of Poseidon, god of the sea. He could hunt any animal on earth. The baby would be a water sign, like Sam, so we thought it fitting.

"Freedom Orion," I said. "I like it."

His first name continued to elude us for a few more months. Sam wanted to name him Illusion, but I said no. He suggested Fistandantilus, after a character in the Dragonlance series, but I said no.

We found it while reading together one night. With further investigation into its meaning, we decided Jasper was the right name for our son. He would be named after a character who was a storyteller: strong, loyal, and giving. Jasper was also a type of stone with properties of protection, emotional security, and stability.

At eight months, my mom hosted a baby shower for me. My aunts, cousins, sister, and family friends gathered to celebrate the life growing inside me. The same people I had turned away from and snubbed when they came for my fourteenth birthday party didn't hesitate to offer their love and support as I joined the ranks of mothers. We played games, ate cake, and opened gifts. In their excitement over the baby, they had not forgotten me. I received new slippers, bras, and pajamas.

On July fourth, we celebrated Sam's nineteenth birthday, watching fireworks at the park and eating cake and ice cream at home. Sam bought his first legal pack of cigarettes. Patrick came over and smoked him up, and I gave him a new Dragonlance book, a Grateful Dead CD, and the new *Final Fantasy* game.

I quit my job at McDonald's on the seventh of July. I cleaned the house, knowing I wouldn't feel up to it after the baby was born. Sam and I went grocery shopping and made sure we had everything we needed for the next few weeks.

My mom had to be out of town for work on my due date. She was worried I would go into labor while she was gone. We talked to my doctor, and he decided to induce labor before she left.

There was nothing in the book about being induced. The first hour wasn't bad. I lay in the hospital bed, waiting. Sam and I had talked about an epidural and decided I would try to go without.

Nicole Lowe

Soon after the anesthesiologist went home, the pain became unbearable. The doctor gave me Demerol, but it didn't touch the pain and only made me feel loopy. The contractions got stronger, and I was crying and yelling for my mom.

Sam didn't know what to do to help, but never left my side. My mom didn't know how to help me, either. She had never been through this; she'd had all three kids by C-section. The nurses tried to get me to breathe, which was the most helpful thing. Finally, my mom told the doctor to have the anesthesiologist come back. They called him at home, and he returned and gave me an epidural.

I fell asleep until twenty minutes before Jasper was born.

reveling in the sun

One-third of teen mothers complete high school and receive their diploma. Less than two percent of teen mothers earn a college degree by the age of thirty.

chapter twenty-two

Judge Cruz never rules from the bench. He goes over the evidence and writes out his findings of fact. He considers everything, and makes sure I have proven my case by the applicable standards of proof: clear and convincing evidence.

It seems like a low standard for something that has the potential to end one family and begin a new one.

I wonder what Jake tells his client in the small conference room while we wait. There is no comfort he could offer Sabrina. He gives her the truth, as he has done throughout the case, as he does for all of his clients.

In my opinion, he has the hardest job of the three attorneys in this courtroom. He sees the potential in his clients and often watches them fail, despite his zealous advocacy on their behalf. He offers not just legal advice, but encouragement and support.

More often than I like to admit, despite his best efforts, we end up in trial, or with the parents relinquishing their rights. Some parents fail to appear at all, and their rights are terminated in a fifteen-minute trial. Fifteen minutes, and their children are gone forever.

I wish I knew what makes the difference for those who are successful and those who are not.

My doctor laid the bundle that was Jasper Freedom Orion into my arms for the first time. He was seven pounds, four ounces, and nineteen inches long. He had on a pink- and blue-striped newborn beanie, and a diaper that was too big. There was a blanket wrapped around his tiny body.

He was so small. I had never held a newborn before. I ran my finger down the bridge of his button nose and my thumb across his chubby cheeks. His skin was so soft. I pushed the beanie off of his head, revealing soft, fine black hair. I brushed my hand softly over his head. He was so fragile.

I reached into the blanket to find his hand. His fingers wrapped around mine. Blue eyes looked up at me and my heart was stolen. The thunder clattered outside, lightning streaked across the sky, and I pulled my bundle a little closer.

The first time his name passed over my lips after he was born, it carried a new meaning. There was an image in my mind, and physical and emotional feelings were tied to his name. Those had not been there before. There were memories and a smell tied to his name. There were sounds that echoed in my mind each time his name was spoken. So much is contained in a name: a past, a present, and a future. In a single word lies the power to change lives.

Jasper was born healthy and strong. We were both released from the hospital after twenty-four hours. He was beautiful and he was mine. I sat in the back of Mom's car with Jasper. I couldn't stop touching him. He was real.

When we got to our apartment, I held him and rocked him the rest of the day. I was still tired from the birth and hadn't slept well in the hospital. I laid Jasper in his crib that night and watched him sleep.

Every four hours. That was what they told me at the hospital. I had to feed him every four hours. If he didn't wake up to eat at night, I had to wake him up and get him to eat.

I set the alarm clock to remind me. I rolled out of bed, pulled on my slippers, and shuffled over to Japer's crib. I rested my hand on him, feeling the rise and fall of his chest. His little grunts as I picked him up made me smile. I took him into the living room to feed him so I wouldn't wake Sam up more than I had to.

I unwrapped Jasper from his blanket, trying to get him to wake up enough to eat. He would latch on, even in his sleep, but he wouldn't suck. I rubbed his little foot and he pulled it away. He whimpered a bit and then began to suck.

Four days after Jasper was born, I called Mom.

"How do I bathe him?" I asked. The hospital had made sure I knew how to feed the little bugger, how to change his diaper, when to walk away from him if I was frustrated, and when to call the doctor—but they neglected to show me how to clean him.

"I'll be right over," she said. I could hear the smile in her voice. She was at my door in fifteen minutes.

We pulled all the windows closed and turned off the fans so they wouldn't blow on him when he was naked and wet. Mom pulled a towel out of the cupboard, laid it on the kitchen counter, and ran the water until it was warm. She wet one of his arms, soaped it up, then rinsed it. I was in charge of drying. Bit by bit, we washed his whole body. He cried the whole time until he was red in the face, but he was finally clean.

"Thank you, Mom," I said. I hugged her as she left.

I knew now that no matter what I had done in the past, Mom always loved me. We may have been enemies for the last few years—at least that's how it seemed from my point of view—but it was never that way for her. Her love for me, like my love for Jasper, was unconditional. She would willingly spend eternity in hell to save me.

I had many everyday questions for Mom. I had never taken care of a baby before. I didn't know what his temperature was supposed to be, or even how to take his temperature. She showed me how to do that, too.

I was scared to cut his fingernails and toenails. He had scratched his face a couple of times, so I knew it was necessary. I took him to Mom and she bit them off, which was what she had done with my siblings and me. She taught me how to swaddle him in his blankets, how to burp him, and what to do when he was tired and couldn't fall asleep.

Sam went back to work after a week. It was summer vacation, so Mom dropped my sister off in the mornings on her way to work and picked her up on her way home. Kara turned thirteen ten days after Jasper was born. She held him and rocked him almost as much as I did. While she held him, I showered and took a nap. Getting up every four hours took its toll.

Kara and I watched movies and ate cookie dough. She told me about school, her friends, and boys she liked. She wore jeans shorts and colorful tank tops. Her golden skin glowed, and her eyes sparkled with happiness and hope. So different from how I had been.

Jasper and I rocked in our rocking chair. It creaked its song. As my thoughts drifted to our life thus far and where it was heading, the sound of the rocking chair faded from my mind.

The plan was for the three of us to hit the road again and travel. We had talked about homeschooling Jasper and getting a VW bus. Many old hippies had done the same. The problem was, I didn't want that for our son. I wanted him to have a stable home, healthy food every day, friends he could run and play with. I had known kids who were homeschooled and they were always a little weird. I wanted him to have medical care if he needed it. On the road, those things were not reliable, and some were impossible.

I didn't know how to tell Sam. Again, I was scared he would leave us. I was tied down, even though I promised myself I never would be. I looked down at Jasper's tiny face cradled in my arm. He sighed in his sleep and the corner of his mouth twitched into a smile. Did I want to see the world, or hold the world in my arms? I knew the answer.

Sam lost his job for insubordination. He quickly found a new job as a cook at a truck stop called Sapp Brothers. They were open twenty-four hours a day, seven days a week, so he always had different shifts, including graveyard.

Mom helped get him to work on Sundays when the bus wasn't running. On nights when he got off too late to catch a bus, he would catch a ride with a friend. He was good at making new friends, and enjoyed the work much more than he had at McDonald's. Money was tight, but we got by. Saving for Europe was no longer an option. I knew that, and I believed Sam knew it too, but we hadn't spoken about it.

When Jasper was six weeks old, I gathered all my strength and closeted my fears. I told Sam I couldn't go back out on the road with the baby.

"I understand if you still want to go," I told Sam, staring down at Jasper as the rocking chair creaked its song, "but I just don't feel right about taking Jasper out there. He's so small and vulnerable. If something happened to him, I just wouldn't be able to forgive myself because there is another option that will keep him safe and healthy."

Sam was silent for a few minutes. He rubbed his left shoulder, closed his eyes, and let out a breath.

"I'm not leaving." He looked straight at us. "I'm not my father. I want to know my son and for him to know me. If that means that our goals and plans get put on hold for now, it's okay."

Relief flooded over me like rain washing the world. I had not dared to hope. I had prepared myself for the worst answer. Instead, what Sam gave me was a gift.

Mom took us grocery shopping every other weekend. When we got home from shopping one afternoon, we found Dusky gone. One of our upstairs neighbors came over and told us that Dusky had bit their four-year-old daughter in the face, and that she had to have stitches. Animal control had taken Dusky to lock-up. With a quick intake of breath, I asked if the little girl was alright. Then I burst into tears.

"Dusky wouldn't bite unless provoked," Sam said. "She has all her shots. There's no reason to quarantine her."

The mother of the child was less than forgiving. "We're going to sue you," she ranted. "You'll have to pay my child's medical bills—she needs plastic surgery! I've already called the landlord and told him he has to evict you, or I'll sue him too."

Sam was furious. "Why didn't you just come talk to us? We could have worked this out!" he said, nearly foaming at the mouth. "We're not paying you one dime. File your lawsuit. We'll see you in court."

Animal control released Dusky after we proved she was up on all her shots. She came home with a nasty case of kennel cough. I had to sit behind her and force the cough medicine down her throat twice a day. We didn't let her outside without one of us being with her.

That evening, one of our elderly neighbors knocked on our door. "I've seen that little girl tormenting Dusky," she said. "She hit Dusky with a stick a couple of times just a few days ago. Dusky is a sweet dog. I'll call the landlord and ask that he not evict you."

Dusky played with her much smaller dog all the time, and was always gentle with him.

Our landlord called the next day. I only heard one side of the conversation.

"We have a one-year lease and have lived here much longer than those people," Sam argued, his voice rising. "We've never been late on rent. We don't cause problems."

Sam fell quiet.

"Whatever, man, you do what you need to do."

He rubbed his forehead and put the phone in its cradle.

It was October, 1997. We started looking for a new place to live. Mom found one first, in a group of eight small houses. Each unit had two bedrooms, one bathroom, a living room, and a kitchen. The yards were all joined and not fenced. One-lane roads led from house to house. There was a bus stop nearby, and Mom was only five minutes away.

They didn't allow pets.

My heart broke.

We didn't have time to find another place. We filled out an application, interviewed, and were approved to move in.

Mom wouldn't take Dusky. She was a digger, and tore up her yard. When we lived with my parents, Dusky ripped up the carpet, jumped out of a two-story window, and shredded the blinds in the process. Mom finally found someone willing to take Dusky. She would be happy there; her new owner had several acres of land, and two other dogs Dusky could chase and play with.

Mom drove us there and sat in the car with Jasper as I said goodbye. Sam said it would be too hard for him to say goodbye, so he stayed home. Beautiful Dusky Rune was my baby girl. I shook as I put my hands around her furry face and kissed her on the forehead. I stroked her from head to curly tail. Tears ran down my cheeks as I told her that I loved her and would never forget her. I rested my hand on the car door and looked back one last time. Dusky wagged her tail. I climbed inside and we drove away.

I buried myself in the care of Jasper to dull the pain of losing Dusky. Pictures of her and Jasper hung on the walls, and I cried any time I stopped long enough to stare at them. Sam worked long hours. All of Jasper's care fell to me. It was a steep learning curve.

Mom picked the three of us up for Thanksgiving Dinner. I helped cook while Mom chewed Jasper's toenails and fingernails down. Grandma came over and tore up the bread for stuffing. Kara helped make pies and yams.

Patrick came in, nibbled on various things, and went back to his reading. Sam didn't interact much with anyone. The last month had been stressful. The dog bite, being evicted, losing Dusky, and moving had all taken their toll.

Some nights, I'd wake to find Sam talking with a coworker on the phone. I had met her once or twice when she drove him home. I didn't like it, but I didn't know how to talk to Sam about it. Telling someone they can't talk to a particular person never turns out well. Up to now, we had never had separate friends—the few friends I had were Sam's friends too. I felt I was being silly. Maybe even a little jealous. I had to trust him.

The daughters of teen mothers are twenty-two percent more likely than their peers to become teen mothers. Sons of teenaged mothers have a thirteen percent greater chance of ending up in prison as compared to their peers.

chapter twenty-three

"As in every case, there is a two-part test in deciding whether or not the state has met its burden." Judge Cruz's grey, overcast eyes meet Sabrina's. They hold no judgement, but his words do.

Her eyes fall to the dark cherrywood table before her. Her small hands clasp together with white knuckles.

"First, the state must prove, by clear and convincing evidence, at least one of the following: you have neglected or abused your child, you are an unfit parent, you have failed to adjust your circumstances despite the state's efforts to assist you, or you have only made token efforts toward completing those services."

Sabrina crosses her bone-thin legs at the ankle and tucks her lace-less, dirty white sneakers beneath her chair.

I knew what his ruling would be even before I walked into the courtroom this morning. I knew because I've prosecuted similar cases many times in the past. But that doesn't stop the ache in my chest as he goes through each finding.

Nicole Lowe

She doesn't lift her head. I think she knows too. Her chin-length, straw-colored hair falls forward so I can't see her face. Maxwell slides another box of cheap tissues onto the table at her elbow.

A barely audible "thank you" escapes her chapped lips.

She's only twenty-two. Her blue and white dress has seen just as many years.

Judge Cruz continues his explanation of the procedure. "Second, the state must prove, by clear and convincing evidence, that it is in the best interests of McCartni to terminate your parental rights, Ms. Hardy."

Everyone is watching her now as she reaches for the tissues. She clutches the thin paper in her fingers, wraps herself in her arms, and waits.

The judge goes through all of the findings of fact and conclusions of law. I don't need to listen to the pages and pages of how she failed to be the mother McCartni needed. They are echoes of the pages and pages of how Sabrina's parents failed her.

But here is where we try to stop the cycle.

"Based upon all of the evidence presented, I find that Sabrina Hardy has neglected McCartni Hardy. Sabrina Hardy is an unfit and incompetent parent. She has failed to adjust her circumstances despite the best efforts of the state to assist her, and it is in the best interests of McCartni to terminate Sabrina's parental rights so that she may be adopted."

Sabrina's shoulders sink and a whimper escapes her lips.

"That takes care of it, then. Ms. Lowe, will you prepare the order?"

The granting of the state's petition for the termination of parental rights is never a win. It is the inevitable result of the collective failure of all involved. It is the loss of a parent. It is the loss of a child. And it is a lost battle against child abuse and neglect, which rips families apart.

The only glimmer of hope is this: McCartni has the chance to dust herself off, pick up the pieces of her past, and soar.

It was the day after Christmas, 1997, when Jasper and I moved out. He was five months old. Sam came to me two weeks earlier and said he had been seeing someone else. I knew in my heart that he was at least emotionally involved with someone.

"We haven't done anything together, I promise," he said, but didn't look at me. "I love you and I love Jasper. I will always be here for you." He stopped to breathe. "No matter what."

The rest just tumbled from his lips. "I can't do this. I'm not ready to give it all up. I'm not ready to be a dad." He looked up at the stars. His breath was visible in the night air.

"I don't want to leave you," he said softly, looking at the glistening snow covering the ground. "I don't want to break up."

"But you are no longer only mine," I whispered into the freezing air.

Nicole Lowe

He took a drag off his cigarette. The smoke tangled with his words as he spoke. "I know."

Through the tears rolling down my face, I said, "I have never flirted with other guys while you were around. I have not worn makeup. I haven't drunk alcohol. I have not married someone I don't love. I will never forget Astarian Silvermoon... But I know I have become tied down. I've broken my promise."

We cried in each other's arms. How could I fault him? We were so young. Our whole lives had changed. All of our plans to travel, to change the world, and to get married at Stonehenge had gone awry.

I was hurt, but not angry. How could I be angry with the person who had given me so much, who'd been by my side for so long, and who I loved and would always love?

Soft, crystalized flakes floated on unseen currents of wind as I watched my father's truck back into the snow-covered driveway. My mom, sister, father, brother, and I loaded up all of Jasper and my belongings. Everything we had fit into the bed of the pickup truck. We moved into my old bedroom at my parents' house. It was crowded, but Jasper and I were together.

If I was going to be all my son had, I was going to be the best I could possibly be for him. I began completing packets through Hunter High School. Each packet was a quarter-credit toward my diploma. I had zero credits when I started. The packets weren't difficult to understand or complete. One after another, I finished them: English, history, math, and science. Everything I'd missed. My education and caring for my son became my only two goals.

As I discovered that I could be successful, I picked up that little girl who used to get straight A's in school. I dusted her off, brushed out her matted, tangled hair, and got her some new shoes. It was going to be a long walk down that road. And I knew I would walk most of it alone. My life had diverged from all those I knew, and even those I didn't know.

When I was pregnant with Jasper, I put on sixty pounds. I had stretch marks on my stomach, calves, arms, and breasts. I had never been overweight before. When I saw other girls at the high school, they were thin and beautiful. They had perfect skin, with lean and athletic bodies. I could lose the weight eventually, I told myself, but the stretch marks were forever. Striped like a tigress. I felt a sense of loss at that realization. I was embarrassed to wear shorts and tank tops. I couldn't even imagine wearing a swimsuit, or being with another man. I was damaged goods. Now my scars were on the outside, too.

Sam didn't come around much. I thought his shame and sorrow were holding him at bay. He would park his car in front of our house and Patrick would go outside to meet him. He and Patrick hung out about once a week. He came into my parents' house only once, months after we'd moved in.

He ruffled Jasper's hair. "Hi, little man," he said, smiling at his son. Jasper brushed his hand away.

My heart ached for Sam's loss and the loss Jasper would certainly come to know. Our separation was not difficult—I took the books and he took all the CDs. I had all the home furnishings and kitchenware. Sam had my heart, but I had the world: Jasper.

Anguish washed over me when I was alone. Jasper's smile and giggles chased it away most of the time, but I had a cavernous hole in my heart that would never be filled. My body convulsed, and my eyes overflowed with tears. I cried in the silent darkness of my room. The moon's glow rested on books and pictures—our books and our pictures. Our songs played on the radio and in my head. Sam's voice and smile were a constant presence in my mind.

Jasper fussed in his crib and I wiped my face with our blanket, breathing in Sam's scent. Tears threatened to spill again, but I held them back. I needed to be strong. Jasper fussed again, this time a little louder. I pushed the blankets off and took the three steps to his crib.

"Shhh, Mommy's here," I whispered to him, picking him up, wrapping him in my arms. I gave up many things when I chose him. And he was worth it all.

Homecoming, Prom, and Sadie Hawkins were all high school experiences I would never have. Football games, driver's education, and first dates—more high school experiences I would never know.

Nicole Lowe

I would have graduated from high school in the spring of 1998, had I never dropped out in the first place. Staying up late, watching movies with friends, and sleeping until noon were not things I could do at seventeen. Shopping at the mall with girlfriends and flirting with boys was not how I spent my weekends. Friends were not something I had. Not many seventeen-year-olds would have wanted to worry about what they were doing or saying in front of a baby. Nor would they want to worry about every object on the floor, or keeping schedules for naptime and bath time. They wanted to live their own lives, not cater to someone else's every need and desire.

I got up a couple of times a night to a little voice in the crib next to my bed. My bedtime was 9:00 p.m. and I got up at 6:30 a.m. to that same little voice, who was now in my bed because I was too tired to put him back in his crib at three in the morning. The only flirting I did was with a blue-eyed, blond-haired little boy who reached his arms up to me or pulled on my pants leg, wanting to be held.

Jasper reached every developmental milestone early and grew twice as fast as I could buy clothing for him. He crawled backward, but not forward—feet first, everywhere he went. One afternoon, I was sitting across the room from Jasper trying to get him to crawl forward to me, but he got upset and fussed because he kept going backward. I set an eight-by-ten photo of him on the floor and he crawled right to it, smiling and showing off the few teeth he had. Walking came much easier. He was toddling around by the time he was ten months old.

I took the GED when Jasper turned one, hoping to start classes at Salt Lake Community College in the fall. The GED gave me five credits toward my high school diploma, which I was determined to achieve even though I didn't need it with the GED. I registered and applied for financial aid at Salt Lake Community College with the thought of going into computer programing or biology.

Mom watched Jasper while I was in school. I took night classes because I wouldn't put him in daycare until he could talk and tell me if someone was hurting him. I finished the semester with straight A's and decided that biology was more interesting than computer programming. I applied my college credits toward my high school diploma and graduated one term behind my class.

I worked two days a week through a temporary staffing agency—nights and weekends, so Mom could watch Jasper. I saved money to take a driver's education class. Mom was driving me to work and to school, and although driving had never been a concern or a priority to me, it quickly became one. I'd always taken the bus everywhere I needed to go, but taking the bus with a young child was difficult, and riding the bus anywhere took twice as long.

When I got home from work at midnight, I would watch Jasper sleeping: a calm, serene expression across his face, the rhythmic rising and falling of his chest, the occasional smile, and the fluttering of his closed eyes. When those sapphire eyes opened, he would stretch his arms out to me and grab me with his tiny fingers, and the most beautiful smile would jump to his lips.

"Mama," he would say, and I would giggle. Sometimes, he peeked at me above the crib bumper and even though I couldn't see the smile on his lips, I could see it in his eyes when he laughed and ducked back down.

What would I have done without you, my son, my rock, my world?

My heart ached and tears welled up in my eyes when I caught just a glimpse, a small taste of how Mom must have felt when I went missing. The thought of Jasper running away from me and experiencing the feelings that I did caused my heart to race with desperation and fear. I decided I never wanted him to know the horrors of who I had been. More importantly, I never wanted him to know the darkness I had felt—the self-hate, and the destruction. I could not imagine anything more painful than losing Jasper to that world.

I once found a sense of belonging, a sense of safety and acceptance, in Sam. I felt complete when I was with him because he embodied those feelings for me. When he left, I had to find those things all over again. I found them in my son. I understood that, in order to find true happiness, I had to find belonging, safety, and acceptance within myself.

Nicole Lowe

reality

i've lost you, you're gone somewhere deep inside
of me
the only friend i had, hidden in fantasy
made my dreams come true, held my hand, and led me
through
reality hit, it knocked me down
my dreams are gone. my whole life falls through
but i'm coming back
coming back to find you
to kick your ass and pull you through.

Statistics will never control my dreams or achievements. My past does not limit my future. Others' beliefs about me do not determine my fate.

Nicole Lowe, 2014

chapter twenty-four

```
It's not about saving them all. It's about saving
the one.
```

    The ability to dream and to have goals is central to who we are and who we will become. Every child deserves a chance to dream. If you walk through life only thinking about where your next meal will come from, where your next fix will come from, where you will sleep that night, or if you will see the next sunrise, you don't have the chance to dream. Children such as these are robbed of their essence. They become fractured children, and then adults who continually seek happiness from the outside world. They are never able to realize that happiness is a choice that comes from within.

    I share my story with great trepidation. I don't wish to cause any more hurt or suffering to my family, who has already lived through one side of this story.

    To now have my side of the story revealed causes me to pause, and has stalled my sharing of this for many years. So why write it now? Maybe because Jasper has now reached the age I was during those years. Maybe because I see so much of myself in my youngest son, Schyler, and I want him to know the strength within himself, and to never give up, even when the world turns its back on you. If my story helps one family or one child to keep hope and keep their dreams, it will be worth it.

My two beautiful sons are polar opposites of one another. They have taught me to love truly and completely, to slow down, maintain my balance, and appreciate the little things in life. I watch each of them go through their own struggles: Jasper, so different from how I was; and Schyler, similar in some ways, but very much his own being.

My sincere wish is that my story will give hope to families who are going through a tough time with a child. To let other girls and women know that strength is at the core of who they are, and to find it, fight for it, and breathe it. Strength and love are not merely emotions, but a state of mind.

Jasper has grown into a strong, intelligent, and compassionate young man. He is very mature and responsible for his age. Any concerns I once harbored that my prior drug use would negatively affect his growth and development have been alleviated. Jasper is in honors, AP, and concurrent enrollment college courses at his high school. He has plans to go on to college and earn an advanced degree. He runs for his high school cross country team, plays Ultimate Frisbee, and takes Tae Kwon Do. He has volunteered at the local peer court program and became the first sophomore judge for our local program.

The way people think and behave fascinates Jasper. He is very observant, and enjoys figuring out what makes them tick before even they know themselves. He is excellent at finding the hidden motivation of others and interpreting their behaviors. He is also very introspective and has a deep understanding of himself and what motivates him in many different situations.

I am not naïve enough to say that my lifestyle and choices have not affected Jasper. They have. Jasper was raised in a single-parent house for most of his life. He felt the loss of his father very early. and again when Sam came back into his life at age eleven, only to leave again. Sam remains very elusive, to this day. Jasper has had to grow up faster than he would have in a two-parent home.

Schyler is currently in junior high school and doing well. He achieves A's and B's in his classes. He is a very compassionate, creative, and straightforward young man. He is the first person to answer the call to action for those in need, whether they are children such as himself or adults.

Sam is married and has three additional children, two girls and another son. He moved to Oregon when Jasper was three years old and did not see him again until Jasper was eleven. He came to visit Jasper for three days and maintained contact for a few months, but that eventually receded to merely birthday and Christmas cards. Despite Sam's pronouncement that he would not become like his father, he has. At least as far as Jasper goes. I believe Sam obtained a bachelor's degree in English.

Patrick has become a wonderful father of two beautiful girls near the ages of my boys. He works full-time, but never did go back and finish high school. He continues his study of Enochian lore and magic. He has completed vocational training for solar energy, but doesn't work in the field. He is married to Bridget, whom he met during our gothic days.

My sister, Kara, never ran away from home. She completed high school with her class. She is married with two beautiful children, a little boy and a girl.

As for the rest of the people in this book, I know very little about who they have become. I had contact with Hunter when Jasper was about six months old. He was living in a halfway house after being released from prison for manufacturing methamphetamine.

I have seen Sandi on and off around town, but don't make contact. When I was pregnant with Jasper, she had her first son and was later involved in a domestic violence relationship. Her son was removed from her custody by the state.

Bill and Mariah moved to Missouri, where Bill's family resided. Their daughter was born healthy. They named her Sage. Child protective services removed Sage from their custody when she was only a few months old and gave her to Bill's parents. Mariah stated that Bill picked Sage up by the arm when he was angry, and it came out of its socket. I don't know if Sage was ever returned to Bill and Mariah.

Where am I now? Who have I become? I am the same girl who you find throughout these pages. I may express myself in different ways, but I am still the girl who does not want to be the center of attention and who, at times, questions her right to be heard.

I graduated with an Associates of Science in 2000 from Salt Lake Community College. I began classes at the University of Utah and completed my Bachelor of Science Degree in Psychology in 2002. After receiving my BS, I went to work as a child abuse investigator for three years.

During that time, I was married, gave birth to my second son, and divorced. I was accepted into the University of Utah S. J. Quinney College of Law in 2005 and graduated in 2008.

I continued working in the child abuse and neglect field during law school, on both a voluntary and paid basis. I bought my first home in 2007. I currently work as an Assistant Attorney General for the state of Utah, trying to help families find the strength to hold onto their dreams. In 2015, I created the Homeless Youth Legal Clinic, which provides free legal services to homeless youth in Salt Lake County, Utah.

It's heartbreaking when parents who are on trial to have their parental rights terminated for drug use, domestic violence, or physical abuse ask me from the witness box, "What would you do in my situation?" Or say, "You could never understand what I've been through." The juxtaposition of our lives serves as a constant reminder to me of how lucky I am.

Children are not one family's responsibility, but are the treasure and responsibility of the world. Each child grows and becomes an adult, contributing to or destroying what is around them. They will become the doctors, teachers, lawyers, waiters, garbage collectors, baristas, and all other things, for each other and us in our old age. If they lose their dreams, we all lose.

As each of us travels down the path of life, life-changing experiences confront us and shape who we become from that moment forward. Some have many such experiences. Others, only one. These moments cause you to ask: Why your life is worth living? And what is important to you? If you don't know your answer, you wander in the darkness, waiting for someone or something to light a flame and illuminate your way. After one of these life-changing experiences, we find our core self has been splintered or completely cleaved in two. It takes us years, if not an entire lifetime, to mend our souls. But once we do, anything is possible.

A remnant of my traveling days is my constant search for somewhere to sleep. I do it to this day. Out on a run through the city or on a drive down the street, I take note of places that would be ideal for sleeping and stashing gear: a group of trees in a field, under a big pine tree, a depression in the ground. I automatically go through the steps of what time I would have to get up to not draw attention to myself, how many days I could probably stay there, where the streetlights are, how the shadows fall, what types of restaurants or stores are around, and the frequency of foot and car traffic.

I work in downtown Salt Lake City. I walk the same streets on nearly a daily basis that I walked when I was tripping, out of my mind with laughter, searching for shelter and food. The same streets I walked in despair and darkness. Sometimes, I see things that transport me back in time. They come with a rush of emotion—some good, some bad. I still have nightmares of the rape, and when I see someone who looks similar to my rapist, my heart races and my stomach turns.

I wonder, how did I get from there to here? *There* and *here* feel eons away from one another, but they're not. They are both right here inside of me at this very moment, side by side, sometimes hand in hand, and at other times staring at one another through a looking glass.

I've played many roles along my journey. I've been a high school dropout, a drug addict, a drug dealer, a teen mom, a homeless youth, a victim of rape and domestic violence, and a member of a cult. Now when people see me, they see an attorney, an ultrarunner, an author, the program director for the Homeless Youth Legal Clinic, and most important of all, a safe and stable mom.

Nicole Lowe

I have often wondered how I made it out when none of my friends did. I do not believe I am special, or that I am different from anyone else. I just had a reason. I had Jasper, who taught me I was a reason of my own.

LSD is still my go-to "drug." Only now, it stands for Long Slow Distance rather than Lysergic Acid Diethylamide. Instead of staying up all night tripping on hallucinations, I'm up all night tripping over rocks and roots, running on single-track trails, mile after mile.

I ran many marathons, but found they didn't feed my need. I began running ultra-marathons of fifty and one hundred miles in 2013. Weaving my way along trails has given me the time and space to piece together the fractured nature of my soul. Step by step.

Running long distance contains many metaphors for life. You choose to get out of bed and face your run, sometimes not knowing the route you are about to head down. At times, it is dark and you can't see what or who is coming at you from the other direction. You come to the foot of a hill or a mountain and you choose the best or worst path to take, up and over.

Sometimes, it's too big and you decide to try to go around, which results in you being lost. Puddles appear, and you happily splash through them or skip around them to avoid the miserableness of soggy feet. At twenty miles, you hit the infamous wall. Your mind is telling your body it cannot go another step, but you do, and you get stronger. You hit another wall at thirty miles, and another at forty. You know they will keep coming, but you know you can keep going because you have done it all before.

Some days, you hit your zone—gliding on top of the world, flying down hills, or floating over the mountains. Some days, you trip over rocks, roots, and your own feet, falling on your face. But you stand back up and keep going. Life has its mountains and walls. It's simply about how you choose to deal with each.

Regardless of how difficult a run is, and no matter how dark the path before me, I know the sun will always rise. I just have to hold on until the darkness is burned away.

about the author

Nicole Lowe lived on the streets between the ages of thirteen and sixteen. She faced many of the challenges that homeless youth still face today, including drugs, hunger, cold, and physical and sexual violence. At sixteen, she became pregnant. A single mother, she returned to high school and graduated in December 1998. She graduated with her Associates of Science from Salt Lake City Community College in 2000 and transferred to the University of Utah, where she graduated in 2002 with her bachelor's degree in psychology.

Afterward, she worked for the Division of Child and Family Services as a child abuse investigator. She was accepted into S.J. Quinney College of Law in 2005 and graduated in 2008. Nicole is currently a Utah Assistant Attorney General in the Child Protection Division. In 2014, she began working with the Utah division of Volunteers of America to create a free legal clinic for homeless youth. She is the program director and chair of the board for the Homeless Youth Legal Clinic (youthlegal.org). In her spare time, Nicole runs 100-mile races. Follow her blogs here:
www.fightingforachancetodream.com
www.ultrarunningmom.com

about the publisher

Glass Spider Publishing is a micropublisher located in Ogden, Utah. The company was founded in 2016 by writer Vince Font to help authors get their works into shape, into print, and into distribution. For further information, visit www.glassspiderpublishing.com.

Made in the USA
Lexington, KY
07 November 2017